SAMAVĀYA FOUNDATION OF NYĀYA-VAIŚEṢIKA PHILOSOPHY

SAMAVĀYA FOUNDATION OF NYĀYA-VAIŚEṢIKA PHILOSOPHY

BISWANARAYAN SHASTRI

SHARADA

1993

SHARADA PUBLISHING HOUSE

DELHI-110052

First Published1993

ISBN: 81-85616-16-7

Published by B.L. Bansal for Sharada Publishing House,
E-239, Shastri Nagar, Delhi-110052
Typeset by Neographics
2/7 Ansari Road, Darya Ganj, New Delhi-110002
Printed at Garg Offset Works
B-76, Naraina Ind. Area, New Delhi

समर्पणम्

पिता मे वेणीकान्ताख्यो भारद्वाजकुलोद्भवः ।
पदे वाक्ये कोषे चैव लब्धविस्तीर्णबोधनः ॥

जननी रूपदा देवी सदा धर्मपरायणा ।
विहाय बालकं पुत्रं या गता त्रिदशालयम् ॥

पितरौ तौ प्रणम्याथ पुस्तकं सामवायिकम् ।
तनयेनार्प्यतें भक्त्या तोषाय सततं तयोः ॥

विश्वनारायणेन

Contents

Preface

Samavāya is one of the six categories, i.e. the sixth category in the *Vaiśeṣikasūtra* and the *Praśastapāda-bhāṣya*. Later on *abhāva* (absence) is added to these six.The Vaiśeṣika system developed independently side by side with the Nyāya system of Philosophy. Both Nyāya and Vaiśeṣika being realist and with causality as the basic theory, came to be regarded as one system, in course of time. The commentators and particularly the authors of the *prakaraṇa granthas* treated them as one.

The Nyāya system has accepted the seven categories of Vaiśeṣika though the *Nyāya-sūtra* enumerated sixteen categories, different from that of the *Kaṇāda-sūtra*. In fact, the sixteen categories of Nyāya are quite different in concept of categories of Vaiśeṣika. The Vaiśeṣika traces the evolution of the physical world to the six categories, which are considered as ultimate reality. Therefore, the pluralist and realist Naiyāyika has got to accept the Vaiśeṣika categories. The Vaiśeṣika theory of emergence of the gross elements in, or from the subtle element, *aṇu* or atom is based on *samavāya*. Without the instrumentality of *savavāya* combination of subtle and unperceptible aṇus cannot be explained. According to Vaiśeṣika system the gross physical entity emerges through the combination of subtle atoms and acquires dimension and perceptibility when atoms are combined in the given process through *samavāya*. Thus for explaining logically the evolution of the world order the role of samvāya in Nyāya-Vaiśeṣika philosophy is omnipotent and overpervading, without which the system cannot stand. It is why *samavāya* is termed as the corner stone of this system of philosophy; while some other describes the function of *samavāya* 'the magic of samavāya'. Even if it is 'a magic' that is to be investigated.

All other systems of Indian philosophy, orthodox and heterodox, have vehemently criticised the concept of *samavāya* and its acceptance as a category. Their opposition to the acceptance of *samavāya* lies in the fact that once the *samavāya* is refuted logically the entire system of Nyāya Vaiśeṣika will collapse.

The main objection, among others, to the concept of *samavāya* as a category by the opponents is that *samavāya* being a relation is quality and comes under *guṇa* like *saṁyoga* and cannot be a category. The Buddhist and Jaina logicians call the concept absurd and illogical.

Though certain aspects relating to *samavāya* are dealt with by a few scholars, no comprehensive treatment of the subject has so far been made.

In this treatise an attempt has been made to trace the origin of the concept of *samavāya*, its development, critique by other schools, and defence by the upholders of the theory. The work is divided into nine chapters including the introductory part.

In the introduction a brief survey is made of the works already done, and the origin of speculative thinking is also discussed.

In the second chapter the emergence of Nyāya and Vaiśeṣika, the development of the two systems, and the basic theory are dealt with. In the third chapter the definition of different types of relation and the difference between *saṁyaga* and *samavāya* are treated. As both Nyāya and Vaiśeṣika are based on the theory of causality, the different causes and their function are defined and concept of part and whole etc. is also discussed.

The fifth chapter deals with the definition of *samavāya* as given by Praśastapāda, and its improvement or modification from time to time by the authors of this system, who were duty-bound to make the definition foolproof. In the chapter that follows the different aspects of *samavāya* with reference to its critique are discussed. In the seventh chapter the refutation of *samavāya* by the Buddhist, the Jaina, the Sāṁkhya, the Mīmāṁsaka, the Vedāntin, etc. are put with all vehemence, which the arguments contain. The reply to the critique, as given by the authors of the Nyāya-Vaiśeṣika, from Uddyotakara to Jagadīśa are quoted and summarised. The strength and the weakness of the arguments, marshalled by the ācāryas of the system to counter and demolish the opposition's argument have been pointed out.

In the concluding chapter the importance of *Samavāya* is shown from the Nyāya-Vaiśeṣika point of view.

Jaina logician Prabhācandra, in his *Prameyakamalamārttanda* makes a scathing attack on *samavāya* in a lengthy passage. Summary of his argument is added as Appendix I.

Quatations are given, under notes and references, at the end of each chapter, in Roman script while short quotations are inserted in the text itself.

This is a revised and abridged version of my thesis entitled "The Concept of *Samavāya* in Nyāya-Vaiśeṣika Philosophy" submitted for the degree of D. Litt. in the Burdwan University. The thesis being a voluminous one remained unpublished for long. Now it has been recast, revised and abridged. I am thankful to the Burdwan University authorities for giving me the opportunity for publishing the present work.

Late Dr. Gopikamohan Bhattacharya, who was dear to me like my younger brother helped me by his valuable suggestions not only in preparing the original thesis but suggesting revision of the work. Without his ungrudging help and valuable suggestions it would have been difficult for me to present the work due to my absorption in political activity. The cruel destiny has snatched a devoted scholar from our midst. He would have been the happiest person today to see the work published.

I acknowledge my indebtedness to all those whose works I have consulted, referred to and quoted.

I thank Prof. Satkari Mukhopadhyaya, who has kindly looked after all aspects of publication of the work.

I must thank my wife Mrs. Mira Devi for providing all supports to me to undertake and complete it. Sri B. L. Bansal of M/s Sharada Publishing House, Delhi deserves my thanks for bringing out the work to light within a short time.

I am fully aware of my limitations and omissions and commissions. I shall feel happy if the publication receives the attention of scholars as it may deserve.

14th January'93 BISWANARAYAN SHASTRI
(Makara Sankranti)
'Ritayana'
Red Cross Road, Guwahati-3

Abbreviations

A.Bh	Aṇubhāṣya
AHIL	A Historical Survey of Indian Logic
Ap. R	Appearance and Reality
AS	Arthaśāstra
AVNDP	Avacchedakatā-vāda-nirukti-Didhīti-Prakāśa
AVNJ	Avacchedakata vāda-Nirukti, Jāgadīśī
Bha	Bhāgavata
BL	Buddhist Logic
Bh. G	Bhagavad-gītā
Bh. M	Bhāmatī
Bh. P	Bhāṣā pariccheda
DPSB	Date of Philosophical Sūtras of Brāhmaṇas
EIP	Encyclopedia of Indian Philosophy
HBNVL	History and Bibliography of Nyāya-Vaiśeṣika Literature
HIL	History of Indian Logic
HIP	History of Indian Philosophy
ILA	Indian Logic and Atomism
IP	Indian Philosophy
INES	Indian Logic in Early Schools
JSD	Jāgadīśa-sūkti-dīpikā
KP	Kiraṇāvalī-prakāśa
KPV	Kiraṇāvalī-prakāśa-vivṛti
MBh	Mahābhārata
MSNL	Materials for the Study of Navyanyāya Logic
MBh. SP	Mahābhārata Śāntiparva
MMH	Mānamanohara
MS	Mahimna stotra
MM	Mānameyodaya
MS	Manusaṁhitā
NNSL	Navyə-Nyāya System of Logic
NM	Nyāyamañjarī
NKa	Nyāyakandalī
NL	Nyāyalīlāvatī
NBA	Nyāya-bhūṣaṇasāra
NDN	Navyanyāya Doctrine of Negation
Ny.P	Nyāyaprakāśa
NP	Nyāyaprakāśa
NK	Nyāya Kaṇikā

NS	Nyāya Sūtra
NSa	Nyāyasāra
NVTP	Nyāya-vārttika-tātparya-pariśuddhi
NV	Nyāya-Vārttika
OST	Original Sanskrit Texts
Pa.D	Pañcadaśī
PC	Padārtha candrikā
PKM	Prameya-kamala-mārtanda
PNVBDS	Philosophy of Nyāya-Vaiśeṣika and its Conflict with the Buddhist Diṅnāga School
PP	Prakaraṇa-pañcikā
PPBh.	Praśastapāda Bhāṣya
PV	Pramāṇavārttika
PLM	Parama-laghu mañjuṣā
PTN	Padārtha tattva-nirūpaṇa
RV	Ṛgveda
SBh	Śāṁkarabhāṣya
SD	Śāstradīpika
SKT	Sāṁkhytatvakaumudī
SLJ	Siddhānta-lakṣaṇa, Jāgadīśī
SP	Saptapadārthī
Spa	Sambandha-parīkṣā
Śr.Bh	Śrībhāṣya
SSP	Six systems of Philosophy
SV	Ślokavārttika
SVTT	Śloka-Vārttika-tātparyaṭīkā
TC	Tattvacintāmaṇi
TCA	Tattvacintāmaṇi-Āloka
TD	Tarkadīpikā
TD	Tātparyadīpikā
TP	Tātparyaṭīkā (by Citsukha)
TS	Tarka-saṁgraha
TV	Tantra vārttika
VBh.	Vātsyāyana Bhāṣya
VeS	Vedānta-sūtra
Vs	Vaiśeṣika-sūtra
KS	Kaṇāda sūtra
Vy.Va	Vyutpatti-vāda
Vy.Va.PM	Vyutpatti-vāda-pañcaka, Māthurī
VV	Vyomavatī
YS	Yoga-sūtra
YV	Yogavārttika

Introduction

The Indian Philosophical Thoughts: Origin and Development of Nyāya-Vaiśeṣika

The Indian philosophical thoughts may broadly be divided into two categories—the *āstika* (theist) and *nāstika* (atheist). Usually those who accept the authority of the Vedas and consider the Vedas as infallible are called *āstikas* and those who reject the authority of the Vedas are termed as *nāstikas.*[1]

However, we find the following distinct schools of Indian philosophical thoughts—the materialistic philosophy, traditionally ascribed to Cārvaka, also known as Cārvaka darśana; the philosophy of the Jainas and the Philosophy of the Bauddhas; and the six systems of philosophy, commonly termed as the Brāhmanical philosophy by the European scholars. These six systems are also clubbed as Nyāya-Vaiśeṣika (N-V), Sāṁkhya-Yoga (S-Y), and Mīmāṁsā-Vedānta (M-V) or Pūrvottara-Mīmāṁsā. Leaving the case of materialistic philosophy all other systems may be divided as idealist and realist, monistic and pluralistic, according to the basic concepts about the origin of the universe and the ultimate reality.

According to Max Mueller the six systems have certain aspects which are common and they agree on them.[2] Radhakrishnan thinks that the acceptance of the Vedas is the common reservoir from which each system has drawn.[3]

Another common characteristic of all the systems is that they protest, in chorus, against scepticism of the Buddhists, the Yogācāra view of the conceptuality of the external world and the theory of universal flux. They establish an objective reality and truth which are quite opposed to the doctrine of eternal, unstable flux. As against this the concept of the six philosophical systems is—that from eternity the stream of the world flows and this flow is not merely mental, but is objective.

> "That in which the world resides, when divested of name and form, some call *prakṛti*, others *māyā*, others atoms."[4]

1.1. *Ānvīkṣikī or the Science of Enquiry*

Philosophy or *adhyātmavidyā* has in course of time been supported or supplemented by *ānvīkṣikīvidyā* or the science of enquiry and inference. This development is more evident with the advent of the Buddhist logic which wanted to prove everything by reasons and valid proof, and hence, they are termed expert in *pramāṇa*.[5]

In the *Mahābhārata ānvīkṣikī* has been mentioned along with *trayī* (Vedas), *vārttā* (the science relating to agriculture) and *daṇḍanīti* (the state policy).[6] In the *Bhāgavata* also *ānvīkṣikī* has been enumerated with *trayī, vārttā* and *daṇḍanīti.*[7] It is clear that along with *trayī, vārttā* and *daṇḍanītī, ānvīkṣikī* was also regarded as a major branch of learning.

Kauṭilya (300 B.C.) while dividing the science of knowledge into four divisions,[8] by *ānvīkṣikī* he includes both philosophy and logic and decides *ānvīkṣikī* as the knowledge consisting of Sāṁkhya, Yoga and Lokāyata (the materialistic philosophy).[9]

1.2. *Origin and Development of Nyāya-Vaiśeṣika*

Of the six systems of Indian philosophy, which are often referred to as the orthodox system or the Brāhmaṇical system of philosophy by the foreign scholars, it is difficult to ascertain the chronology, or which system preceded which. Nyāya and Vaiśeṣika stand in the name of Gotama or Gautama and Kaṇāda respectively. But it is not correct to say that they were the originators of the respective systems. At least they are the redactors or formulators of *sūtras*, because the thoughts were there since long. It is generally accepted that doctrines of the six systems of philosophy are older than the *sūtras* of the systems.

Finding similarity in thoughts and expressions in some of the *sūtras* of these systems some scholars are prompted to assert that some of them are original and others borrowed. Originality or indebtedness cannot be decided on the ground of similarity of expressions. Since the thought and discussions on the theories were there before the formulation of the *sūtras*, it is quite likely that there were cross references, and, hence, it is not safe to put the finger on a particular expression to term it either as original or borrowed. It is rather safe to presume that each system developed independently and had its own concept. In this context the observation of Dr. Muir and Prof. Monier Williams definitely holds good.

> "Earnest thinkers of a subject, equally interesting to all, will often think in the same way and there is nothing to wonder at, if the truth flushing on their minds from a common source, find similar expression in both."[10]

It has been stated that the philosophical schools are older than the systematic exposition of them by the *sūtras*. Therefore from the *sūtras* alone one cannot decide the relative dates of the schools. For instance, it is the generally accepted view that the Sāṁkhya school is the oldest of all the philosophical schools, but the *Sāṁkhya sūtras* are decidedly of later date, might be the latest of all the philosophical *sūtras*. Similarly, Yoga as a school of meditation might be an oldest one but its *sūtras* are not so old.

The *Vaiśeṣika sūtras* are considered to be later than the *Brahmasūtra* on the ground that the former seems to have borrowed certain terms from the latter. However, that does not lead to the conclusion that the school itself is of later origin. The doctrine of the Vaiśeṣika is older than both the Mīmāṁsā schools. The Nyāya system is the latest of all the orthodox systems of Indian philosophy and, the time gap between the flourishing of the doctrine and the formulation of the *sūtras* is perhaps less. Anyway, the *Nyāya-sūtra* of Gotama or Gautama is later than the *Vaiśeṣika sūtra*.[11]

The Nyāya and the Vaiśeṣika, the two systems of Indian philosophy, which are very often referred to together as one school, though have many things common, originated and developed independently. From the nature of treatment about the creation of the world and its acceptance as a reality and also from the stand point regarding the proof the two systems appear to be similar in their have emerged as one school and the later writers wrote their treatises taking both the systems as one.

When the process of syncretism started and completed is not clear. The process of syncretism started, according to some,[12] before the redaction of *sūtras* and a close link, they say, had been between the two systems since the days of the *Mahābhārata*.[13]

Nyāya has been identified with *ānvīkṣikī* which means the science of reasoning and enquiry and that it has been accepted as such is clear from the commentary of Vātsyāyana on the *Nyāya-sūtra*.[14] He also further asserts that the Nyāya is an independent school.[15] That the Nyāya is a separate school has been proved from the reference to Nyāya as a separate system *(pṛthak prasthāna)*.[16]

However, scholars have traced the germ of reasoning and inference in the Ṛgveda. "I saw at a distance smoke coming from burning cowdung. Yonder by means of this I inferred the netherlying, and spreading Agni by which, afterwards I cooked sacrificial food."[17]

The Nyāya-Vaiśeṣika system has been considered as unique on account of their cardinal doctrines and radical views.[18] Of the two systems Nyāya is more compact and systematic dialectics than any other philosophy. Gotama or Gautama enumerates sixteen categories which are wrongly called *padārtha*, in fact, these are topics only.[19(i)] The sixteen categories of Gautama are not *padārtha* in the strict sense of the term, some of them are logic while others are false logic.[19(ii)] On the other hand the Vaiśeṣika is essentially a system of metaphysics and the logic has been skillfully dovetailed into it by the later writers. Kaṇāda enumerates six categories or *padārtha*[19(iii)] which contain the entire universe in themselves and whenever they come across with an unanalyzable irreduceable concept they seek to purge it as *svarūpa* or *akhaṇḍopādhi*.

The six categories of Kaṇāda are divided into two groups, viz. the first three, namely, *dravya* (substance), *guṇa* (quality) and *karma* (action) possess the common inhering character *sattā-sāmānya* and termed as *artha*[20] and the other three are, namely, *sāmānya* (universal), *viśeṣa* (particular) and *samavāya* (inherence) exist on their own and termed as *svātma-sat*. The sixteen categories of Nyāya are different from the six categories of Vaiśeṣika. But the commentators have made an all out effort to include the sixteen categories in the six categories. Vātsyāyana, in the *Bhāṣya* has referred to the six categories.[21]

The two systems, Nyāya and Vaiśeṣika, take almost similar stand as to the creation of the universe and the objective reality of the world. Thus the two systems have developed by mutual support, and, in course of time, emerged as one school. Though the process of syncretism has started long before, the *bhāṣyas, vārttikas* and other commentaries had been written on the two systems separately. It is only in the independent treatises the two systems have been dealt as one.

A SHORT ACCOUNT OF THE BASIC LITERATURE ON SAMAVĀYA AND ITS CRITIQUE

1.3. *Vaiśeṣika Literature*

The *Vaiśeṣika sūtra*[22] is the earliest literature where *samavāya* is enumerated as one of the six *padārthas* (categories) of that system. The Vaiśeṣika system of philosophy is known as *ṣaṭpadārthī*, the treatise based on six categories, viz. *dravya* (substance), *guṇa* (quality), *karma* (activity), *sāmānya* (general or universal), *viśeṣa* (special) and *samavāya* (inherence). The theory of *aṇu* (atom) involving formation of gross elements from the subtle and discrete atoms is based on the concept of *samavāya*, which inherently combines the atoms and makes the gross element. This provides a logical explanation of the process of formation of the gross elements. It is believed that *asatkāryavāda*, the doctrine of pre-absence of effect in the cause, of *Vaiśeṣika* is the basis of some of the Buddhist doctrines.[23] Perhaps it is why Ācārya Śaṁkara has denounced the *Vaiśeṣika* system as *ardha-vaināśika*[24] (half-nihilist).

Padārtha-dharma saṁgraha[25] known as *Praśastapādabhāṣya* by Praśastapāda, who is also called Praśastamati and Praśastācārya is a commentary on *Kaṇāda-sūtra*. Unlike others this is not a running commentary on *Kaṇāda-sūtra*, rather an independent treatise on the system. It is generally believed that there were other commentaries[25] on *Kaṇāda-sūtra* before Praśastapāda had written his commentary. These were older than *PPBh.* All these works were lost and hence the views expressed on *samavāya* in those works were not available to us. It is said that the *PPBh.* was written to remove the atheistic tendency of *Rāvaṇabhāṣya.*[27] Between the period from the date of *Kaṇāda-sūtra* to *PPBh.* the *Vaiśeṣika* system and for that matter the concept and definition of *samavāya* was criticised by the opponent of the system particularly the Buddhist. Praśastapāda had to take note of this criticism and in order to refute it and defend the concept of *samavāya* redefined it by introducing element like *ayutasiddha* (inseparably connected) as the basis of *samavāya.*

He is believed to be posterior to the Buddhist philosopher Diṅnāga and his indebtedness to Diṅnāga is accepted by the scholars. He is placed in 4th century A.D.

Vyomaśiva is the earliest known commentator on *Padārtha-dharma-saṁgraha* of Praśastapāda. His commentary is known as *Vyomavatī.* Vyomaśiva adds *śabda* (word) to the list of *pramāṇas* and admits three *pramāṇas* as against two, *pratyakṣa* (perception) and *anumāna* (inference) by Kaṇāda. Kaṇāḍa includes *śabda* under *anumāna.* He is placed in early 10th century A.D. Vyomaśiva has been eulogised as the incarnation of Śiva.[28]

Bhāsarvajña is one of the earliest commentators on the *Vaiśeṣika* system of philosophy. His work *Nyāyabhūṣaṇa* with a self-gloss *Nyāyabhūṣaṇasāra* is also commented by a few scholars. Bhāsarvajña is placed in the early part of the tenth century A.D.

Śrīdhara, the author of *Nyāyakandalī* is an accomplished scholar, and his commentary *Nyāyakandalī* on *Padārthadharma-saṁgraha* was accepted as the standard work of the Vaiśeṣika school. The opponents of the Vaiśeṣika school have very often quoted from *Nyāyakandalī* to illustrate the doctrine of Vaiśeṣika. Citsukhācārya of the Vedānta school, and Prabhācandra of the Jain school of Philosophy have quoted *Nyāyakandalī* while refuting the Vaiśeṣika theory. Śrīdhara can be placed in late 10th century A.D.

Śrīvallabha or Vallabha is a celebrated author of this school and he wrote a commentary on *PPBh.*, named *Nyāyalīlāvatī.* According to D.C. Bhattacharya Śrīvallabha lived and wrote in the second half of the eleventh century A.D.

Vardhamānopādhyaya, Śaṅkara Miśra, and Bhagīratha Ṭhakkura wrote commentaries on *Nyāyalilāvatī* of Vallabha. All these Vaiśeṣika works have dealt with *samavāya* and refuted the criticism against it.

1.4. *Nyāya Literature*

The *Nyāya-sūtra* or the aphorism of Nyāya is ascribed to Gotama or Gautama. Gautama is known as Akṣapāda.[29] Scholars are of opinion that Gautama, Kāśyapa, etc. are not individual names but surname or the name of a *gotra*.

Vātsyāyana, known also as Pakṣila-svāmin and Ḍramila wrote a commentary on *Nyāyasūtra*. His commentary is known as the Vātsyāyana-bhāṣya or the *Nyāyabhāṣya*. This is the earliest available work which explains the *Nyāya-sūtras*. His *Bhāṣya* is the spring hoard from whence the Nyāya theory developed. He may be placed in 3rd century A.D.[30]

Uddyotakara wrote a commentary on the *Nyāya-bhāṣya* of Vātsyāyana, known as the *Nyāya-vārttika*. By writing this *vārttika* he wanted to "dispel the darkness caused by the pseudo-logicians in the Nyāya-Vaiśeṣika realm of philosophy".[31] Uddyotakara ably defended the Nyāya-Vaiśeṣika theory from the attack of Diṅnāga and his followers. Subandhu, the great prose writer hails Uddyotakara as the embodiment of Nyāya. *"Nyāya-sthitimivoddyotakara-svarūpām'*[32] Uddyotakara might have flourished in sixth century A.D.

Vācaspati Miśra wrote a commentary on the *Nyāya-vārttika* of Uddyotakara. His commentary is named as *Nyāya-vārttika-tātparyaṭīkā*. At the time of Vācaspati Miśra the *Vārttika* of Uddyotakara was considered as a very old work and he, by writing this commentary, tried to infuse new blood in it.[33] Vācaspati Miśra's date is supposed to be the first part of the eleventh century.

Jayanta Bhaṭṭa (A.D.10)[34] of Kashmir wrote an independent treatise of Nyāya system known as *Nyāya-mañjarī*, a compendium of Indian speculative logic. Jayanta Bhaṭṭa proceeded to defend the views of Vātsyāyaṇa expressed in his *Bhāsya* from the attack of the opponents, the Buddhists and the Mīmāṁsakas. While defending and explaining the views of Vātsyāyana he has introduced new matters. *Nyāya-mañjarī* being the first independent treatise on the system has the freedom of selecting subjects and topics. He does not claim originality and humbly submits: "How can we discover new fact or truth in philosophy? Hence one should only consider our charming way of expressing the old theory."[35]

Udayanācārya lived in the eleventh century A.D. and he infused new blood in the Nyāya-Vaiśeṣika system of philosophy. Śivāditya in his *Saptapadārthī* includes *abhāva* into the categories (*padārtha*) and thus enumerates seven categories. Prior to Śivāditya Udayana speaks about *abhāva* and explains that *abhāva* is deemed to be a separate category.

The new school of Navya-nyāya might be said to have originated with the treatises written by Udayana, although Gaṅgeśa has been accepted as the father of the Navya-nyāya system, who wrote his epoch making treatise *Tattvacintāmaṇi* several centuries after (A.D. 1400) Udayana. By Udayana's time both the systems of Nyāya and Vaiśeṣika had emerged as one school. Of the five works of Udayana, the following deal with *samavāya*: (a) *Nyāya-kusumāñjali,* (b) *Nyāya-vārttika-tātparya-pariśudhi,* and (c) *Kiraṇāvalī.*

1.5. *Nyāya-Vaiśeṣika*

Vācaspati, Jayanta and Udayana have written their treatises dealing with both the systems as one. Their works have been referred to in the foregoing paras under Nyāya, though they belong to the syncretic school of Nyāya-Vaiśeṣika.

Śivāditya is one of the foremost scholars, who wrote an independent treatise on the syncretic school of Nyāya-Vaiśeṣika, which he aptly named *Saptapadārthī.* Śivāditya has also authored some other works such as *Lakṣaṇamālā, Hetukhaṇḍana,* etc. He might have flourished in the twelfth century A.D.

Keśava Miśra is the author of *Tarkabhāṣā*, a small handbook on the Nyāya-Vaiśeṣika system. The work is handy but suffers from being brief and terse. Keśava Miśra's date is between c. 1225-1275 A.D.

Gaṅgeśa, the celebrated author of *Tattvacintāmaṇi*, created a new epoch not only in thought but in approach too, in the field of Indian logic. With new terminology and new mode of expression he created a new methodology in Indian logic which revolutionised the entire gamut of logical argument. *Tattvacintāmaṇi* is divided into four parts, namely *pratyakṣa, anumāna, upamāna* and *śabda khaṇḍas*, i.e. the four means of valid knowledge as stated by Gautama.

Vardhamanopadhyaya wrote a commentary on *Kiraṇāvali* of Udayana and *Nyāyalīlāvatī* of Vallabha. He lived in the last part of the 14th century.

Pragalbhācārya is one of the commentators of *Tattvacintāmaṇi*. He wrote a commentary on all the four parts of *Tattvacintāmaṇi* and on *Kiranāvali*, and on *Nyāyalīlāvatī* of Vallabha. He lived upto the middle of the sixteenth century A.D.

Jayadeva Miśra known also as Pakṣadhara Miśra wrote commentaries on *Dravya-prakāśa* and *Līlāvatī-prakāśa* of Vardhamāna. These two commentaries were considered most important thesis in the Navya-Nyāya school. He belonged to the sixteenth century A.D.

Raghunātha Śiromaṇi of Bengal wrote a commentary on *Dravya-kiraṇāvalī-prakāśa, Guṇa-kiraṇāvalī-prakāśa* and *Nyāya-līlāvatī-prakāśa* of Vardhamāna Upādhyāya. His commentary is known as *Dīdhiti*. His *Padārthatattvanirūpaṇa* is an important treatise. Raghunātha differs, on many points, from the traditional views.[35] He lived in the later part of the 15th century A.D.

Jagadīśa and Mathurānātha are two celebrated writers on the Navya-Nyāya system in the late sixteenth century. The commentary on *Dravya-kirāṇāvalī* and *Guṇa-kiraṇāvalī* written by Mathurānātha are known as *Rahasya*. He also wrote a commentary on *Nyāyalīlāvatī*.

Jagadīśa wrote a commentary, named *Dravyasūkti* on *Padārtha-dharma-saṁgraha*.

Viśvanātha's independent work *Bhāṣāpariccheda* deals with the seven categories systematically. The *kārikas* of *Bhāṣāpariccheda* together with author's own gloss, called *Siddhānta-muktāvalī* is a popular handbook of the Nyāya-Vaiśeṣika system and widely studied. The work has two famous commentaries, Rāmarudrī and Dinakarī. Viśvanātha wrote in early seventeenth century A.D.

There is a good number of commentaries on the standard works of Navya-Nyāya and some of them have sub-commentaries. In all these works and their commentaries the question of *samavāya* has been dealt with in the traditional way with the methodology of Navya-Nyāya. The question has assumed added dimension on account of the fact that Navya-Nyāya is an empire built on the concept of relation of which *samavāya* is one of them. In fact it is called 'Relational Logic'. Yajñapati Upādhyāya's *Tattvacintāmaṇi-prabhā*, a commentary on T.C. (anumānakhaṇḍa) is an important work of Navya-Nyāya.

The discussion on *samavāya* mainly veers round the accuracy of the definition, its non-pervasion *(avyāpti)* and over-pervasion *(ativyāpti)*, non-one sideness of the reason *(hetu)*, defect of probandum, etc. of the inference of *samavāya*. In most of the discussions the original concept of *samavāya* as a cardinal principle for the emergence of the world from the descrete atoms has been overlooked and relegated to the background.

1.6. *Critique of Samavāya*

The school of Pūrva-Mīmāṁsā criticises *samavāya*. Kumārila in his commentary *Ślokavārttika* on *Śabarabhāṣya* criticises and refutes the concept of *samavāya*. The commentaries of *Ślokavārttika* have discussed the question without throwing much light on it. Pārthasārathi Miśra, a follower of the Kumārila school of Pūrva-Mīmāṁsā, in his work *Śāstradīpikā* discusses this subject in some detail and tries to strike a compromise.

In *Bṛhatī* of Prabhākara while there is a passing reference to it, Śālikanātha, his disciple, has dealt with *samavāya* in *Dīpaśikhā* and *Prakaraṇapañcikā* in detail. Nārāyaṇa in his work *Mānameyodaya* says that *samavāya* can neither be perceived nor inferred, and as such it is not proved and there is no ground for admittance of *samavāya*.

Bādarāyaṇa in *Vedāntasūtra* while rejecting *paramāṇu-kāraṇa-vāda* refers to *samavāya*. Śaṁkara in his commentary, *Śārīraka-*

bhāṣya discusses and refutes the concept of *samavāya* on two different occasions. Ramānuja in his *Śrībhāṣya* tries to replace *samavāya* by *apṛthak-siddhi.* Citsukha in his work, *Citsukhī* rejects *samavāya.* Vallabhācārya in his commentary *Aṇubhāṣya* and Puruṣottama in the subcommentary, named *Bhāṣya-prakāśa* have criticised and refuted the concept of *samavāya.*

Of the Sāṁkhya school, in *Sāṁkhyakārikā* and *Sāṁkhya-tattvakaumudī* there is only indirect reference to *samavāya* in the context of the discussion on the cause-effect-relation vis-a-vis *satkāryavāda.*

The Jaina school takes great pain to criticise *samavāya* and rejects the concept of *samavāya.* Māṇikyanandin in his *Parīkṣāmukha-sūtra,* which is after the pattern of *Laghīyastrayī* of Akalaṅka, touches the subject. It is Prabhachandra, who in his *Prameya-kamala-mārttaṇḍa* deals with *samavāya* in great detail and demolishes the argument of the Nyāya-Vaiśeṣika.

The strongest opposition to the concept of *samavāya* is from the Buddhist. None of the four schools of Buddhist philosophy admits relation, and, as such, all of them oppose *samavāya.* In *Samabandha-parīkṣā* of Aśoka[37] the very concept of relation is criticised and rejected. Following Diṅnāga Dharmakīrtti[38] criticises and rejects relation and for that reason *samavāya* stands rejected. Śāntarakṣita in his *Tattvasaṁgraha* and Kamalśīla in his commentary, *Tattvasaṁgraha-pañjikā,* on the said, criticise *samavāya* and refute all the arguments of the Nyāya-Vaiśeṣika.

1.7. *Survey of the Works: Works Already Done*

There is so far no complete study on the concept of *samavāya* in all its aspects, the origin of the concept, the development and changes it had undergone, its critique and defence, etc. The subject is casually dealt with by a few scholars who had written on Nyāya-Vaiśeṣika system.

D.N. Shastri in his work *The Philosophy of Nyāya-Vaiśeṣika and its Conflict with the Buddhist Diṅnāga School,* devotes a chapter on the import of *samavāya.* He speaks about the "magic of *samavāya*" and also "the miracle of *samavāya*" which make the "inherent cause to retain its essence to itself in its entirety". He further describes *samavāya* as "a unique device to meet all the predicament and contradictions involved in the metaphysical structure of the Nyāya-Vaiśeṣika".

According to him the argument advanced in support of *samavāya* by the mediaeval authors of the Nyāya system are the outcome of lack of proper understanding of the import of *samavāya*. He has not taken note of the argument in support of *samavāya* in *Tattvacintāmaṇi* and other works of Navya-Nyāya and also the critique of *samavāya* in the Jain philosophy. The dissertation seems to be weighing heavily on upholding the Buddhist view.

D.C. Guha in his *Navya-Nyāya system of Logic*[39] while dealing with the 'relation' discusses the scope of occurrence of *samavāya* and points out its difference from *svarūpa* (selflinking) and *paryāpti* (relation of completion). Since the scope of the work being limited to Navya-nyāya, the works of Gaṅgeśa and his predecessors had not been consulted for tracing the concept and the occurrence of *samavāya*.

N.S. Jhunakar in his work, *Gautama* : *The Nyāya Philosophy*,[40] refers to *samavāya* in different contexts. While giving an account of six kinds of sense-object-contact he refers to the occurrence of *samavāya*. In the course of discussion on the nature of inference he throws light on the subsistence of inherence in the entity which can be inferred. Finally he states that inherence is an inexplicable proposition since its existence in an entity cannot be logically explained with the help of four kinds of *pramāṇas*.

In Sadananda Bhaduri's work, *Studies in Nyāya-Vaiśeṣika Metaphysics*[41] though the concept of *samavāya* of the Nyāya-Vaiśeṣika literature is not discussed separately, he had thrown light on the nature and occurrence of *samavāya* in the course of his discussions, more particularly, under the headings "Whole and Part" and "Causality". He had taken great care to prove the necessity of *samavāya* in upholding the theory of whole as distinct from its parts and that of causality as a necessary principle for the Nyāya-Vaiśeṣika doctrine of realism.

B.K. Matilal in his work *Navya-Nyāya doctrine of Negation*[42] in the course of discussion on relation deals with the concept of *samavāya.* He points out the relevancy of the doctrine of *samavāya* as connected with the metaphysical background of the traditional Nyāya-Vaiśeṣika school which assumes that qualities like *guṇa*, *karma*, etc. inhere in their locus, i.e. the substance. And for their subsistence in the substance the relation of *samavāya* is conceived as a separate category by the school. He says that this proposition is further strengthened by the ontological commitment of the school such as universal (*jāti*) as different from the individual (*vyakti*), the whole *(avayavin)* as distinct from the part (*avayava*).

He observes that the acceptance of *samavāya* in Nyāya-Vaiśeṣika system is "a peculiar instance of construing a relation as a separate category".

The discussion, though brief, is precisely to the point of importance and the character of *samavāya.*

G. Patti's *Der samavāya in Nyāya-Vaiśeṣika system*[43] is the only monograph on the subject. The author makes an effort to explain the concept of *samavāya* as is conceived in the system and the importance it enjoys. The work has not yet been rendered into English, and as such, not available to the scholars in general.

S.S. Barlingey in a short essay[44] on *samavāya* makes an attempt to explain the significance of the subject in the light of western philosophy. He tries to prove his points with the help of diagrams and symbols. He has neither discussed nor taken note of any of the problems relating to *samavāya* as has been posed by the traditional authors. The essay being non-textual nature has not thrown much light on the concept of *samavāya*, as it is developed in Nyāya-Vaiśeṣika system.

K.C. Varadachari in a short essay,[45] *Samavāya : a Critique*, analyses the nature of *samavāya.* He points out the main objection to the admission of *samavāya*, by the opponents i.e. the defect of *ad-infinitum.* That *samavāya* is also a cause and distinct from the other causes, is also stated. The essay has not gone beyond that. It thus touches only the fringe of the subject.

Hiriyanna in an essay on *Samavāya and Apṛthaksiddhi*[46] deals with one aspect of *samavāya.* He poses the question if *samavāya* can be accepted as an entirely internal relation? He had taken great pain to prove his point that though the traditional writers on Indian philosophical systems have held *samavāya* as an internal relation different from *saṁyoga,* it has also certain characteristics of an external relation.

Bodas in his introduction to *Tarkasaṁgraha*[47] writes a few paragraphs and points out the salient features of the subject. In an explanatory note he terms *samavāya* as "the corner stone of the Nyāya philosophy". He observes that it is *samavāya* that explains the phenomenon of causality as conceived by the Naiyāyikas.

The discussion of *samavāya* by S.C. Vidyābhūṣaṇa,[48] S. Radhakrishnan,[49] S.N. Dasgupta[50] and by a few others in their works on the history of Indian philosophy is of preliminary nature.

It is stated in "the scope of the present work" that the concept of *samavāya* had undergone changes since it was conceived by Kaṇāda. New definitions along with new concepts have made it more and more complex with the passage of time. Almost all the writers on the Nyāya-Vaiśeṣika system have got to discuss *samavāya* and defend the concept by refuting the criticism levelled against it by the Mīmāṁsaka, the Vedāntin, the Jain and the Buddhist critics. To trace these all for presenting briefly, the arguments for and against *samavāya*, and also to assimilate them, means discussion of the cardinal doctrines of Indian philosophy. In view of the absence of any comprehensive work on the subject the present work is undoubtedly justified. The investigation into the subject will throw light not only on the subject proper but its allied aspects too.

1.8. *The Scope of the Present Work*

The edifice of Nyāya-Vaiśeṣika system, the theory of the objective reality of the world and its emergence from the atoms stand on admission of *samavāya* as one of the categories distinct from the others. Therefore, an in-depth study of the subject is of importance to the study and understanding the doctrine of Nyāya-Vaiśeṣika philosophy.

The concept of *samavāya* is a unique one, which, as I have pointed out elsewhere is not acceptable to other systems of Indian philosophy including that of Buddhist and Jaina. All of them have challenged the concept of *samavāya* and attacked Nyāya-Vaiśeṣika stand. The Buddhist, who does not admit relation, offered the strongest criticism. The Jaina, though is not averse to relation, does not admit *samavāya*.. He also rejects the concept of *samavāya* with vehement objection. The Mīmāṁsaka, the Sāṁkhya and the Vedāntin also criticise *samavāya*. The Nyāya-Vaiśeṣika had to defend their fort from the onslaught by their opponents. In the process new concept, new ideas have been added to the original one.

The concept of *samavāya* seems to have originated in connection with the theory of causation. That *samavāya* explains that an effect subsists in the cause. The theory of causation as inunciated in Nyāya-Vaiśeṣika is closely connected with the concept of *samavāya*, hence a brief discussion of the theory of causation is necessary for proper understanding of the subject.

According to Nyāya-Vaiśeṣika *samavāya* subsists in the part and the whole, and both are related through *samavāya*. The unique position maintained by the Nyāya-Vaiśeṣika as to the existence of a separate identity of the whole, quite distinct from the parts, in which it resides, can only be explained with the help of *samavāya*. In view of this position the concept of whole as visualised and supported by the Nyāya-Vaiśeṣika, and its critique by the Buddhist, had got to be discussed in some detail. The discussion of the concept of the whole has become all the more important for the reason that without the admission of *samavāya* the concept of whole becomes illogical.

It is a fact that once the relation of *samavāya* is established in respect to the causation theory, its scope is extended to the subsistence of quality, movement and the universal in their respective locus. This involves the relation between the universal and the individual. In fact the concept of universal, according to Nyāya-Vaiśeṣika, is dependent upon the concept of *samavāya*. The Buddhist by their opposition to *samavāya* refuses to admit the concept of whole (*avayavin*). The Mīmāṁsaka like the Buddhist is equally emphatic in repudiating the concept of *samavāya*, but unlike the Buddhist he admits *samavāya* or *jāti* (universal). Thus he strikes a middle parth and maintains that while the universal *(jāti)* is identical with the individual (*vyakti*) it also differs from the individual. By admitting the identity-cum-difference of the two, the Mīmāṁsaka does away with the concept of *samavāya*. This aspect is discussed in the said background.

The relation of the word and meaning has been discussed in the light of the school of grammar. The nature of relation that exists between the word and the object of its connotation has been defined differently by the Naiyāyika and the Mīmāṁsaka. The Buddhist seeks to replace that relation by the theory of *apoha* (exclusion). Since this aspect means relation, some discussion of it, seems well within the scope of the present dissertation. In fact, the concept of relation and the refutation of relation by the Buddhist are dealt with only to that extent as the subject demands.

The scope of the present work is thus wide enough to be covered by a work of single dissertation. However, those subjects and the aspects of the subjects having direct bearing on the investigation proper, have been brought in for discussion, while other aspects simply referred to.

Coming to the subject proper it may be said that the development of, and the change in the concept of *samavāya* is due to the criticism offered by the different schools. This is a historical process. Attempt has been made to trace the development of the original concept of *samavāya* in historical perspective, which will reveal the debate that was going on in the field of philosophical thoughts by the scholars during the period of more than one thousand years beginning from Kaṇāda to Gaṅgeśa on one side, and Nāgārjuna to Kamalśīla on the other side.

In the present work while the arguments in support of *samavāya* have been summarised from a large number of works on Nyāya-Vaiśeṣika system the critique of *samavāya* by the Jaina and the Buddhist are given somewhat in greater detail.

In the course of discussion while picking up the main points of the opposing views the soundness or otherwise of the respective arguments has been stated. The stand of the Nyāya-Vaiśeṣika with regard to *samavāya* and the ground of compelling necessity for its admission are mentioned in the conclusion.

Notes and References

1. "nastiko vedanindakah"—*MS*.2.11
Bhīmācārya in Nyāyakoṣa terms those who believe in other world (paralokādyastitvavādī) as *āstika*, and those who do not follow the path of Vedas (vedamārgam ananurundhānāḥ) as *nāstika*. Kumārila in *Tantravarttika* (1.3.4) expresses similar views.
2. "The longer I have studied the various systems, the more have I become impressed with the truth of the view taken by Vijñānabhikṣu and others that there is behind the variety of the six systems a common fund what may be called national or popular philosophy, a large Mānasa Lake of philosophical thought and language far away in the distant North and in the distant past, from which each thinker was allowed to draw for his own purpose."
—Maxmüller, S.S.P. XVII
3. IP. Vol. II, p.25
4. nāmarūpa-vinirmuktaṁ yasmin saṁtiṣṭhate jagat /
tamāhuḥ prakṛtiṁ kecin māyāmanye pare tvaṇum //
—Quoted by *Vijñānabhikṣu* from *Bṛhadvāsiṣṭha* in *YV*.
5. bauddhā buddha iti pramāṇapaṭavaḥ kartteti naiyāyikāḥ. —*Mah. S.*
6. trayī cānvīkṣikī caiva vārttā ca bharatarṣabha /
daṇḍanītiśca vipulā vidyāstatra nidarśitāḥ // —*MBh*. S.P. 59.33.
7. ānvīkṣikī trayī vārttā daṇḍanitis tathaiva ca /
evaṃ vyāhṛtayaścāsan praṇavo hyasyodāhṛtaḥ // —*Bha*. 3.12.44.
8. ānvīkṣikī-trayī-vārttā-daṇḍanītiśceti vidyāh / —*As*. 1.2.
9. —sāṁkhyaṁ yogaṁ lokayātañceti ānvīkṣikī / —Ibid.
S.N. Dasgupta interprets Kauṭilya's definition as "Sāṁkhya, Yoga, Lokāyata and Ānvīkṣikī are four systems of philosophy". He further explains his point by saying that at Kauṭilyas's time Nyāya was composed of philosophy and logic. "The fact that Kauṭilya was not satisfied by counting *ānvīkṣikī* as one of the four *vidyās* but also named it as one of the philosophies side by side with Sāṁkhya seems to lead to the presumption that probably even in Kauṭilya's time Nyāya was composed of two branches, one as *adhyātma-vidyā* and another as science of logic or rather of debate." *HIP*., p. 278. D.N. Shastri considers it as a misunderstanding of a simple passage by Prof. Dasgupta. See. Ph. Ny. V. p. 90. fn. 37.
10. *Original Sanskrit Texts*, Vol. iii, p. 133.
11. Jacobi, *Date of Philosophical sutras of Brahmanas*, *JAOS*, 1911. also:
    (a) Bodas, *A Historical Survey of Indian Logic*, printed as Introduction to *Tarka-saṁgraha*.
    (b) Stcherbatsky, *Epistemology and Logic as thought by Later Buddhists*.
    (c) Faddegon, *The Vaiśeṣika System*, 1918.
    (d) Keith, *Indian Logic and Atomism*, 1921.

(e) Vidyābhūṣaṇa, S.C., *A History of Indian Logic*, 1921.
(f) Kabiraj, G.N., *History and Bibliography of Nyāya-Vaiśeṣika Literature*, S.B. Studies, Vols. III, IV, V & VII.
(g) Randle, *Indian Logic in Early Schools*, 1930.

12. *PNYVa.*
13. The *Mahābhārata* describes Nārada as proficient in Nyāya and some other topics, including *samavāya*.
nyāyavid dharma-tattvajña ṣadaṅgavidanuttamḥ /
aikya-saṁyoga-nānārtha samavāya-viśāradaḥ // —*MBh.* S.P. 5.3.
14. pratyakṣāgamaśritam anumānaṁ sa ānvīkṣikī tayā
pravarttata iti ānvīkṣikī nyāya-vidyā nyāya-śāstram. —*VBh.* 1.1.1. p.2.
15. tasyāḥ pṛthak prasthānaḥ. —Ibid.
16. *HIP.* Vol. I, p. 278 also, *imāstu catasro vidyāḥ pṛthak* prasthānāḥ .... yāsāṁ caturthīyam ānvīkṣikī
nyāyavidyā, tasyāḥ pṛthak prasthānam. —*VBh.* under *sūtra*, 1.1.1.
17. Ṛgveda 1.154.20.
18. Bodas, Introduction to *TS.* p. xiv.
19. (i) "The sixteen *padārthas* of Nyāya are not an analysis of existing things, but are list of central topics of logical science."
—*IP.* Vol. II, pp. 184
(ii) "Gautama begins by enumerating 16 topics, which have been erroneously are called padarthas." —Introduction to *TS.* p. xiv.
(iii) "*Padārtha* means literally the meaning of a word. A *padārtha* is an object which can be thought (*artha*) and named (*pada*). All things which can be cognised and named, in short, all sort of experience and not merely the things of the physical world, are *padārthas*."
—*IP.* Vol. III, pp.184
20. *KS.* VIII, 2.3.
21. astyanyadapi dravya-guṇa-karma-sāmānya-viśeṣa-samāvāyāḥ padārthāḥ.
—*VBh.* 1.1.1.
22. *Vaiśeṣika-sūtra* is ascribed to Kaṇāda, known as Kaṇabhuk also. The real name of the author of *Vaiśeṣika-sūtra* is Kāśyapa. The *sūtras* were formulated before 300 B.C. Kauṭilya refers to the system under Ānvīkṣikī. See *Indian Philosophy*, Vol. II. pp. 177-180.
23. See, Ibid. p. 177.
24. *BS. Śāṁkarabhāṣya*, 1.
25. *Padārtha-dharma-saṁgraha* is placed in the fourth century A.D. See, Dasgupta, *History of Indian Philosophy*, Vol. I, p. 351; *ILA*, pp. 25 and 93; Ui, *Vaiśeṣika Philosophy*, p. 17, n. 3; Bodas, *Tarkasaṁgraha*, p. xxxvii.
26. *Rāvaṇabhāṣya* and *Bhāradvāja-vṛtti* are the two works referred to in *Prakaṭārtha-vivaraṇa*.
27. *A primer of Indian Logic*, pp. xxvi-vii.
cf. prāyeṇaiva hi mīmāṁsā loke lokāyatīkṛtā /

tāmāstikya-pathi kartum ayaṁ yatnaḥ kṛto mayā //

—*Mimāṁsā-śloka-vārttika*, i.i.10.

28. siddhānteṣu maheśa eṣa niyato nyāye'kṣapādo muniḥ
gambhīre ca kaṇāśinastu kaṇabhuk śāstre śrutau jaiminiḥ
sarvajñaḥ sphuṭameṣa ko'pi bhagavān anyaḥ kṣitau śaṁkaraḥ
dhatte kiṁtu na śāntadhīr viṣamadṛg raudraṁ vapuḥ kevalam.
—Quoted in the introduction (Hindi) *to Prameyakamala mārttannḍa*, pp. 9-10
29. There are controversies regarding identification of Gautama. S.C. Vidyabhusana believes that Gautama wrote only the first chapter of *Nyaya-sūtra* and he is identified with the author of a *Dharma-Sūtra*.
30. Regarding the date of Vātsyāyana, see *His. I.Ph.*
31. kutārkikājñāna-nivṛttihetuḥ. —*Ny. Va.* .1.1.1
kutārkika has been identified as Dignāga and his followers by Vācaspati Miśra.
kutārkikair Diṅnāga-prabhṛtibhiḥ. —*Nya. va. ta. ti.* 1.1.1.
Diṅnāga-prabhṛtibhirarvācīnai kuhetusaṁtamasā-samuthānena ācchāditaṁ śāstraṁ na tattvanirṇayāya paryāptam iti Uddyotakareṇa sva-nibandhena tadapanīyate. —Udayana, *Ny. V. TP.* i.i.i., p. 27
32. Subandhu, *Vāsavadatta-kathā*.
33. icchāmi kimapi puṇyaṁ dustara-kunibandha-paṅka-magnānām uddyotakaragavīnāṁ atijaratīnāṁ samuddharaṇāt.
—*Nya. va. ta. ti.* v. 4, p. 22.
34. For the date of Jayanta Bhaṭṭa, see Dasgupta, *His. I. ph.*
35. kuto vā nūtanaṁ vastu vayam-utprekṣitum kṣamāḥ /
vāco vinyāsa-vaicitryamātram-atra vicāryatām.. —*Nya. m.*v.8
36. Raghunātha, for instance, holds that *samavāya* is many as against one held by others.
See J.V. Bhattacharya, 'Navya-Nyāya', *Cultural heritage of India.*
37. Paṇḍita Aśoka, *Sambandhaparīkṣā*, Six Nyāya-Buddhist tracts, ed. H.P. Shastri.
38. *Pramāṇavārttika*, with the commentaries of Manorathanandin and Prajñākaragupta, and also *Nyāyabindu* with *Nyāyabinduṭīkā* by Dharmottara. Dharmakīrtti's *Sambandha-parīkṣā* in original Sanskrit is lost; it has now been restored into Sanskrit from its Tibetan version. In this work DK criticises the very concept of relation *samavāya* including.
39. Bharatiya Vidya Prakasan, Varanasi.
40. Motilal Banarsi Dass, Delhi.
41. Bhandarkar Oriental Research Institute, Poona, 1947.
42. Harvard Oriental Series, 1960.
43. Scripta Pontifici Institute Biblica 109, Rome.
44. Published in a modern Introduction to Indian Logic, National Publishing House, Delhi.

45. Published in "Essays in Philosophy" by Ganesh & Co. Madras.
46. Indian Philosophical Studies.
47. *Tarkasaṁgraha*, notes on samavaya, pp. 96-98.
48. *History of Indian Logic*, Calcutta.
49. *Indian Philosophy Onward.*
50. *History of Indian Philosophy*, Cambridge.

Chapter 1

The Nyāya-Vaiśeṣika Theory of World and its Creation

1.1 . *Objective Reality*

The Nyāya-Vaiśeṣika is an uncompromising realist, who holds that the object of our cognition is real and independent of it, i.e. not conceptual. To the common sense the external object appears as real and that experience *(saṁvid)* is taken as the means for the assumption of the object as real.[1] Beginning with this experience the Nyāya-Vaiśeṣika puts it on logical plane and applies the criteria of valid knowledge to testify to the objects as real. The premise is, every unerring knowledge generated by perception or otherwise, has an object behind it on which our knowledge takes its definite shape. In other words, we cognise an object which is real and objective and that is at the bottom of our knowledge about that object. If we analyse logically our cognition we find that what stands as the object of our cognition is not the concept, it is something real. These reals are responsible for our knowledge.[2]

The Nyāya-Vaiśeṣika repudiates the theory of conceptualists by saying that even those who believe in ideas and not the objective reality have to admit the ideas as real which have a subjective reference to the objects. The ideas, only when stand referred to the objects, generate knowledge and not by themselves. Thus some sort of reality is inevitable, hence it is better to admit the external object as real, says the Nyāya-Vaiśeṣika.

The 'realistic' character of Nyāya-Vaiśeṣika philosophy may also be stated, according to the criteria of modern logic, from the following points of view:

(a) The epistemological thesis of Nyāya-Vaiśeṣika holds that it is possible to have a direct knowledge of the objective world.

(b) The Nyāya-Vaiśeṣika system maintains reality of the relations, such as *samavāya,* which is a distinct category in Nyāya-Vaiśeṣika scheme. It is as real as the substance. From the logical point of view this doctrine is based on realism, and it is against the concept of subjectivism.

(c) If a philosophical system concedes reality to the intrinsic entities like universal, the system is usually termed as 'realistic' according to the standpoint of modern logic, and this view is in contrast to conceptualism. The Nyāya-Vaiśeṣika holds that universal is real and this reality is based on the fact that universal is a category.

The acceptance of universal as real is necessitated for explaining the applicability of the general term. The Nyāya-Vaiśeṣika explains the applicability of the general term such as "cow" by positing the existence of a generic unity, which the system calls universal *(jāti).* The general term "cow" is applicable to the universal "cowness", i.e. where it is manifested. However, the concept of universal *(jāti)* had undergone some changes in course of time.[3]

Like all other philosophers the Nyāya-Vaiśeṣika wants to understand the world order and explains it from the premise that the experience is the sole criteria for the assumption of the objects which are real. But the objects are innumerable which cannot be experienced and analysed individually as all words cannot be derived and learnt individually. Therefore, the Nyāya-Vaiśeṣika has attempted to reduce the entire universe into a number of categories which include every conceivable entity.

In the process of finding out the basis of the universe the Vaiśeṣika has traced six different categories *(padārtha)* which are objectively real and also ultimate real. They are real not because we conceive them, or in other words, they are not subjectively real. They are real whether or not we conceive and cognise them. They are real not because we conceive them as objects, but on their own right.

2.2. *The Six Categories (Padārtha)*

The Vaiśeṣika admits six categories *(padārtha),* namely, substance *(dravya),* quality *(guṇa),* action *(karma),* universal *(sāmānya),* particular *(viśeṣa)* and inherence *(samavāya)*[4] which are real. The Naiyāyika however enumerates sixteen categories, but accepts the six categories of the Vaiśeṣika and says that the sixteen categories are included in the said six. Later on, absence *(abhāva)* has been added to the above-named six.

Padārtha (category) literally means the meaning of a *pada* (word). It has been defined variously by the scholars. In short *padārtha* means not only the object and subject of the thought, but the process of thought itself. According to Praśastapāda "whatever is, is knowable and nameable *(astitva jñeytva abhidheyatva)* is *padārtha.*[5] By the term *padārtha* Śivāditya understands the objects of valid cognition.[6] Radhakrishnan following the concept of Praśastapāda explains *padārtha* as all objects of experience and points out the difference between the six categories of the Vaiśeṣika and the sixteen categories of the Naiyāyika. The categories characterised by 'isness', 'knowability' and 'nameability' maintain their distinct character, which prevents them from being confused. Thus each of the categories exists as a distinct reality and the objective reality is covered by these categories. This means the object also possesses 'isness', 'knowability' and 'nameability', therefore, the objects are not mere forms but reals.

The character of 'isness' of a category is entirely individualistic and different from the character of existence. The existence *(sattā)* is a common characteristic which being a class character resides in a group of categories, while 'isness' *(astitva)* is the nature of the particular object. Śrīdhara explains that whatever the distinctive character of an object that is its 'isness'.[7] This 'isness' is not different from the object itself and the presumption of such a state is fraught with the danger of conceding the object as unreal,[8] while the 'existence' being the common characteristic of substance, quality and action is to be admitted as different from the real where it resides by inherence. The intention is that only on a real object the existence *(sattā)* resides. From the above characteristic it appears that the real of the Nyāya-Vaiśeṣika concept is the real which possesses self-identity, i.e., it is different from the others. Śrīdhara says that self-identity is to be construed as it 'otherness'.[9] Thus the character of 'isness' implies distinctness which the real can only possess.

The other two characteristics, namely, knowability and nameability, in fact, are not the additional criteria for reality of an object, but two aspects of reality.[10] That is, the conscious knows an object, and as such, the object is a thing knowable *(jñeya)* by valid cognition. Then the object which is endowed with the character of knowability must expose itself to the verbal expression, i.e. the name. To be precise, when an object is known by the faculty of mind it is to be associated with an expression and that is nameability. This three-fold criteria laid down by Praśastapāda for cognising the external object as the real entity puts the Nyāya-Vaiśeṣika concept of the world-order as objectively real.

The matters qualified by their attributes stand as the object of our cognition. When we cognise an object we do not cognise it as the unique particulars, but the qualified individuals. The individuals qualified by their properties—some generic properties, some qualities, activities, etc. are cognised. Our cognitive state must accord with its content *(viṣaya)* and the structure of the external world is reflected in the structure of our cognition.

When I cognise a certain thing as a blue pot, I naturally differentiate it from others, which are not blue, by cognising the blueness in the pot. In the same way, when I cognise a certain thing as a chair I differentiate it from a table and this differentiation is due to some generic properties occurring in the object of our cognition, which according to the Nyāya-Vaiśeṣika is universal or *sāmānya.*

The universal is objectively real and occurs in all individuals of the same class by which we can put together all individuals possessing that attribute in one class, as well as differentiate those particulars from the individuals belonging to other class. The class and the individual both are real, the former occurring in the latter. So also the quality and substance, the part and the whole, all are reals, one qualified by the other.

From the above statement an absolutely pertinent question arises how one subsists in another or, how this occurrence is possible? Nothing can occur in other unless the two are intimately related. Thus for proper understanding of the emergence and the nature of this world the question of relation is all the more important which we shall discuss in the following chapter.

2.3. *The Emergence Of The World*

In the history of Vaiśeṣika philosophy Praśastapāda for the first time has introduced a coherent theory of creation and destruction.[11] This creation is a continuing process of the ultimate finest to the gross susbstance through the different stages.

To the Nyāya-Vaiśeṣika the external world is a constituent whole—the whole that exists comprising matters categorised into eternal and non-eternal. Those objects which are products are of complex structure comprising their immediate parts. And when a matter is divided into parts and the process of dividing the parts is continued it will ultimately come to the final stop. At this stage the ultimate particles of matter, called *paramāṇu* (atom) which is not further divisible, remains. The process of destruction thus rests on atoms. Again the process of creation begins on atoms.

2.4. *The Theory of Atoms*

The Nyāya-Vaiśeṣika wants to translate the external world into its system. The external world is produced by combination of elements of which the atom *(aṇu)* is the ultimate particle. Two atoms combine and produce dyad *(dvyaṇuka)* and three such dyads combine to produce the gross element. Atom is not perceptible and when two atoms combine that combination is also not perceptible. When three dyads combine, the combination is the first gross element, and, by further combination of which the universe is created. The process is of production of the magnitude from the atom *(aṇu)*, which has no magnitude.

Let us explain it with the help of three straight lines. If three lines stand neither contiguously nor in the same plane but related, they will produce a thing having dimension and magnitude.

a + b + c = B

a, b, c have no magnitude but being related they produce B which has magnitude.

In the above illustration a, b and c may be taken as dyad (combination of two *aṇus*) and such three dyads *(dvyaṇuka)* can produce the gross element which has magnitude. Again, two atoms when combine cannot produce a gross element of magnitude. We may take two atoms having been combined producing something lesser than the gross element. Suppose two atoms combine they produce a line only, which has no magnitude, as shown at (A) above, but when such three dyads *(dvyaṇuka)* combine produce the gross element. Three has the plurality, this plurality is responsible for grossness in the triad, but individual atoms cannot produce the gross element. Two atoms must combine first for the combination of three.

The gross element that is produced by the combination of subtle elements, is quite different, in its nature and content, from its component parts. The elements combine and produce a new object. This can be formulated like this.

A number of separate elements can produce a single new element, which is other than, and different from, the aggregation of the elements responsible for its production.

The process continues and the universe is created, which is different from its components. Therefore, in the theory of creation of the universe in the Nyāya-Vaiśeṣika system the relation has got the vital role to play, without which the subtle elements cannot combine and the universe also does not come into existence. It also leads to the theory that things of no magnitude cannot be conceived of as having component parts, and, as such they cannot be produced. They are considered to be existents, they exist eternally, and cannot be divided leading to its destruction.

Notes and References

1. "Saṃvideva hi bhagavatī vastūpagame naḥ śaraṇam"—quoted by Śaṅkara Miśra; see, pp. 3-33.
2. *Nyāya-mañjarī*, pt. 1, p. 124.

3. On an examination of the concept of universal in the historical perspective it may appear to the earnest followers of the system that though the early school of Nyāya-Vaiśeṣika subscribed to this view of universal without reservation the latter school of Nyāya-Vaiśeṣika in order to avoid many a logical paradoxes and inconsistencies restricted the scope of universal to some extent by the introduction of *upādhi* (imposed property) which is different from *jāti* (generic property). The Buddhist attacked the concept of *jāti* and the Nyāya-Vaiśeṣika was obliged to maintain it by building up strong defence and in the process the scope of *jāti* was narrowed down. Udayana, in order to defend *jāti* lists six different situations, which prevents occurrence of *jāti*.

vyakterabhedas-tulyatvaṁ saṅkaro' thānavasthitiḥ
rūpahānirasambandho jātibādhaka-saṁgrahaḥ.

4. dharma-viśeṣa-prasūtād dravya-guṇa-karma-sāmānya-viśeṣa-samavāyānāṁ padārthānām ... — *VS.* 1.1.4
Vātsyāyana commenting on *NS.* 1.1. says:
astyanyadapi ḥ dravya-guṇa-karma-sāmānya-viśeṣa-samavāyāḥ prameyāḥ.
Of the six categories the first three are grouped together and called existential *(sattāsamavāyin)* and the last three are grouped separately and termed as other-than-existential *(svātmasat).* This may be stated like this:

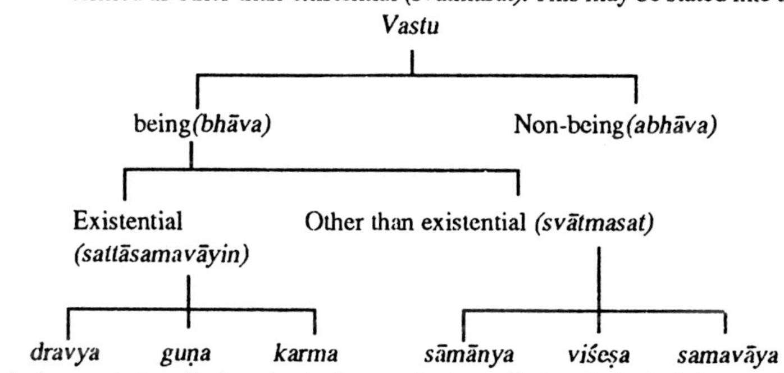

5. *PPBh.* on *K.S.* 1.1.4.
6. pramitiviṣayatvam padārthaḥ. —*SP.*
7. yasya vastuṇo yat svarūpaṁ tad eva tasya astitvam. —*NK.* p. 16.
8. na api astitvaṁ ānarthakaṁ niḥsvarūpe sattāyāḥ samavāyābhāvāt. —Ibid., p. 16.
9. *NK.* p. 620
10. abhidheyatvaṁ padārtha-sāmānya-lakṣaṇam. - *TD.* p. 2
11. pārthivebhyaḥ paramāṇubhyo dvyaṇukādikrameṇa mahā pṛthivī *samutpannā saṁhatāvatiṣṭhati.* —*PPBh.*, p. 133
tathā pṛthivyudaka-jalapavanānāmapi mahābhūtānām anenaiva krameṇa uttarasmin ca sati pūrva-pūrvasya vināśaḥ. —Ibid., p. 132

Chapter 2

The Concept of Relation (Sambandha)

3.1. The concept of relation or *sambandha* has been introduced in Indian philosophy to explain the theory of creation. The school of grammar also has its own concept of relation and the grammarians have dealt with the subject to prove as to why a particular word denotes a particular object, in other words, the kind of relation that exists between the word and its meaning. In this context the question of reality of otherwise of the external object has also come up for consideration. If the external object is real what is the relation between the object and the word that denotes itñ If the object is conceptful, how a word can denote It ?

When we visualise an object could we see the whole or a part or parts of it ? If we see only parts of it how the whole is conceived ? What is the relation between the parts and the whole ? When we see a cow, how do we cognise that is a cow ? By cognising cowness? Where does the cowness reside? In every cow or cow as a whole ? These and similar questions are intimately connected with the question of relation and these have been discussed in Indian philosophy in great detail. The question of relation has received somewhat an elaborate treatment in the Nyāya-Vaiśeṣika system of philosophy. Under compelling necessity the theory of relation was dealt with in an elaborate manner—the necessity of defending the Nyāya-Vaiśeṣika theory of creation *(paramāṇuvāda)* from the attack of the other systems of philosophy. For instance, the Nyāya-Vaiśeṣika stand has been attacked on the one hand, by the Buddhist and Jaina logicians, and on the other hand by the Sāṁkhya, Vedāntin and Mīmāṁsaka.

3.2. It has been pointed out that the concept of relation has played an important role in explaining the theory of creation as propounded by the Nyāya-Vaiśeṣika system. The relation is also a very important factor for the Navya-Nyāya doctrine of *abhāva* (absence). The Navya-Nyāya system of logic is so much dependent on relation that it is called 'Relational logic'.

> "Indeed the conception of relation is so interesting and pervasive that on account of its application the Navya-Nyāya safely be called 'Relational Logic' even in the most modern sense of the term. Anything which has most precisely been enunciated in the Navya-Nyāya has been done so with the help of relation."[1]

The exponents of the Navya-Nyāya are so much obsessed with *sambandha* that they are humorously called *'sambandhin'*, which means, literally, a related person; but in Bengali (the Navya-Nyāya developed in Mithila and Bengal) the term is used to mean the brother of one's wife. Ridiculing the obsession of Naiyāyika in relational aspect of logic a lampoon was composed (apparently by a Vedāntin), which was widely popular among the pandits.[2]

3.3. The Navya-Nyāya logicians recognise several kinds of relation which will be stated in the following paragraphs. They employ these relations to explain their theory. Usually a relation exists between two objects, but it may occur between two or more substances, between two or more classes or between a class and its members. The Nyāya-Vaiśeṣika terms the relation *saṁyoga* (contact) as *guṇa* (quality) and *samavāya* (inherence) as a category by itself.

The relation, in the light of modern logic can be explained as follows:

Suppose R represents relation, X and Y represent two entities, the two relata. The relation of X to Y will be like this.

X-R-Y = X is related to Y.

The relation itself is related to its relata as in the case of *saṁyoga;* to indicate this the following signs will be helpful.

' + R +' represents that it is being related to its relata. Hence, we may put it like this:

X + R + Y = X is related to Y, and + R + is related to X on the one hand, and on the other hand to Y.

A varieties of formula can be used to explain all the relations which Indian logic admits.

The Western logic has classified the terms as absolute general term and relative term. For instance, terms like 'man', 'red', etc. are called absolute general terms, and as against this, terms like 'father', An 'opponent' etc. are called relative terms.

An absolute general term is true of any object of knowledge: say, X, Y, Z, that is, such terms are true of the objects in all context. But a relative term is true of the objects in pair only. That is, a relative term is not true of an object, say, of X, when X is alone, but true of X in respect to some other, say Y.[3]

The relative terms presuppose relation. For instance,

(a) Father (A is father of B)

(b) Head (head of Y)

(c) Opponent (X is opponent of Z)

(d) Taller (Y is taller than Z).

It is seen that a relative term stands in relation to another term. Without being related to another term a relative term cannot convey the full import.

The relation which exists between such relative terms is to be understood in the secondary sense of the term, relation, so far our investigation is concerned. We are discussing the relation in its primary sense that relates two objects which are cognised in the external world.

4. *Relation : What It Is*

4.1. In the world of reality the objects are related and the relation between the objects is described according to the nature of its function.

> "In the real world there are substrata *(dharmin)*, properties *(dharma)* and relation *(sambandha)* each having appropriate sub-divisions. The entities combine in this world so as to produce further entities; they are also related so as to constitute what we may call facts. The minimal form of a fact, call it an 'atomic fact', if you will, consists of substratum connected by a relation to a property. The 'sentences' of the

system are linguistic entities which reflected the form of such facts."[4]

In the Nyāya-Vaiśeṣika system the relation has been explained with the help of technical terms such as *pratiyogin* (adjunct), *pratiyogitā*[5] (adjuncthood), *anuyogin* (subjunct), *niyāmaka* (governor), *nirūpita* (conditioned), *nirūpaka* (conditioner), *avacchedakatā* (limitorship), *prakāratā* (qualifierness), *vṛtti* (occurrent), etc. which have enabled the school to define everything precisely.[6]

First of all, a relation when it relates two objects, it has a direction, i.e. it may be taken as pointing from one relatum to other. For instance, when it is said that X is related to Y, X's relation is directed to Y. Thus the two relata of a relation have been specified, one being distinguished from the other. When a relatum is mentioned with its distinguished character it indicates the direction and the relation, too. In Navya-Nyāya terminology one of the relata is called *pratiyogin* (adjunct) and the other *anuyogin* (subjunct) of the relation. "X is related to Y" here the relatum X is *pratiyogin* and the relatum Y is *anuyogin.* If we take the illustration, *"Rāmasya pitā Daśarathaḥ*— Rāma with sixth case-ending stands as adjunct *(pratiyogin)* and Daśaratha as subjunct *(anuyogin)* of the relation (which directs to Daśaratha). If we take the illustration *"Daśarathasya puttraḥ Rāmaḥ"* Daśaratha is adjunct and Rāma is subjunct of the relation (which directs Rāma). The relation that obtains between the two relata in the last sentence can be specified as *"Rāma-nirūpita-pitṛtvaṃ Daśaratha-vṛttiḥ".*

Let us now examine the general concept of relation, in the primary meaning of the terms i.e. the relation that exist between two objects of knowledge the relation between a *pratiyogin* (adjunct) and an *anuyogin* (subjunct).

A relation relates two or more than two objects or in other words, it subsists or exists on two or more objects, which it relates. This relation has been defined by the different schools differently and also it is divided into a number of classes.

4.2. Nāgeśa Bhaṭṭa defines relation as : That a relation is different from its two relata, which it relates, subsists on both and has a qualified object as its content, which causes a qualified knowledge.

This is the realisation of the knowledgeable persons. For instance, when we say "there is a pot on the ground", i.e. the ground is with a pot, we cognise a relation of the pot with the ground. This relation is the relation of contact *(saṁyoga)*. This contact is different from its two relata i.e. the ground and the pot and at the same time it subsists on both. Now we have three objects before us – the ground, the pot and the relation (contact) between the two. But we do not have three separate cognitions or the cognition of three objects separately. We simply cognise the ground as qualified by the pot, or in other words, we have a qualified content of our cognition.[7]

The relation between the ground and the pot is determined by the pot. The ground is the substratum *(ādhāra)* of the contact and hence we have a qualified object as the content of our qualified cognition *(viśiṣṭa-buddhi)*. Without the relation of the contact the ground and the pot cannot cause the qualified cognition *(viśiṣṭa-buddhi)*, hence the relation is the determining factor for such a qualified knowledge.

4.3. The Naiyāyika defines the relation in his own way. According to some, the definition of relation is as follows:

(i) "A particular determinant of a qualified knowledge is called relation."[8]

The underlying meaning of this definition is that every knowledge has a content in the external world for its cognition and that content determines the knowledge. In case of relation the particular knowledge of relation has a qualified object as its content.

However, the above definition of relation is considered defective by others. The *niyāmaka* (governor) which presupposes a *vyāpti* (invariable concomitance) is included in the definition of *sambandha*. It, therefore, stands that the definition of *vyāpti* would not be intelligible, because it requires the knowledge of *sambandha* for its comprehension and thus leads to the defect of self-dependence *(ātmāśraya)*.[9]

(ii) That element is called relation if it governs a qualificative cognition (*viśiṣṭa-dhīniyāmakatvaṁ sambandhatvam)*.

The content of a qualificative cognition must have a qualification, *vaiśiṣṭya* or relation. "If it is found that some thing is cognised as qualified by some other entity, or, in other words, if in a cognition some entity appears as qualified by some other entity, then the natural conclusion will be that one is related to the other. Thus a relation accounts for their being so cognised, and hence, a relation can be said to govern such a qualificative cognition.[10]

On a close examination the above definition of relation is found to be inaccurate. Because in a qualificative cognition the relation as stated above is not the governing factor, but all the three, namely, the qualifier *(viśeṣaṇa)*, the qualificand *(viśeṣya)* and the element which joins the two (the relation) are jointly governing factors of the qualificative cognition. The reason for taking them jointly is that all of them are separate and independent concepts. The concepts of a qualifier presupposes the existence of a qualificand as well as qualification, *vaiśiṣṭya* or relation. (The relation is as real as the relata).[11]

Further, the term *'niyāmaka'* leads to complicacy and, therefore, Raghunātha Śiromaṇi prefers to do away with *'niyama'* and says that existence of relation can be defined without bringing the concept of '*niyama*' (governance).[12]

Jagadīśa also attacks the concept of '*niyama*' and says that in the relation which is beyond perception, the factor of governing the cognition becomes impossible *(atīndriya-sambandhe janakatva-rūpa-niyāmakatvāsambhavāt)*. Therefore another definition of relation is given:

(iii) That element is the relation if that is the object of a qualificative cognition and at the same time is neither qualifier nor a qualificand.

Though this definition seems to be perfect and convincing it also exposes itself to the criticism of self dependence *(ātmāśraya)*. Because without taking recourse to the qualification *(vaiśiṣṭya)* qualificative cognition is not possible.

In order to obviate these difficulties Jagadīśa has defined *sambandha* in a different phraseology. His definition is:

(iv) That relation is contentness *(viṣayatā)* other than qualificandness *(viśeṣyatā)* and the qualifierness *(viśeṣaṇatā)* of a qualified knowledge *(viśiṣṭadhī)*.[13]

The object of this definition is to exclude the qualificand *(viśeṣya)* and the qualifier *(viśeṣaṇa)* from the content of the qualified knowledge *(viśiṣṭadhī)*. (However, in case of an erroneous cognition this definition will be found inadequate. To avoid this some scholars want to insert 'valid knowledge' in place of 'knowledge' and others still revise the definition).

In the example of "daṇḍī puruṣaḥ" (the man is with the staff) the meaning is this that the man is qualified by the staff and hence the knowledge of that man also is a qualified knowledge *(viśiṣṭadhī)*. Here three objects are the contents of qualified knowledge, namely, the man, the staff and the relation of the man with the staff. If the man, the qualificand *(viśeṣya)*, the staff, the qualifier *(viśeṣaṇa)* are excluded, as they stand without being related from the content of the qualified knowledge, only the relation exists between the two and remains as the content of the qualified knowledge. Hence in a qualified knowledge the relation is the content of cognition.

4.4. But whether the relation is a real entity, as real as the objects it relates ? Views differ on this question. According to the Nyāya-Vaiśeṣika school the relation between two facts is a third unit possessing reality and existence, but the further relation between this third unit on both its sides and the two objects connected by it, has no separate existence; it possesses *svarūpasattā* (self-same existence) which is *viśeṣaṇa-viśeṣyabhāva* (qualifier-qualificandness) but not the universal existence *(sattā-sāmānya)*.

That an inference is based on relational construction is pointed out by Stcherbatsky as follows: An inference is nothing but the necessary inter-relation between two facts and their necessary reference to a point of reality. The inter-relation of three terms of an inference has been settled by the theory of the three aspects of the logical reason. They are the formal conditions which every logical reason must necessarily satisfy. But we are not told either in what inter-relation consists, nor whether the relations themselves are real, as real as the objects inter-related; or whether they are added to objects by our productive imagination. What indeed are relations to the things related? Are they something or are they nothing ? If they are something they must represent a third unity between the two units related. If they are nothing, the two things will remain unrelated, there will be between them no real relation at all.[14]

He further quotes Bradley: "If relations are facts that exist between facts, then what comes between the relations and other facts ? The real truth is, that units on one side, and on the other side, the relation existing between them, are nothing actual."[15]

5. *The Types of Relation*

5.1. It has been pointed out that relation may be classified as primary relation and secondary relation, i.e. a relation in its primary sense and secondary sense. In the previous paragraphs we have pointed out that some of the terms are relative and as such the objects denoted by them are supposed to be relative. These are the cases of relation in the secondary sense of the term and they are innumerable.[16] Each and every object may be considered as related to some other object or is a component part of a relation, and since the number of objects of knowledge is unlimited the relation between them is bound to be unlimited. The relation is usually divided into two groups according to the nature of its occurrence, viz.

(a) *Vṛttiniyāmaka* or occurrrence-exacting, and

(b) *Vṛttyaniyāmaka* or non-occurence-exacting.

D.C. Guha in his *Navya-Nyāya System of Logic* speaks about these two types of relation and includes *viśeṣaṇatā* (qualification) relation, *saṁyoga* (contact), *samavāya* (inherence) and *tādātmya* (the relation of identity) in *vṛttiniyāmaka* category. He states that these are the relations in the primary sense of the term.[17] At the same breath he states "the relation of identity or essential identity *(abheda tādātmya)* is not an occurrence exacting relation *(Vṛttiniyāmaka sambandha)"*.

Let us try to understand the character of these two types of relations.

The first type, i.e. *vṛttiniyāmaka* means, the relation which governs the occurrence of the superstratum in the substratum *(ādhāra)*.[18] This may be illustrated like this :

'A' is related to 'B' and 'A' resides or rests on 'B'; hence 'B' is the substratum of 'A'. The state of occurrence of 'A' in 'B' is governed by the relation—this relation is *vṛttiniyāmaka*.

On the other hand, say, 'A' is related to 'B' but 'A' does not occur or reside in 'B'. Now in such cases the concept of the relation will be different from that of the first one. This type of relation does not determine the occurrence of one entity on the other, still it is called a relation because it generates qualified cognition *(viśiṣṭadhī).* In other words, it is the content of the qualified knowledge hence, it is called relation. Since it does not determine or state the occurrence it is called non-occurrence-exacting relation, which is innumerable.

The occurrence may also take place in another way. Both the relata of a relation may have a common substratum. For instance the fire and the smoke are related and both have a common substratum, in which they occur.[19]

6. *Saṁyoga (Contact)*

6.1. *Saṁyoga* is an important relation of *vṛttiniyāmaka* (occurrence-exacting) class, but it can be *vṛttyaniyāmaka* (non-occurrence-exacting) also. While a pot is on the floor, or berries are in the basket, the conjunction between the pot and the floor on the one hand and berries and basket on the other is *vṛttiniyāmaka.* For, here the relation delimits the *ādhāra-ādheyabhāva* of the two related things; the floor and the basket are *ādhāra,* the pot and the berries are *ādheya.* In such instances the *ādhāra-ādheyabhāva* is expressed by the locative case-ending. The conjunction between the palms held (together) vertically is *vṛttyaniyāmaka,* for here there is no *ādhāra-ādheyabhāva* (substratum-super-stratum-hood) and one does not say 'hand on hand' *(haste hastaḥ)* in this instance.

Contact does not mean physical contact alone. It need not be presumed that contact relation may exist when two objects are in the closest proximity. Without coming into contact physically, there may be contact *(saṁyoga).* In the visual process of perception there is the contact between the eyes and the object that is visualised, but that is not physical.[20]

That there cannot be contact between two all-pervading things, such as between Time and Space. However, Navya-Naiyāyika holds that everything rests in *Mahākāla* (eternal Time) delimited by an *upādhi* (imposed property).

6.2. Saṁyoga is one of the qualities and it subsists on a substance.[21] It is capable of relating two substances at least one of which is material *(mūrta)*. On the analogy of *saṁyoga, vibhāga* (disjunction), *pṛthaktva* (separatedness) are qualities and they reside in a pair of separate substances. Similarly *saṁkhyā* (number), higher than 'one', resides in a pair of substances or in more than one substances.[22]

The conventional examples of *saṁyoga* are:
daṇḍī puruṣaḥ (the man is with the staff);
bhūtale ghaṭaḥ, ghaṭavat bhūtalam (the pot is on the ground).

Saṁyoga subsists on a substance through the assistance of a relation. Therefore the question arises by which relation *saṁyoga*, a quality, subsists on the two relata, which it relates? In other words, what is the relation between *saṁyoga* and its relata? Because for its subsistence on the substance the quality requires the assistance of a relation, other than the self. That relation according to Nyāya-Vaiśeṣika school is *samavāya* (inherence).

It appears to be absurd that in order to be related to its relata *saṁyoga* (contact), which itself is a relation, needs the assistance of another relation. It is true, but no other postulation can explain the relation of quality with a substance and hence the assistance of *samavāya* is a must.

Though *saṁyoga* and *samavāya* both are relations the Nyāya-Vaiśesika maintains difference between the two and says that *samavāya* needs no other relation.

How inherence subsists? Is it in the need of the service of another relation? The obvious reply is that inherence does not require the agency of any other relation for its subsistence. If it is presumed that one inherence, for its subsistence, needs the assistance of another inherence then it will lead to the ad infinitum *(anavasthā)*. Of course, it may be said if *saṁyoga* needs the assistance of another relation, why not *samavāya*? The Nyāya-Vaiśeṣika says that due to the peculiar nature of *samavāya* it relates and subsists as well.

The relation is also to be classified on the basis of occurrence as:

(1) *Vyāpyavṛtti* (complete occurrence); and
(2) *Avyāpyavṛtti* (incomplete occurrence).

When the contact occurs covering the two, it means complete occurrence *(vyāpyavṛtti)* and when it does not it is incomplete occurrence *(avyāpyavṛtti)*. *Saṁyoga* is usually a relation of incomplete occurrence, because when two substances are connected the contact takes place on only one part of both the relata. *Saṁyoga* does not cover the two objects entirely; hence, *saṁyoga* is a relation of incomplete occurrence *(avyāpyavṛtti)*.[23]

(i) *Saṁyoga* is again divided by some scholars into two:
  (a) *saṁyogaja saṁyoga* (contact born out of contact)
  (b) and *karmaja saṁyoga* (contact by action).

(ii) Viśvanātha in his *Bhāṣāpariccheda* divides *saṁyoga* into three subdivisions:
  (a) The first one is generated by the action of either of the two relata which are being connected;
  (b) the second one is caused by the action of both; and
  (c) the third is caused by the action of contact itself *(saṁyogaja)*.[24]

(i) *Saṁyoga* :
  (a) contact by action,
  (b) contact from contact *(saṁyogaja) (Karmaja)*

(ii) *Samyoga:*
  (a) contact by the action of either of the two relata *(anyatarakarmaja)*.
  (b) Contact by the action of both the relata *(ubhayaspandajanya)*.
  (c) Contact caused by the contact *(saṁyogaja)*.

7. *Samavāya (Inherence)*

7.1. *Samavāya*, though relation, unlike *saṁyoga* is a category by itself. *Samavāya*, as conceived by Kaṇāda and developed in the Nyāya-Vaiśeṣika school is an inseparable relation. It is conceived as a permanent relation between two inseparable *(ayutasiddha)* things related as located to the locus. It is permanent in the sense that it connects adjunct, to the subjunct in such a way that the adjunct can never occur or exist as separated from the subject.

To understand the nature of *samavāya* relation let us illustrate it.

The pot is on the ground;
The cow is in the shed.

In the above statements one understands that the ground is the container of the pot, and the shed is the container of the cow. Similarly in the statements

The potness is in the pot;
The cloth is in the yarns

One understands that the potness is contained in the pot, and the cloth in the yarns. Here is a container-contained state, but this container-containedship differs from the above stated container-containedship. In the former the two relata exists independently and separately but in the latter independent existence or separate existence of both is not possible and the relation between the two cannot be realised unless the inseparable relation is accepted. *Samavāya* is a necessary relation of substance (whole) to its parts, quality or action to substance, and generic character to real thing.[25]

Samavāya is restricted to five pairs of entity on the basis of cause and effect *(kārya-kāraṇabhāva)*, substratum-superstratum *(ādhāra-ādheyabhāva)*, property and property-possessor *(dharma-dharminoḥ)*. They are between the part and the whole *(avayava-avayavinoḥ)*, universal and the individual *(jāti-vyaktyoḥ)*, particular and eternal substance *(viśeṣa-nityadravyayoḥ)*.[26]

Inherence has no universal inhering in it, nor any individuator individuating it. This follows from the fact that inherence is one,[27] and eternal *(nitya)*.[28]

8. *Svarūpa Sambandha (Self-Linking Relation)*

8.1. *Svarūpa sambandha* (self-linking relation is) often termed as *tādātmya sambandha*, self-linking connector. Except contact and inherence all other relations are either complexes of the simple ones, or instances of self-linking relation. This relation is not over and above the relata and it occurs without the medium of other relations *(sambandhāntaram antareṇa viśiṣṭa-pratyaya-janana-yogyatvasyaiva svarūpa-sambandhatvāt)*.[29]

The relation between knowledge and known (*jñana* and *jñeya*) may be cited as an instance of self-linking relation. This relation is also termed as, *viśeṣaṇatā sambandha,* the relation that occurs between qualifier and the qualificand.

iv. *Viśeṣaṇtā Sambandha (Particular Qualification Relation)*

This relation may further be subdivided as follows:

(a) *Kālika-viśeṣanatā-sambandha* (the temporal *svarūpa* relation)
(b) *Daiśika-viśeṣaṇatā-sambandha* (the spatial *svarūpa* relation)
(c) *Abhāvīya-viśeṣaṇatā-sambandha* (the absential *svarūpa* relation).

The first category can be noticed in the case of an occurrence of an object in a portion of time, while the second category in respect of occurrence of an object in a portion of space, and the third category in case of an occurrence of an absence *(abhāva)* in its locus. How an object can occur in eternal time or endless space and also a negative entity *(abhāva)* in its locus is explained with great care in Navya-Nyāya.

It may be stated briefly like this: everything occurs in time *(janyānāṁ janakaḥ kālaḥ),* and hence, each entity is supposed to be tied to the time by a relation, which, ontologically cannot be different entity from its subjunct. Though the time is eternal and indivisible for convenience we refer to the imposed division or calibration of Time *(kālopadhi).* Any such finite time or *kālopādhi,* according to the Nyāya-Vaiśeṣika, may be construed as the subjunct in which other entity may occur.

Any *kālopādhi* may be looked upon as a time segment of the four dimensional material world, exhaustive spatially and perpendicularly to the Time axis.

It can be realised that each entity, spatial or temporal has the potentiality to be considered as occurring in another finite entity i.e. the time segment through *svarūpa* relation. To be precise, it may be stated that a thing in a place can be related to a temporal entity if the duration of both coincides. Thus a time segment *(khaṇḍakāla)* may be the subjunct of an adjunct.

D.C. Guha sums the position: "When all entities eternal and non-eternal are supposed to exist directly in the Universal Time *(Mahākāla)* the Universal Time itself is considered as the relation without any other medium whatsoever."[30]

Kālika-sambandha (temporal relation) is again two, direct *(sākṣāt)* and indirect *(paramparayā)*. When some entities are supposed to exist directly in a portion of Time *(khaṇḍakāla)* which is nothing other than imposed property *(upādhi)* on universal Time, the particular imaginary portion of time is also conceived as the direct temporal relation *(sākṣāt-kālika-sambandha)*.

Through indirect temporal relation *(kālika-paramparā-sambandha)* one entity is qualified by another entity, when those entities reside in the same portion of time *(khaṇḍe kāle)*.

8.2. *Daiśika-viśeṣaṇatā* (the spatial *svarūpa* relation) is explained in the same way. The space is considered as finite by *upādhi* (imposed property) and the finite space in respect of an entity is subjunct and thus *svarūpa* relation. However, the atom (eternal object) cannot be accepted as the calibration of space, because only the object of limited size and magnitude can constitute this.[31]

Abhāvīya-viśeṣaṇatā (the absential *svarūpa* relation) is explained in this way: we have seen positive entity occurring in some locus, following the same logic the absence of that entity is also regarded as a single whole property occurring in same locus. In the case of the positive entities the relation may differ according to the character of the subjunct-adjunct situation of the entities, i.e. it may be contact, inherence, etc., but in the case of absence it is always *svarūpa*, which is referred to as *viśeṣaṇatā* relation. *ghaṭābhāvavad bhūtalam* (there is absence of the pot on the ground)—here "the absence of the pot" on the ground is the qualifier *(viśeṣaṇa)* and the "ground" is qualificand *(viśeṣya)*. As such the absence is identical with the qualifier and it qualifies the ground, hence it is called *abhāvīya-viśeṣaṇatā-sambandha* (absential particular qualification relation). However, if it is stated like this that "there is no pot on the ground" *(bhūtale ghaṭo nāsti)* then 'absence' will be the qualificand.[32]

The relation between inherence and its relata is also self-linking according to some school.

v. *Paryāpti Sambandha (Relation of Completion)*

8.3. The relation of completion may be mentioned as a separate relation and from its nature it comes under *vṛttiniyāmaka* relation (occurrence-exacting). Raghunātha Śiromaṇi has classified it as a separate class of relation.[33] Other scholars would like to include the same in inherence, while others say that *paryāpti* is not proved by any means of valid knowledge.[34]

9. *Kārya-Kāraṇa Sambandha (Causal Relation)*

9.1. According to Nyāya-Vaiśeṣika the causal relation is between individuals, and some of the individuals are momentary, but not all. The Nyāya-Vaiśeṣika agrees on this point with Sāṁkhya that all individuals are not momentary, but continuants. However the two systems differ on the question of relation between continuants which are causes and those which are effects.

The Nyāya-Vaiśeṣika holds that only plethora of causal factors can produce an effect, the effect is neither causal factor nor it is included in the cause. The causal factors, according to their function, are classified as *pradhāna* and *gauṇa* (prominent and accessory respectively) while only non-eternal things can be produced (effect) both eternal and non-eternal may be the cause for production of an effect. Causality is a relation between two groups of individuals coming under two classes. The Nyāya-Vaiśeṣika holds that the cause must exist prior to its effects and he defines causality as "belongingness to class which is regularly connected with an earlier time *(pūrva-kālaniyata-jātīyatva)* ". This means that the relation between cause and effect is a relation of temporal precedence together with constant conjunction.

The casual factors may be classified into three—*samavāyikāraṇa* (inherence cause), *asamavāyikāraṇa* (non-inherence cause) and *nimittakāraṇa* (instrumental cause).

Vyomaśiva divides non-inherence cause as minor *(laghvī)* and major *(bṛhat)*. The minor non-inherence cause can be illustrated by the example of "*ākāśe śabdāḥ*" one sound preceding the other sound inheres in the same ether and the first sound is non-inherence cause (minor) of the second sound. The major *(bṛhat)* non-inherence cause is the colour of the threads to the colour of the cloth, because the non-inherence cause and the effect both inhere in the same substance.

These two varieties, i.e. *samavāyikāraṇa* and *asamavāyikāraṇa* are absent in *abhāva* (absence), hence, a third variety of cause in causal relation is considered more important, which is called instrumental cause *(nimittakāraṇa)*. All the accessory causes are included in instrumental cause.

But according to Sāṁkhya theory causality is a connection between " a cause which contains the effect in a potential state" and the effect, the same cause is being manifested *(vyakta)*. For instance, the oil of the sesame seeds, here seeds are the material cause of the effect, oil, but oil is not different from the seeds, it is only the manifested form of oil in seeds.

10. *The Buddhist Rejection of Relation*

10.1. (i) The Buddhist does not admit eternal atom and the theory of emergence of the gross element from the combination of atoms. According to him the so-called atoms cannot be related, and as such, they cannot produce the gross element.

The Buddhist questions the very concept of relation. Dharmakīrti in *Pramāṇavārttika* and Aśoka in *Sambandha-parīkṣā* have criticised the theory of relation and refuted all arguments advanced in support of it.

What is meant by relation, which is supposed to exist between two entities, i.e. the relata ? Does it mean the dependence *(pāratantrya)* of the relata for their being into existence ? Or, does it mean the mutual clinging *(rūpaśleṣa)* of the two entities?

On an examination of the two alternatives, the first one may convey the sense that the two entities which are yet to come into existence *(aniṣpanna)*, by being related come into being. However, this is not possible, because when the relata themselves are non-existent how the non-existent things can be related ? Presumption of the relation between non-existent entities will make the horns of an ass or the horns of a horse related. But this is quite absurd.

If, on the other hand, it is presumed that two entities which are already in existence, are related, then where lies their dependence for coming into existence due to the operation of relation ? The relata being existent do not depend on the relation for coming into existence.

"The relation means dependence of the relata, when they are existent, the question of dependence does not arise, like the mountains of Sahya and Vindhya. In fact, there is nothing like the relation of entities."[35]

In the second alternative, the mutual clinging of the terms of the relation is not possible. Because the relata of a relation have their own individual characters and they cannot assume the character of one. If the two be taken as one, then there will be no relation at all. The relation for its existence requires at least two, and it exists in two; in the absence of the second one the concept of relation would be absurd.

10.2. (ii) *Is Nirantaratā a Relation* ?

However, it may be argued that there is nothing between the two relata which intervenes, and this state of non-intervening *(nirantaratā)* is a relation. But the state of non-intervening being a negative one cannot be the basis for a relation. Moreover, if the state of non-intervening be taken as the basis for a relation, by the same logic, the state of having intervening *(sāntaratā)* should also be taken as the basis for a relation. Both *nirantaratā* and *sāntaratā* are equally in need of the two for their existence.

Again, the Buddhist says, if the "mutual clinging" *(rūpa-śleṣa)* of the two relata is supposed to cover the both in their entirety, then the combination of atoms itself will be another atom and not anything bigger than the atom. On the other hand, it cannot occur by part (i.e. to say, clinging of one part of an entity to one part of another entity), because, the atoms have no parts. Consequently if two partless entities are said to be related the position would be like this:

The relata are related by an outside agency partly or wholly. This presupposes that one agency is in need of another agency for its relation to the relata, and that needs another, thus it will lead to the state of regressus ad infinitum *(anavasthā)*. If by "mutual clinging" it is meant that the two relata assume one characteristics also retaining their own characteristics, the very notion of "mutual clinging" will be absent. The atoms being divergent in their character cannot themselves constitute the relata of a relation, because to be the relata of a relation they must cling to some identical characteristics. Hence, no relation can unite two atoms.[36]

It may, however, be said that the state of dependence on the other *(parāpekṣā)*, a quality residing in two, may be taken as a relation. This assertion is exposed to the criticism that if this state of dependence *(parāpekṣā)* is a negative one, it cannot constitute a relation, because, a non-existent thing like the horn of an ass cannot have dependent state. On the other hand, if it is taken to be a positive entity, the positiveness of an entity not being dependent on anything else for its being the state *(parāpekṣā nāma yadrūpa)* is not a relation.[37]

10.3. (iii) *How Relation Exists in the Relata* ?

The question is, whether the relation is something different from its two relata or identical with them ? If it is said that the relation is identical with the relata, then there should have been only the relata, and not the relation at all, or, only the relation should have existed, not the relata. If, on the other hand, the relation is taken to be a separate entity different from the relata, how the relata, left to their own, stand related?

Let the relation be a separate entity, but what is the relation between the said relation and the two relata? The relation, without the assistance of some other relation, cannot be related with the relata, as the two relata are not related on their own. Assumption of the assistance of another relation will lead to *anavasthā*. Thus the cognition of relation, which is supposed to exist in the relata, is not real. Neither they can be related on their own, nor through some other relation. The relata and the relation which are mutually different, reside in their own state and they appear to be related only due to our imagination.

11. (iv) *The Word-Meaning Relation*

11.1. The Buddhist from this premise of imagination asserts that there is no real relation between the word and its intended meaning. When we say 'cow' it means something other than 'non-cow' *(anyāpoha-agovyāvṛttir gauḥ).* Similarly, there is no relation between the subject and the verb. The subject being a momentary entity (instant particular) cannot function as the cause of the verb, because at the second moment after it was born, it is destroyed. Therefore, in the instances, such as "Devadatta! drive the white cow with the stick." The subject, and the verb etc. and their relation is based on imagination.

11.2. (v) *Rejection of Cause-Effect Relation*

The Buddhist rejects the cause-effect relation also. No relation can exist between the cause and its effects because both are instant particulars *(kṣaṇika).* The cause and its effect being in the nature of universal flux both do not exist at a particular point of time. Hence, the relation not residing in two cannot be termed as relation.

However, one may argue, says the Buddhist, that in order to be a cause the entity must be in existence before the emergence of the effect *(niyatapūrva-vṛttitva),* therefore, there is nothing wrong if the effect is non-existent when the cause exists, and when the effect emerges, the cause is destroyed. In both the cause and the effect do exist at the same point of time, the position will be like the two horns of a cow. It is obvious, neither the left horn of a cow can be the cause of the right horn, nor the right horn the effect of the left horn.

This argument suffers from the defect as follows; says the Buddhist.

The relation, which exists in two, presupposes the existence of the two relata at a given point of time, and it must reside in both. Otherwise, the very character of the relation, viz. *dviṣṭhatva* will be negated.

Further argument by the supporter of relation may be like this: The relation may exist first in the cause and then in the effect, thus the relation, by turn, exists in both, the cause and the effect, and the characteristic of the relation viz. *dviṣṭhatva* is not violated.

This is just a false argument, says the Buddhist. The relation when resides in the cause is not dependent on effect, and when it exists in the effect does not depend on the cause. Thus it is being independent of either the cause or the effect resides only in one of them, and therefore, it lacks the character of "being in two" and cannot be called a relation.

Further, hairsplitting argument may be made that the relation in question, though resides in one at a time is deemed to have existed in both, the cause and the effect, since the cause awaits the emergence of the effect and the effect also presupposes the existence of a cause. Thus, the relation by residing in either of the two, by turn, fulfils the required condition of "being in two" and can be termed a relation.

This statement is not correct, says the Buddhist. The cause and the effect, whichever is awaited by the either, must be one of the deciding factors in the cognition of the relation. Now the question arises, how a non-existent (at a given time) entity (the cause or the effect) can be a factor in the process of cognition of a relation?[38] It is an admitted fact that when the cause exists, the effect does not emerge, and when the effect comes into existence, the cause disappears.

11.3. (vi) *The Cause-Effect Relation is neither Perceptible nor Inferable*

The Buddhist further reacts to the cause-effect relation on the ground that the cause-effect state of the entities can neither be perceived nor inferred. There is no other means of valid cognition. The cause-effect state of the two entities, and for that matter, the cause-effect relation is not perceptible. The fire is the cause of the smoke, and the smoke is its effect, as such, the cause-effect relation is to exist between the two. Now let us examine, if this relation can be perceived.

There may be a particular perception through which either the fire or the smoke or both can be perceived. By the perception of fire, one can cognise the fire only, not the smoke. The smoke not being perceived cannot be cognised as the effect of the fire, and also the fire as its cause. It is seen that in the absence of the counter-positive *(pratiyogin)* nothing can be cognised as its (the counter-positive) cause. In other words, if in the absence of the smoke (when smoke is not cognised) the fire is accepted to be its cause, by the same analogy, one may accept the fire as the cause of the 'sky-lotus' *(gaganāmbhoja)*. Nobody is competent to say that this is the cause of the 'sky-lotus' or, this is like the 'sky-lotus'.

On the other hand, when smoke is perceived, the fire is not perceived in that particular perception, hence at the time of cognition of the smoke the fire is not perceived. As such, nobody is able to perceive the cause-effect relation between the fire and the smoke (i.e. to say one relatum is perceived while the other is not). It is thus evident that the cause-effect relation may become perceptible when both the relata i.e. the fire and the smoke, in question, are perceived together.

There is another danger in the perception of the cause-effect relation even if the two are perceived at a time. When one perceives both fire and smoke (i.e. cause and effect) that process of perception is confined to the two objects only, and it does not go beyond that. The implication is, by the perception of fire and smoke, the cause-effect relation, which subsists between the two, cannot be perceived. Hence neither the fire can be perceived as the cause, nor the smoke as its effect.

It is to be noted that two entities having distinct shape and form may appear as the objects of a single cognition, but that does not lead to the cognition of them as the cause and effect, otherwise, the cloth and the pot will also appear as the cause and effect. It is just like the cognition of the cloth after the cognition of the pot. Both are the objects of a single cognition but they are not cause and effect. Similarly, the fire and the smoke by becoming the objects of one single perception do not render themselves as cause and effect.

Moreover, when two objects are cognised, the cognitions must be mutually different. Simply because the two objects are cognised in close sequence, the knowledge cannot be said to be one. The knowledge is bound to differ from object to object, which are cognised.

11.4. (vii) Here the Mīmāṁsaka may say the *pratyabhijñā* (recollection) may come to the rescue. The knowledge of fire and that of the smoke is not one, but two. When we perceive the two, one after another, we have the cognition of the two in close sequence. Thereafter we remember that one precedes the other. Thus, though the fire and the smoke are the objects of two different knowledges, they on account of their having appeared in close sequence, should be regarded as cause and effect.

This view is erroneous, says the Buddhist. What cannot be perceived as cause and effect by the sense organ, taking recourse to recollection for cognising them as cause and effect is highly improper. For instance, when I visually cognise a sandal wood and recollect the smell that does not prove that I visually cognise the sandal paste as fragrant.

An argument may be advanced as to the perception of the fire and the smoke as cause and effect on the basis that these two objects appear as cause and effect in the visual perception, after the visual organ is assisted by the recollection that the smoke comes out from the fire. Thus it is a matter of determinate perception *(savikalpa pratyakṣa)* and we need not take recourse to recollection.

This argument is not sound. On the strength of this argument it would be possible to assume that the smell will also be the object of the visual perception. It implies that we might have the cognition of the smell by the visual perception, because it is associated with recollection of smell. The cognition " the sandal paste is fragrant" may occur on that premise, to a person by the process of the visual perception of the sandal paste, because the function of the visual organ is followed by the recollection that "the sandal paste is fragrant". If the recollection is made an auxiliary factor for the perception of an object, then we must perceive the fragrance of the sandal paste by our visual organ. But nobody admits this. Therefore, taking recourse to "recollection" for the perception of relation is of no avail.

After having refuted the possibility of the perception of relation, the Buddhist asserts that it cannot be determined by "perception and its absence" *(pratyakṣa-anupalambhābhyām)* also. That the absence of perception, like the perception, operates in those objects which are prohibited as the object of that perception. "Where there is fire, there is smoke, where there is absence of fire, there is absence of smoke." This logic does not prove the cause-effect relation between the fire and the smoke. Dharmakīrtti has raised the question of existence of a property in an object and cites the example of the flame of the fire. He says that if the flame of the fire *(śakrasya mūrdhā)* possesses the property of the fire, it is fire itself, and if it is of non-fire character, how smoke can be emitted from it.[39]

Moreover, the cause-effect relation of the fire and the smoke can be inferred when "all fires" and "all smokes" of all time and space *(sakala-deśa-kālāvasthita-akhila-agni-dhūma-vyakti)* are included, but neither by the determinant nor by the indeterminant perception all of them can be cognised. By the perception and its absence also all these instances of fire and smoke cannot be comprehended.

11.5. The view of the Mīmāṁsaka regarding the cause, in this context, has been refuted. The Mīmāṁsaka says that an object can be treated as a cause, if it possesses effect-producing power. And the said power is not perceptible but can be cognised on seeing the effect. Kumārila asserts that the power of all the positive entities is to be proved by implication *(arthāpatti)*.[40] The most important point here is, after the cause-effect state of the fire and the smoke is known, then only, through inference, it could be known that the fire has got the power of producing the smoke (effect). But the cause-effect relation between the power of the fire and the smoke cannot be perceived. (That both cause and effect cannot be the objects of a single perception has been discussed above).

Taking recourse to inference for the cognition of the relation between the power of the cause and the effect will lead to the regressus as infinitum (*anavasthā*) or, to mutual dependence (*itaretarāśraya*). In other words, in order to cognise the relation between the smoke-producing power of the fire and the smoke, another inference will be needed. Or, after knowing the cause-effect relation between the fire and the smoke, the relation between the power of the cause and the effect could be known; this again is the basis for the cognition of the cause-effect-state of the two. Thus it is a case of mutual dependence.

It is now clear that the relation of one and all description cannot be cognised by inference. Hence, relation is not proved.

11.6. An attempt is made to justify the cause-effect relation by an interpretation of the definition of the relation. The intended meaning of the definition is that both the cause and the effect revolve round one thing, and, therefore, both are related as cause and effect. This interpretation will cover the concept of the number "two", etc. says the Buddhist. The number "two" is reckoned in one entity with reference to another, and both are factors for the cognition of "two". Similarly, right horn is cognised with reference to the left and vice versa, but nobody cognises the cause-effect relation between the two horns.[41]

The cause-effect relation is criticised further. When either the cause or the effect exists, the state of cause-effect exists, in absence of either of the two, that state does not exist. Thus, the existence and the non-existence are the imposed property *(upādhi)*. It appears that this *upādhi* is the determining factor between the two, and, therefore, what is the use of assuming a relation?

The Buddhist further questions what is the cause-effect state *(kārya-kāraṇabhūta)* ? Are they mutually different or identical? If presumed to be different, there cannot be a relation *(bhinne kā ghaṭanā)*. If identical, there cannot be cause-effect state, because for the existence of that state it requires two.

From the above postulation another argument is advanced in support of relation by the opponent. That the relation is one, and the relata are related to it. Hence the question of difference and identity of the cause and effect is irrelevant.

This view is not logical, says the Buddhist. If the relation is separate from the two (cause and effect), how they can be taken as cause and effect? If identical, how there can be the relation of contact, inherence, etc. No relation seems possible in one entity.

In the case of inherence, the yarns are the inherent cause which produce the effect, i.e. the cloth. The test of the relation, therefore, depends on the beneficial character of the cause. In absence of the beneficial character, there cannot be any relation between the two. It is be noted that the cause though helps emergence of the effect, on that count it cannot be termed as the inherent *(samāvayin)*, because the effect is yet to be emerged. Nothing can be accepted as the inherent simply because it generates the effect. If it is presumed to be so, the potter who creates the pot, will also have to be cognised as the inherent cause of the pot.

On further examination it is seen that though the yarns and the cloth are *samavāyin* of the relation they are not mutually benefactors of each other. The inherence being eternal cannot be caused by the two inherents *(samavāyin)*. The inherence cannot effect anything in those two inherents, and for that matter, in other relata.

Notwithstanding this, if the relation of inherence is presumed to exist in such cases, then everything in this world, without being related will appear as the inherent of the other.

The contact being an act is to be caused, which is caused by the two relata. There is nothing to object. But simply because the contact is caused by them, they cannot be accepted as the contact-possessors *(saṁyogin)*, that is, they are not related by the relation, named contact. If it is so presumed, the action, which unites, will also have to be regarded as the contact-possessor *(saṁyogin)*. This is against the accepted norm that contact occurs between two substances *(dravya)* and not in other categories. Therefore, the entities which are united, cannot be termed as having the relation of contact simply because they generate the contact.

However, it may be said that the two entities are to be admitted as possessing the property of the relation of contact *(saṁyogitā)* on the ground that they establish contact, though do not cause it. This also stands refuted. It has already been stated that the contact can only be caused and the relata do not generate it, hence there cannot be the cause-effect relation between them. The state of being established and the establisher, which is said to be existing between the contact and the contact-possessors *(saṁyogin)* is also not acceptable, because the said state is not different from the cause-effect state.[42]

11.7. From the above discussion it becomes clear that neither inherence nor contact can be proved logically as a relation. This also refutes all other conceivable relations. Stcherbatsky says: "Causality is a relation superimposed upon reality by our understanding." He arrives at this conclusion on the assertion of Dharmakīrtti that all necessary relations are one of three kinds:

(a) relation of contradiction,
(b) relation of identity, and
(c) relation of causality.

That is to say, that everything in this world is either opposed to it, or is identical or casual. The position may be stated briefly like this:

(a) The past and the future which are unknown, on which present is dependent. The past and the future are simply notional and hence the temporal distinction is 'constructions and not real'.

Therefore the notion of continuation, that is, something did exist and will go on existing in notional.

The Nyāya-Vaiśeṣika also admits that the non-eternal things are subject to destruction. Now, by your own admission, says the Buddhist, it is the necessary characteristic of non-eternal thing, then why do you presume that for its destruction it depends on the casual factor ? It is better to accept, without depending on casual factor, that destruction occurs to a non-eternal thing as soon as it is produced.

Thus the question of casual relation has been dealt with on different plane. The Buddhist says that the things stand in a principle of future, *pratīya-samutapāda* (of dependent origin), everything is born in a chain succession.[43]

12. JAINA REPLY TO THE CRITIQUE

12.1. All the arguments of the Buddhist against assumption or relation are countered not only by the Nyāya-Vaiśeṣika and

Mīmāṁsaka but by the Jaina also. Prabhācandra picks up every point of the Buddhist objections and replies them.

Prabhācandra asserts that our cognition is the proof for assumption of relation. For instance, we cognise the cloth as being related to the yarns, the colour of the cloth as being related to the cloth—all such cognitions are due to the cognition of the relation that holds between the cloth and the yarns, cloth and its colour. In the absence of a relation we would have cognised the cloth as separate from the yarns and vice versa. Thus it is the relation, which is at the root of the cognition of such entities as connected *(saṁśliṣṭa).* Had there been no relation the atoms would not have combined and no body could have carried water with the pot (combination of earth-atoms), because without being combined, the atoms as they are, cannot retain the water.

Moreover when a person pulls the head of a bamboo pole the entire pole moves, when he pulls one end of the rope, the whole rope is pulled. In the absence of a relation the other parts of the bamboo pole or the rope would have appeared disjointed, and consequently nobody would have been able to pull a piece of bamboo or a rope etc. This clearly proves that there is a relation, which by holding between the parts, connects them and makes them appear as one.

Thus establishing the relation Prabhācandra counters the argument of the Buddhist as to whether relation occurs partly or wholly. He says that the relation occurs in certain cases covering the two entities, which you may call, occurring wholly, such as the relation between the rice powder *(śaktu)* and water. The rice powder and water are two different entities with their distinct character, when mixed the two give up their identity and appear as one *(viśliṣṭa-rūpatā-parityāgena hi saṁśliṣṭarūpatayā kathañcid anyathātva-lakṣaṇa-ekatva pariṇatiḥ sambandhaḥ).*[44]

12.2. In some other instances the relation occurs partly i.e. it covers only a part of the relata. The instance of joining two fingers of the hand may be cited to illustrate this point. However, from the above statement the Buddhist cannot say that the atoms have *aṁśa* (parts). He asks what is meant by *aṁśa*? Does it mean the character of the entity itself, or *avayava* (part) ? If the first alternative is preferred we are glad to accept it, if the second is intended, we would say it is not probable. The atom on account of its indivisibility *(abhedyatva)* cannot have *aṁśa* (parts).

That the atoms have their own character and one atom is different from the other in its character cannot be used against the notion of indivisibility of atoms, because indivisibility means "one which cannot be divided and not without characteristic" *(yato' vibhāgitvaṁ bhedayituṁ aśakyatvaṁ na punar niḥsvabhāvatavam).*[45] He says that the Buddhist postulation, "whether the relation, which is of dependent nature, holds between two existent entities, or between two entities which are yet to come into existence *(niṣpannayor aniṣpaṇṇayor vā)* " is meaningless. The relation occurs between two entities which exist in some form. For instance, the cloth exists in the form of yarns before the cloth is produced, though it does not exist in the form of cloth; the yarns also though exist in their proper form, do not exist in the form of cloth, which they constitute. The same way the two fingers exist as they are, but do not exist as the constituents of contact which occurs. Thus the relation holds between two entities which exist in some form or other. The argument of the Buddhist against the cause-effect relation is countered by Prabhācandra from a number of points of view.

He says that the Jaina has never stated that the cause and effect should either co-exist and one must succeed the other, hence the objection by the Buddhist is only a semblance of logic and has no force. What is stated by us is that if the production of an entity is assured by the presence of the other entity, the former is the effect and the latter is the cause of it, and a relation between them is inevitable. Thus some of the causes co-exists with the effect, while other exists prior to the production of the effect. This state of co-existence and prior existence can be cognised by perception and non-perception.

Notes and References

1. *NNSL.*, p. 57.

2. *bhāvād-abhavād yadi nātiriktaḥ*
sambandhibhiḥ svīkriyate padārthaḥ /
janyāvināśi-pratiyogi-śūnyaṁ
śrīlakṣmaṇa-kṣauṇīpater-yaśaḥ kim //
—MM. Phanibhūṣaṇa Tarkavāgīśa, *Introduction to Nyāya-paricaya* (Beng.).
3. W.V. Quine, *Word and Object*, p. 105.
4. *Encyclopedia of Indian Philosophy*, Vol. II, p. 48.
5. Etymologically the term *pratiyogitā* means
prati = *pratigata* or *svīkṛta*, meaning accepted; *yoga* = *sambandha* or relation, meaning inpossessor;
tā = *bhāva*, nature, thus the term stands for "the nature of being relation-possessor".
6. For being more engrossed in such polemics the main objects are very often over-shadowed or forgotten, it has been alleged. "During this period it is the hair-splitting style of writing which has engrossed the attention of the scholars at the cost of the subject matter of the system itself. Students of Nyāya and Vaiśeṣika are not aware of the entire work of Gautama and Kaṇāda and have fixed their attention on the commentaries of the single *sūtra* of Gautama—*pratyakṣānumānopamānaśabdāḥ pramāṇam.*
"They do not know what is the aim of Nyāya and Vaiśeṣika as philosophical system of Indian thought. They are lost in *avacchedakatā-prakāraratā* only."
—Umesh Mishra, *Introduction to Nyāya-Kaustubha.*
7. sambandho hi sambandhidvaya-bhinnatve sati dviṣṭhatve ca sati āśrayatayā viśiṣṭabuddhiniyāmaka ityabhiyukta-vyavahārād ghaṭavad bhūtalam ityādau saṁyogarupaḥ sambandhaḥ sambandhibhyāṁ bhinnaḥ, dviṣṭhaḥ ghaṭanirūpita-saṁyogāśrayo bhūtalam iti viśiṣṭa-buddhiniyāmkaśca.
—*PLM.* p. 28
8. viśiṣṭa-pratīti-niyāmaka viṣesaṣya eva sambandhatvāt. —Vyadhikaraṇa dīdhiti, p.135
viśiṣṭadhī-niyāmakasyaiva tathātvāt. —*SL. Jāgadīśī*, p. 252
9. nanu svarūpa-sambandhātmaka-pratiyogitvasya viśiṣṭa-dhī-janak-niyam-ghaṭitatvād ātmāśrayatvam. —Ibid. p. 255
10. The Navya-Nyāya Doctrine of Negation, p. 35. —*BL.* Vol. I. p. 246
11. Regarding perception of relation Uddyotakāra says:
"The perception of the connection of an object with its mark is the first act of sense-perception from which inference proceeds."
—What Uddyotakra means to say is that connection is perceived by the senses as well as the connected facts. —*NV.*
12. darśitaṁ ca niyamaghaṭitatvam api sambandhatvam. —*PTN.* p.
13. viśeṣya-viśeṣanatvānya-viśiṣṭadhī-viṣayatvam eva sambandhatvam iti bhāvaḥ. —*SL. Jāgadīśī*, p. 256
14. *BL.* Vol. I, p. 247.

15. Ibid. p. 96.
16. *Materials for the Study of Navya Nyāya Logic*, p. 74.
17. *Navya Nyāya System of Logic*, p. 58.
tacca tādātmya-viśeṣaṇatā-saṁyoga-samavāyeṣveva mukhyam
—Anantakumar Nyāya-Tarkatīrtha on *Jñāna-lakṣaṇa-vikāsarahasya*, p. 3.
18. Substratum means the physical entity which contains certain other entity, but the notion of it is extended to the temporal locus also. To understand the reason behind this expansion of meaning we must go to the Nyāya-Vaiśeṣika concept of physical entity. A physical entity according to this school has both temporal stretch and spatial stretch. Though the time is eternal and endless *(mahākāla)* it is referred to as divisible by imposing property on it. Such division of time is mentioned as covered by the duration of a physical entity, is a division of time *(khaṇḍakāla)* and such time segment constitutes the temporal substratum of an entity.
19. The relation conveys the sense that one thing, the attribute, belongs in some way to another thing, the subject; in the sense both Godhead and conch are attributes of Viṣṇu, who is their subject.
20. Praśastapāda speaks about six kinds of sense-object relations. Viśvanātha enumerates them with illustrations. *PPBL*. p.
BLP. Kārikā, pp. 59-61.
21. *dravyāśraya-guṇavān saṁyoga-vibhāgānapekṣa iti guṇa lakṣaṇam.*
—*VS*. 1.1.10.
22. *NV*. p.
23. M.M. Phaṇībhūṣaṇa Tarkavāgīśa states (*Nyāyadarśana*, Vol. p.) that *saṁyoga* may also become *vyāpyavṛtti* (contact of complete occurrance). Because *saṁyoga* may also occur between two ojects which have no parts or are incapable of having parts and contact in such cases must be taken as the contact of complete occurrence. For instance, when two atoms combine the contact subsists on two in their entirety, because atom has no parts, it is being the ultimate particle. Again contact of mind with the soul is another instance of *vyāpyavṛtti saṁyoga*. Both mind and the soul are incapable of having parts and hence the contact that occurs between mind and the soul is supposed to cover them entirely.
24. kīrttitas trividhas teṣām ādyo' nyatara-karmajaḥ /
tathobhaya-spanda-janyo bhavet saṁyogajo' paraḥ. //
—*BLP*. Kārikā, pp. 115-116.
25. Samavāya of generic character corresponds to the predication or membership relation of Western logic. For instance, when we say "it is a pot" we mean it is a member of the class of pot. "*ayaṁ ghaṭaḥ*" means "*ghaṭatvavān*".
26. *avayava avayavinoḥ, guṇaguṇinoḥ, kriyākriyāvatoḥ, jātivyaktyoḥ, viśeṣa-nityadravyayoḥ ca samavāyaḥ sambhavati.* —*PC*., p. 101
—*BLP. Kārikā*, p. 11.
27. samavāyas tveka eva —*PPBh*. p. 8

28. nityasambandhaḥ samavāyaḥ —*SP*., p. 51, xxxix
samavāyatvaṁ nitya-sambandhatvam —*NSM*., p. 86
29. Kālipāda Tarkācārya observes: "*vastastu nitya-sambanddhatvaṁ samavāyatvam, ayutasidhānām ityādikantu svarūpa-paricayāka-mātram.*"
—*Jagadīśa-sūktidīpikā*, p. 37
30. Jayadeva, *Tattvacintāmaṇi-Āloka*, p. 715.
The purpose for which *svarūpa* relation is assumed may be stated like this: The property of an entity indicated by an adjective is intrinsic. Such property is conceived of any substantivised term, which is a separate entity. This is indicated by adding the suffix *tva* or *tā*. This property is to be related to the substantive term by a relation, which means involvement of multiplicity of relations. In order to avoid this the Nyāya-Vaiśeṣika assumes *svarūpa* relation for relating such abstract property to the substance, except in the cases where such abstract properties are construed as of generic character *(jāti)*. *Jāti* is related through *samavāya*, because it is a separate real possessing class character.
30. *Navya-Nyāya system of Logic*, p. 65.
31. nityānām avyāvarttakatvāj janyānām eva mūrttānāṁ digupādhitayā grahaṇam. —*CTDJ*., p. 110.
32. bhūtale ghaṭo nāsti ityatra abhāvasya viśeṣyatvaṁ draṣṭavyam.
—*TSD*., p. 43.
33. *Materials for the Study of Navya-Nyaya Logic*, p. 77.
34. *atha paryāptyākhya-vilakṣaṇa-sambandha-aprāmāṇikaḥ, tat kathaṁ tatsambandhatā?* —Vyutpattivāda, p. 162.
35. pāratantryaṁ hi sambanddhaḥ siddhe kā paratantratā /
tasmāt sarvasya bhāvasya sambandho nāsti tattvataḥ. // —*SPa*. V. No. 1
Kumārila while rejecting inherence of inseparably connected entities raised this question.
na-niṣpannasya sambandhaḥ niṣpattau yutasiddhatā. —*SV*.
36. *rupaśleṣo hi sambandhaḥ dvitve sa ca kathaṁ bhavet /*
tasmāt pratiti-bhinnānāṁ sambandho nāsti tattvataḥ. // —*SPa*. V. No. 2
37. *parāpakṣā hi sambandhaḥ so' as ati kathamapekṣate /*
saṁśca sarva-nirāsaṁśo bhāvaḥ kathamapekṣate // —*SPa*. V. No. 3
38. *yadyapekṣyā tayorekam anyatrāsau pravartate /*
upakārī hyapekṣyaḥ syāt kathaṁ copakarotyasau // —*Spa*.V. No. 9
39. *agnisvabhāvaḥ śakrasya mūrdhā yady-agnireva saḥ /*
athānangni-svabhāvo' sau dhūmas tatra kathaṁ bhavet // —*PV*. 3.35
40. *śaktyaḥ sarvabhāvānāṁ kāryārthā-pattigocara.* —*SV*. 5.254
41. *yadyekārthasambandhāt kāryakāraṇatā bhavet /*
prāpta-dvitvādi-sambandhāt savyetara-viṣāṇayoḥ // —*SV*. 5.110
42. *saṁyogajanane' pīṣṭau tataḥ saṁyoginau na tau /*
karmādiyogitāpatteḥ sthitiśca prativarṇitā // —*SPa*. 22

43. This theory may, vaguely, be compared with the notion of Kant, who says: "The relation between two things one of which is cause, the other is effect, is not "analytic" since the things are two; yet it is a priori true that the first thing has an effect and that the second has a cause."

—*Critique of Pure Reason*, p. 62

44. *PKM.*
45. Ibid.

Chapter 3

The Theory of Causation

3.1. The Nyāya-Vaiśeṣika concept of realism stands upon the theory of causation of that school. The theory of causation is so formulated that it explains its theory of realism. The causation theory anticipates the synthetic principle of *samavāya* which is at the bottom for the appearance of gross elements, which are objective and real. Therefore, an examination of the causation theory will provide us the ground for under standing the concept of *samavāya.*

Causality is the universal feature of reality. That means a thing, which is real is also capable of causing something. How it causes and what is the relation between the cause and the effect has been explained in various ways in Nyāya-Vaiśeṣika literature.

The primary concern of all philosophical system is to provide an explanation supported by logic as to how this universe has come into existence and how it functions. The Nyāya-Vaiśeṣika holds that the external objects are real and these gross elements are produced by the atoms (*aṇu*) which are the ultimate discrete particles of the substance. The process of combination and their existence are based on the theory of causation.

The common sense view demands an explanation of the happening or the event that occurs, and in the attempt for providing a logical explanation for it the causation theory or the causality principle has been formulated in accordance with the basic doctrine of a system. It is like this:

That every happening or event in this world has an antecedent which acts as the cause for the production of the effect. This common sense realisation is taken as the basis by the Nyāya-Vaiśeṣika and is placed on a logical plane.

3.2. *Every Event Has a Cause*

An event presupposes a cause for its happening, i.e. the cause exists prior to the event, thus it is a priori necessity of the causality principle. In other words, the cause and events are antecedent and consequent respectively. The question arises: Can all antecedents be the cause of consequents? If not, what are the conditions that make the antecedent a cause of a consequent?

3.3. *Cause : The Sceptical View*

Cārvāka says, no. He argues that the sequence cannot establish the law of causality. That simply because one event precedes the other, the former cannot assume the role of the cause. Such sequence might be accidental.[1] Even if we observe the sequence in hundreds of such causes the law of causation cannot be established, because there is the probability of a good number of exceptions.[2] The notion of linking one event with the other as the cause and effect is due to our repeated observation, and there is no logic behind it.[3] Hume also speaks in the same language.[4]

The sceptical analysis of the causation theory and some of the arguments against it are reproduced in the *Nyāyamañjari*, the *Nyāya-kusumāñjali* and other standard works of the Nyāya-Vaiśeṣika school only to refute them. This shows that the theory of causation had been challenged from early times.The opposition by the Sāṁkhya and the Buddhist will be discussed in the following pages.

Udayana refutes the sceptical arguments against the theory of causation. He suggests that the sceptic might formulate his theory in four different ways, namely, (i) There is no cause of an event; (ii) no event happens at all; (iii) if an event happens, it is by itself; and (iv) the event is produced from nothing. Udayana refutes all these postulations and terms them as absurd.[5]

He further asserts, if an event is admitted as not caused, then it is to be assumed that the event does not happen at all or it happens all the time. In either case, the contingency (*kādācitkatva*) of the events cannot be logically explained.[6] However, the sceptic goes on arguing and the Nyāya-Vaiśeṣika counters them and asserts from his standpoints that the events are caused.

3.4. *What is Cause?*

The cause has been defined as that which causes the event.[7] Some others, however, do not consider the productive power as the necessary condition for being a cause. They emphasise the sequence and somewhat independence of the cause in its relation to the event. Accordingly they define cause as an invariable antecedent and independently necessary of an event (which is not taken up in bringing about of something else).[8]

In conformity with the definition of cause the event is defined as an invariable consequent independently necessary of the cause (which is not brought about by any other cause).[9]

In the above definition of cause one may notice two important points, namely, (i) the cause must be an invariable antecedent (*niyata-pūrvabhāvitva*) of an event, and (ii) it should necessarily exist as without being the cause of other event, that is, its existence in relation to the event is obligatory.

The cause being termed as the antecedent of an event implies that the cause is different from the effect. We can have the notion of antecedence and consequence between two things when the two are distinct and there is a sequence. It leads to the conclusion that the effect being different from the cause, cannot be regarded as some other form of the cause itself, but it originates completely anew. In other words, it is *ārambha* (origination) and not *pariṇāma* (change).

3.5. *The Invariable Antecedent*

The invariable antecedent, the cause, is not always followed by invariable effect. Had it been so, the clay would not have been regarded as the cause of the pot, because the invariable presence of the clay is not followed invariably by the pot.

Now the question arises: What is meant by invariability? It means the cause never fails to be the antecedent of the effect, or, in other words, when there is an effect, there is a cause, which is invariably antecedent. Where there is no cause, there cannot be an effect.

Another question follows the heels of the former. Is it to be presumed that the invariability of antecedence of cause is invariably followed by the effect whenever the cause is present? The reply is, no; the effect does not. If it is so, how the relation between the two and the production of the effect can be explained? The reply would be that the cause which is in your mind, is not the only cause of an effect. For example, the clay is not the only cause for the production of the pot. There are other causes too. These are also as necessary for the production of the pot as the clay is. Hence, the antecedents are classified as three types of cause:

(i) *Samavāyikāraṇa* (inherent cause or the constituent cause),[10] (ii) *asamavāyikāraṇa* (non-inherent cause), and (iii) *nimittakāraṇa* (instrumental cause or accessory cause).

An effect is produced by the concerted operation of these three causes. For instance, for the production of the cloth (i) the yarns are the inherent cause, (ii) the conjunction of the yarns is the non-inherent cause, and (iii) the loom, shuttle, etc. are the instrumental cause.

There are certain other antecedents to an effect which resemble a cause, but they are not cause. For example, an ass is an antecedent for the production of the pot (as the carrier of clay) but it is not invariable. The non-causal antecedents, such as the colour of clay for the pot, is also to be excluded from becoming a cause. Therefore, the Nyāya-Vaiśeṣika terms such antecedents as *anyathāsiddha* (proved to exist antecedently otherwise) and distinguishes them from the cause. And hence, the cause is defined as *ananyathāsiddha* (conditional or proved to exist antecedently without another factor). In order to fix the relation between the cause and the effect, *anyathāsiddha*[11] is to be separated from the cause.

3.6. *The Relation between Cause and Effect*

The invariable antecedence of the cause to the effect presupposes many things, such as, (i) the event must have a cause, (ii) the event of a particular type must have particular cause, (iii) there must be uniformity between cause and effect, (iv) there must be a sequence.

For example, the pot and the clay. The pot has a cause in the shape of clay and in a given circumstances the pot is seen to be produced in clay; now, if the same circumstances prevail, similar pot will be found to be produced from the clay; on the other hand, if all the conditions are fulfilled and the circumstances are the same the pot will not fail to be produced from the clay. This means there is uniformity, and the event and the cause are determined by each other.

The Locus of the Relation

Now one question arises: Where the causal relation exists? Between a particular clay and a particular pot or, between the two classes? The relation is between individuals of two different classes. The particulars are characterised by the universal; the invariable antecedence is between two sets of individuals determined by two universals. That is, the causal relation is between two classes, clay and the pot. The particular is cognised when it is qualified by the universal, otherwise nobody can have a uniform knowledge, because every individual is unique and one differs from the other.[12]

The underlying meaning of the above assertion is this: that a cause, say clay, being a substance is possessed of substancehood and is of existential nature (*sattā*). Now these two characteristics of clay are not uncommon. The potter's wheel has also these. Then clay cannot be the exclusive cause of the pot. But clay is the inherent cause of the pot, not anything else. Therefore it is presumed that apart from substance-hood clay has another generic character, i.e: clayness. Such generic characters are called proximate universal or *avāntarajāti.* This proximate universal, clayness is the determining factor of potness, the proximate universal of the pot. Hence the sequence is between clayness and potness. In other words, the *causal* relation that connects clay with the pot, is a connection between the nature of the cause, clay, and the nature of the effect, a pot.

3.7. *Co-existence of Cause and Effect*

The antecedence of the cause to the effect does not mean that the cause disappears as soon as the effect is originated. The cause (inherent) is real and as such exists not only for the origination of the effect but for its existence also.

The causation theory as conceived by the Nyāya-Vaiśeṣika implies co-existence of the cause and the effect and also of a relation between the two. The ground for the existence of the relation between the cause-effect and their co-existence is provided by the fact that both share the same locus. But mere sharing the same locus does not prove the relation that exists between the two, because many entities may reside in the same locus without being mutually related. Without the relation, co-existence of the cause and the effect cannot be established. For example, clay is the inherent cause of the pot, and the pot is the effect, a new entity, which is different from its cause. Though the cause and the effect are mutually different entities, they are not like the horse and the elephant; there is a close relation between the two, which unites them. The relation that relates aninherent cause with its effect is *samavāya*. Through that *samavāya* relation the effect subsists in the cause; in the case of clay and the pot, the pot subsists in the clay, the inherent cause of the pot. Thus, the clay is the locus of the pot. In that locus the pot subsists through *samavāya*. Now clay must have also a locus and that locus is clay itself. Clay subsists in its locus by the relation of *tādātmya* (self-sameness). The position may be stated like this:

'A' is the inherent cause of 'B'
'B' resides in 'A' through *samavāya* relation.
'A' resides in 'A' through *tādātmya* relation.
Thus, 'A' and 'B' sharing the locus 'A' are mutually related.

Now this relation of self-sameness of the inherent cause to its locus, in which (locus) the effect subsists through *samavāya* relation, is the determining factor regarding the relation between the cause and the effect. In other words, there must be a relation of the inherent cause with the locus of the effect, and that relation iss the determinant of the cause and the effect.

3.8. *The Function of the Cause*

That the Nyāya-Vaiśeṣika admits three kinds of cause has been mentioned above. A little more discussion on the distinct nature of the three will throw light on the necessity of assuming the three for the causation theory.

Keśava Miśra[13] defines *samavāyikāraṇa* as that in which the effect is produced by inhering in it. The effect abides in the inherent cause through the relation of *samavāya*, without which the effect cannot come into existence and cannot exist. The inherence of the effect in that particular cause makes it different from other causes. If we take the conventional example of cloth and yarns, the yarns are the inherent cause of the cloth and they are the components of the cloth; as such the yarns are both the inherent cause and the substratum of the cloth, because when the yarns, the inherent cause, are destroyed the cloth has no substratum to subsist.

Viśvanātha[14] speaking in the same tone states that the inherent cause of an effect must be a substance, while the effect may be a substance, a quality, or an action. In the above-quoted example of cloth and yarns, the yarns, says Viśvanātha, are the inherent cause of the cloth as well as that of its own colour.

Asamavāyikāraṇa (non-inherent cause) has been defined as that which by being in close proximity inheres in the inherent cause and possesses causal efficiency for the production of an effect.[15] For example, the conjunction of the yarns is the non-inherent cause of the cloth. The conjunction of yarns being a quality of the yarn inheres in yarns, which is the inherent cause of the cloth. It has its causal efficiency for the production of the cloth because with the conjoining of the yarns cloth appears and with the destruction of the conjunction the cloth disappears.

Nimittakāraṇa (instrumental cause or accessory cause) is that which is neither an inherent cause nor a non-inherent cause, but yet a cause of an effect. For example, the shuttle is an accessory cause for the cloth. The shuttle is neither the locus of the cloth (the characteristic of an inherent cause) nor it has the close proximity (*pratyāsannatā*) to the inherent cause (the characteristic of a non-inherent cause) i.e. for unlike non-inherent cause it does not inhere in the yarns, but has the causal efficiency for the production of the cloth.

An effect is produced in its inherent cause when the other two causes, namely, non-inherent cause and the accessory cause are in operation. The effect i.e. the whole inheres in its cause i.e. the components. To be inhered means, something to be contained in it and also to support it by serving as its locus. Therefore, the inherent cause is the originating and sustaining factor of the effect. From this it becomes evident that though the effect is a new entity and separate from its inherent cause it cannot exist apart from the cause. Herein lies the notion of *ayutasiddha*, the foundation stone of *samavāya*. This peculiar doctrine of the Nyāya-Vaiśeṣika that the effect, i.e. the whole is different from its cause i.e. the parts, makes him heavily lean on *samavāya*, which is the factor responsible for providing an intimate link between the two and presenting the two different entities as one.[16] Thus we cognise the whole in the parts without the cognition of all the parts of the whole, because the whole is a different entity.

The Nyāya-Vaiśeṣika does not admit that the inherent cause is the stuff matter for the origination of the effect or the whole. That is why this cause is termed in *Nyāya-Vaiśeṣika* terminology as the *samavāyikarāṇa* (inherent cause) and not as *upādānakāraṇa* (material cause). This difference in terminology from Sāṁkhya is in accordance with the causation theory of the Nyāya-Vaiśeṣika. Unlike Sāṁkhya the Nyāya-Vaiśeṣika says that an effect is originated and not emerged. Since the effect is originated anew in the cause neither its stuff nor its essence can be determined in the cause before it is produced.

Therefore, neither the yarns are the constituent cause of the cloth nor the clay that of the pot. They are considered as constituent because the cloth subsists in the yarns and the pot in a lump of clay through *samavāya*. From this it follows that neither the yarns nor the colour of the yarns are the constituents of the colour of the cloth. The quality of the effect is different from the quality of the cause. In other words, the cause does not transmit its quality to the effect.

That alone can be produced, which has a cause, and whatever is produced is to be taken as non-existent before it is produced. The intention of this is not to suggest that non-existent entities are produced, but it is non-existen' in the cause. The non-existence is not to be construed as a cause, it is just a state.[17]

In order to produce a whole a number of entities are to combine themselves, but they are to combine in a given order. Mere combination or holding together the entities does not produce a whole i.e. a new entity. For instance, if the yarns combine in a given order then only the cloth is produced and not otherwise. When a bunch of yarns is taken in hand or tied together they do not conjoin in the required order and the cloth is not produced there. And for that matter the yarns, though come in close proximity of each other do not turn out to be a new entity.

One may pointedly ask this question—why this happens and that does not? This happening and the absence of happening is explained by the Nyāya-Vaiśeṣika by assuming a non-inherent cause which inheres in the inherent cause of the effect. Here lies the logical necessity of assumption of the non-inherent cause.

3.9.A relation between two entities is determined by *anvaya-vyatireka* (presence-absence-agreement) and the relation between a cause and its effect can precisely be established by *vyatireka* (agreement in absence). The relation of a non-inherent cause to its effect is just the position of agreement in absence. For instance, when there is absence of conjunction of the yarns, there is no cloth, and when the conjunction is destroyed by taking out the yarns, the cloth disappears; thus there is a negative-pervasion (*vyatireka-vyāpti*) of the non-inherent cause in the effect. It means that even when the inherent cause is present, in the absence of non-inherent cause the effect is not produced; again when the non-inherent cause is destroyed, the effect disappears though the inherent cause remains intact. The logical conclusion, therefore, is that conjunction of the yarns has the causal efficiency for the origination and survival of the cloth. Hence, this is an important factor in the Nyāya-Vaiśeṣika causation theory.

The non-inherent cause determines not only the character of the effect, but its origination too. In the instance of the cloth and the yarn, the conjoining of the yarns, in a given order is the factor responsible for the production of the cloth, and, in its absence the cloth is not produced though the yarns might conjoin.

Another example may be taken up to explain the logical necessity and importance of assuming the non-inherent cause. Let us take the colour of the cause and the colour of the effect i.e. the colour of the part and the colour of the part and the colour of the whole. A piece of blue cloth is produced in the blue yarns. According to the Nyāya-Vaiśeṣika doctrine the blue colour of the cloth is essentially different from the blue colour of the yarns. Neither the cause transmits its quality to the effect nor the effect can inherit the same from the cause, nor the quality of the effect is a changed or modified form of the quality of the cause.

The quality of the effect originates anew in the effect and inheres in it; the effect in its turn subsists in the cause through *samavāya* relation, wherein its quality resides. Thus the colour of the yarns is the non-inherent cause of the colour of the cloth.[18] Let us take up the following example:

'A' is the inherent cause; 'C' is the quality of it and subsists in it through the relation of *samavāya.*

'B' is the effect; and 'D' is the quality of it and subsists in it through *samavāya.* Again, 'B' being the effect subsists in 'A'. Hence 'C' shares the same locus with 'B'. Thus 'C' is related to 'D' through the locus.

A question may arise: Since the colour of the cloth is different from that of the yarns what is the necessity of assuming a *causal* relation between the two? It is true, that the two are not the same but the colour of the yarns creates a similar condition for the origination of a similar colour in the cloth. If such a relation is not admitted then there would be no determining factor for the origination a quality in the effect i.e. the whole, say, colour in the cloth. A red cloth might be produced from the blue yarns, or, a coloured cloth from the white yarns. In other words, the cause material by serving as the inherent cause provides the locus of the effect, the *nimittakāraṇa* by serving as the cause efficient sets the origination of the effect into being, but it is the non-inherent cause which determines the nature and quality of the effect, the new entity.

Like *samavāya* the *asamavāyikāraṇa* (non-inherent cause) is also a special feature of the Nyāya-Vaiśeṣika school, the assumption of which has been necessitated by its unique theory of causation, according to which the whole is not produced by or from the parts, but in the parts, which are represented in the whole. The non-inherent cause determines the nature of participation of the parts in the whole. Thus, apart from participation in the whole, so long the whole exists, the parts have no special significance. We reserve further discussion on this aspect for the chapter on "Whole and Parts".

Nimittakāraṇa

Any other extraneous cause which is independently necessary for the production of an effect is *nimittakāraṇa* (instrumental cause or accessory cause), such as the shuttle, weaver, etc. for the production of the cloth. It is on the one hand different from the inherent cause and on the otherhand from the non-inherent cause. It is entirely extraneous but has a specific *casual* efficiency and indispensability for the production of an effect. Its indispensability is open to be determined by the circumstances and the nature of the effect that is going to be produced.

Some of the camp-followers of the sceptics have raised objection to this theory and questioned the validity of *causal* relation on a different ground. They say there is plurality of causes of an effect, hence cause-effect relation is not logically valid. For instance, the fire is seen to be caused by a plethora of causes, such as, by rubbing two pieces of woods, by concentrating the rays of the sun on a lense and so on. Hence we do not know which is the cause of the fire and which is not.

The above objection lies in the fact that the theory of causation rests entirely on the invariable relation between the cause and the effect i.e. the relation between the two is to be uniform, exceptionless and of sequence of time. In the foregoing discussions we have shown that a relation of this character can exist only between two individuals belonging to their respective universals (*avāntarajāti*) only. In other words, the relation is not between two particulars, but between two sets of individuals determined by the respective class-characters. It means the class-character is the determinant of the relation. But this class-character is not seen in certain cases of causal relation such as the fire and its causes. Hence the relation between the cause and the effect is neither uniform nor exceptionless. It being so, the very foundation of the causation theory seems to be shaky.

The objection pinpoints that if a particular effect is capable of being produced by a number of alternative causes there cannot be a uniform relation between the class-character of the effect and that of the cause, because the class-character of two pieces of wood (in the case of production of fire) is not the same with that of the solar rays. Therefore the relation is not exceptionless. The conclusion of this hypothesis would be that the class-character of the effect is not determinable by the class-character of the cause. It is supposed to occur independently. In other words, the antecedent is not always the cause and the cause has nothing to do invariably in shaping the form of the effect. Thus the *causal* relation is untenable.

Udayana in his *Nyāya-Kusumāñjali* meets all these objections squarely. While defending the Nyāya-Vaiśeṣika position he also criticises the view of the Prabhākara school of Pūrva Mīmāṁsā. The Prabhākara school admits *causal* relation. According to this school the relation between the cause and the effect is not variable, though this might be by more than one cause for the production of an effect. The invariable relation between a cause and an effect is maintained by them by introducing a new notion—the notion of power of the cause (*śakti*) or the casual power. The Nyāya-Vaiśeṣika rejects this saying that the remedy is worse than the disease.

The Prābhākara maintains that every existential entity serving as a cause has a latent potency or power (*śakti*) of its own.[20] This power acts behind all the cause of the production of an effect. Since this power is one and the same in all the causes of an effect, the plurality of the cause is only apparent. It is the power of the causes, not the causes as such, is responsible for an effect, and hence the relation is to be between the power and the effect. For example, one may say the fire is caused by a number of causes. Of course, apparently there might be a number of causes from which the fire is capable of being produced, but in fact neither an individual cause nor the plethora of causes is responsible; it is the latent potency of the cause(s) which we call *śakti*, is responsible.

The Prābhākara Mīmāṁsaka further maintains that *śakti* is a supersensible entity, its existence can only be inferred (*kāryeṇānumīyate*). The existence of the power can be inferred this way: On seeing an effect we infer a cause behind it and under certain circumstances the effect is produced. In other words, when the cause is present, the necessary circumstances prevail and the condition for the production of an effect is satisfied, the effect is seen being produced. But this always does not hold good. Even when everything necessary for the production of an effect, as stated above, is present the effect is not produced. The production of an effect is seen negated by the application of a counterproductive (*pratibandhaka*) agent. From this *śakti* is inferred.

Śālikanātha says: That the fire has an action, it burns. But when an antidote is associated the same fire is seen bereft of action, i.e. it does not burn.[21] Here what is taken as the cause of the action (i.e. burning), it is evident, is not the cause, because there is no difference in the fire which is seen not to burn. Had the fire been the real cause of burning, the burning fire would have been different from the non-burning fire. Hence there should be some characteristic of the cause which produces an effect. It is to be qualitatively different from the cause which does not produce an effect. For instance, the sharp axe, which cuts is different from the blunt axe in the form of sharpness.[22] But no such difference is observed in the case of the fire which burns and that which does not.

Śālikanātha says, there must be some difference, otherwise no effect could be produced, and that difference is beyond our perception, therefore, we cannot cognise it. The burning power, which is beyond perception, is thus inferred when that difference, the burning capacity in the cause of fire, is destroyed by using an antidote, no effect is produced. It also cannot be said that by the use of antidote no quality beyond perception is destroyed, but only the presence of antidote is the cause of non-production, because that will lead to the position that without any deficiency in the cause, there is no effect. The underlying meaning of this argument is this, that the antidote by mere presence cannot stop the effect in view of the fact that it does not effect change in the cause. Hence, it is to be assumed that some quality in the cause is destroyed.

If, however, it is said that the non-application of the antidote is also a cause of an effect and when it is applied the state of non-application is removed; thus it brings deficiency in the cause and hence there is no effect.

To this the reply would be; that the non-application is the absence of application (*aprayogasya ca prayogābhāvarūpatvāt*) and being an absence it cannot be a cause for an effect, because every existential effect should have an existential cause (*sarvabhāvakāryāṇāṁ ca bhāvakāraṇaniyatatva-darśanāt*).[23] The absence cannot be the *cause* for the production of any effect. Thus it is proved there is the *causal* power in the fire which cannot be perceived, but inferred. That when the *causal* is present but there is no effect, the absence of the effect is either due to the suppression of the *causal* power or due to its destruction. When casual power is destroyed there will be no effect for ever, but when it is suppressed, with the removal of suppression, the effect is produced.

The power as the cause of the effect is illustrated by further example, such as, the fire is not produced when the moon-gem is present along with the cause of the fire. The counter-productive agent neither block the way of origination of the fire nor physically alter the cause of the fire. Even thing seems to be intact. Then why in spite of the presence of the cause the effect (fire) is not produced? The logical explanation of the situation would be that the power of the cause (*śakti*) which is responsible for the production of the fire has been qualitatively effected by the power of the counter-productive agent.

It is also experienced that when that counter-productive agent, i.e. the moon-gem is withdrawn the effect, i.e. the fire, originates. Moreover, when a positive-productive agent, say, the sun-gem, is introduced, the negative capacity of the counter-productive agent (moon-gem) is neutralised and the effect (fire) is seen to be produced. Thus it proves that inspite of the presence of the cause, and other conditions being satisfied, the effect (fire in the example) at times, is not produced because the power is negated. Hence, it is not the cause, as an entity, is responsible for the production of the effect, but its underlying power, which being rendered ineffective by a counterproductive agent, does not respond, and responds when the counterproductive is withdrawn the power is restored to its original capacity. The power being one, the question of plurality of the cause of an effect is no longer fraught with danger. The Prābhākara concludes that the assumption of power of the cause as the factor responsible for the production of an effect is just a logical consequence of the causation theory.

3.10. *The Refutation by the Nyāya-Vaiśeṣika*

The Nyāya-Vaiśeṣika neither accepts plurality of the causes nor admits a mysterious power lurking behind the cause as its potential factor. Therefore the Nyāya-Vaiśeṣika offers his own solution of the problem consistent with the theory of causation, i.e. invariable relation between the cause and the effect. However, before providing a convincing reply to the question he once again pinpoints the defect in the assumption of the notion of power.

The Nyāya-Vaiśeṣika states that from the effect, if the power is assumed as the factor responsible for the production of an effect, the cause cannot be inferred. If the cause cannot be inferred from the effect a relation of uniform nature cannot be established between them. The power that lies in different causes of a particular effect must be one and the same which is responsible for the production of the effect. If it be so, no particular cause can be fixed as the cause of an effect, because the productive power is equal to all causes as regards to that effect. For example, the fire may be caused by rubbing two wooden pieces, by concentration the solar rays on cottons through a lens etc. but from the fire nobody can infer and fix a particular one among the potential causes as the cause responsible for the fire, because the power is present in all the causes. The existence of the fire, according to this view, is not precisely indicative of a particular cause for the reason that one cause is not more potent than the others. On the other hand, the absence of a particular cause will not be followed, because other causes possessing the same potentiality might be present there for producing the effect. This means there is no invariable relation between a cause and an effect.

Moreover, where plurality of causes is not seen, on the analogy of plurality, nothing can be said with certainty that this particular antecedent and not something else, is the cause of this particular effect, because invisible causes with the productive power might be at large. This leads to the position that an effect has no determinant antecedent and it can be produced by any of the antecedents. This cuts at the root of the causal relation.

Of course, the Prābhākara may go on arguing his case by saying that power is not such an entity that it will be indiscriminately present everywhere and confuse the causes. In fact, the position is quite different from as sought to be presented. When a sequence between some antecedents of different kinds of entities and a consequence is detected, and, further the causal relation between antecedent and consequent has been established, then only the power can be regarded as the latent factor responsible for the production of the effect lying in all the causes in regard to that effect. In other words, the assumption that the causal power is possessed by all the different kinds of causes of a single effect follows the causal relation, and does not precede it. Hence, in no way the assumption of power disturbs the causal relation, rather puts it on a firm footing.

The Nyāya-Vaiśeṣika is not convinced by this argument. According to him the causal relation is to be determined first. In the presence of plurality of causes how can the causal relation between a particular effect and a particular cause be fixed? The problem is of linking an effect with a cause, when there is plurality of causes. The causal power is dependent on the relation and the relation can be established when a particular cause is singled out from the rest. The power of cause does not fix the cause. Therefore, the doctrine of causal power is untenable.

Moreover, the Nyāya-Vaiśeṣika rejects the causal power doctrine on another ground. The causal power being a product of the things where it resides must be many which, in another way, is the plurality of causes. If it is held to be a non-product, it would simply be an absurd proposition. With a definite origin in time nothing can be non-caused.

The Nyāya-Vaiśeṣika offers his own solution. Sticking to the causal relation he asserts straight way that the effect of each cause is different in kind from that of the other cause. Each particular effect has a particular cause of its own, hence the question of plurality of cause does not arise. From this premise it follows that the fire that is produced by rubbing two wooden pieces is, in kind, different from the fire produced by concentrating the solar rays on the cotton through a lens. But we perceive all the fire as the same and one, because our perceiving faculty fails to perceive the distinction between them. That the apprehension of fires of different origins as one does not prevent the logical conclusion that they are different. To him who has the faculty for close observation, the distinction will appear.[24]

Further, the Nyāya-Vaiśeṣika refutes the argument regarding the counter-productive agent. That the presence of a counter-productive agent, say, the moon-gem, takes away the causal power from the cause is not correct. For the production of an effect apart from the presence of the cause, the condition necessary for the purpose must be satisfied. The absence of the counter-productive (*pratibandhakābhāva*) is a part of the condition necessary for the production of an effect. It is the totality of the condition that is responsible for the production and the absence of the counter-productive is included in the totality of the condition. That when the moon-gem is present it is to be viewed that the totality of the conditions for the production of the fire has not been satisfied. Hence, it is not to be interpreted that the absence of the counter-productive as the determining factor for the presence of the causal power and thus to make it responsible for the production of an effect.

An objection regarding smoke as the reason (*hetu*) for inference of fire is raised, i.e. the smoke as such is not a *hetu* but its invisible characteristic, because one smoke differs from the other. Udayana refutes this by saying that the Nyāya-Vaiśeṣika does not admit invisible for supersensible entity.

3.11. *The Cause-Effect Relation : Sāṁkhya View*

The Sāṁkhya school holds a different view on the cause-effect relation. The Sāṁkhya theory of causation differs from that of the Nyāya-Vaiśeṣika mainly on two points: (i) a cause itself changes into its effect and the essence of the cause is present in the effect, or in other words, the essence of the cause is the same with that of the effect; and (ii) both cause and effect, so far as they are substance (*dravya*), are identical.

In order to point out that difference in the causation theory between the two schools, the Sāṁkhya view and its refutation by the Nyāya-Vaiśeṣika should be discussed. The views of the two schools are embodied in different terminologies. First, causation may mean *āvirbhāva* (emergence) or *ārambha* (origination). While the Sāṁkhya school holds that it is *āvirbhava,* i.e. the effect is a pre-existent thing and appears in a changed form, the Nyāya-Vaiśeṣika maintains that it is *ārāmbha* i.e. the effect is absolutely a non-existent thing which emerges. Hence, the theory of causation of the Nyāya-Vaiśeṣika is called *ārāmbhavāda* (the theory of origination). The effect, the Nyāya-Vaiśeṣika holds, comes into existence by negating its previous non-existence. The theory is termed as *asat-kāryavāda* that the effect is non-existent prior to its production, because the effect is non-existent before it is produced.

The Nyāya-Vaiśeṣika says that the fiction like the hare's horn is not produced not because it is non-existent, but there is no cause of it. Whatever is produced has an antecedent to it and, therefore, in order to come into being there must be a cause. The thing whichever is seen produced, is invariably non-existent before it is produced. However, non-existence of a thing is not to be taken as the cause of production, it is simply a condition,[25] which is negated by the production.

The Sāṁkhya tries to assail the Nyāya-Vaiśeṣika position on his causation theory. He says: the causation theory as conceived by the Nyāya-Vaiśeṣika demands the causal relation, the determinate relation between the inherent cause and its effect, in the absence of which there would be no determining factor for the production of a particular effect. All effects being non-existent and in the absence of a determining relation, might be produced from any cause or from all the causes without discrimination, when the causes operate.[26] Hence, the relation, according to the Nyāya-Vaiśeṣika, is the only determining factor, and for holding a relation two relata are required. How there can be a relation between an existent cause and a non-existent effect? The denial of existence of the relation, on the other hand, would be a strong contradiction of the causation theory. Since if only one of the two relata is present, no relation is capable to relate a non-existent effect.[27] Hence it is to be admitted that the cause and the effect must exist together, i.e. both are identical in their essence.

Herein lies the difference of the theories of causation of the two schools. Since the Sāṁkhya considers the effect as identical with its cause, he does not stand in the need of the relation of *samavāya* for connecting effect with the cause. He takes both of them identical and the effect resides in the cause by its own right, i..e in the unmanifested form. The Nyāya-Vaiśeṣika holds that the effect originates afresh, which is non-existent before production, is a quite distinct entity; hence he needs the service of a relation for intimately connecting the cause with the effect. This is why the Nyāya-Vaiśeṣika conceives *samavāya* as an intimate relation for operating between cause and effect, whole and part etc. *Samavāya,* in the real sense, is the saviour of the causation theory of the Nyāya-Vaiśeṣika and for that matter all other doctrines connected with it.

The Sāṁkhya does not admit *samavāya* and he explains the inseparability of cause and effect in terms of identity. The Nyāya-Vaiśeṣika holds that for the existence of a relation the contemporaneity of the effect with the cause is not a necessary condition, hence the determinate causal relation does exist between the two. What is needed is the agreement between the two in presence and absence (*anvaya-vyatireka*). It is there. The efficiency of a thing is its class-character and that class-character produces the effect. As stated above the relation between these two class-characters is always possible and seen. Therefore, the co-presence of the two is not necessary for the causal relation.

The Sāṁkhya puts more arguments in support of his theory i.e. the cause and effect are identical. The presence of the cause presupposes the existence of the effect. To prove the identity between the two the following arguments are made:

(a) That the effect is some aspect of the cause, such as, the cloth is some sort of arrangement of the yarns. Such a notion is possible when the two are identical. No one can have the similar notion in respect of a horse and a cow, because the two are different.

(b) *Upādānakāraṇa* (material cause) is the substance stuff of the composite whole and the relation of *upādāna-upādeyabhāva* exists between the cause and effect i.e. part and whole. Such a relation is unthinkable if the two entities are numerically different. For instance, there cannot be such a relation between a cow and a man.

(c) An effect cannot be conjoined with or disjoined from the cause. A whole also cannot be taken either in conjunction with or disjunction from its parts, because the conjunction (*saṁyoga*) and separation (*vibhāga*) can occur between two distinct entities.[28]

All these arguments, says the Nyāya-Vaiśeṣika, are not at all convincing. The things should not be taken as pole apart, simply because they are distinct. On the otherhand, identity of the cause and the effect cannot be thought of. Does anybody consider a pot identical with a lump of clay? Had it been so, we would have a lump of clay for bringing water. In fact, they differ in their concept, nomenclature, structure and utility. They occur at different times and there is a sequence between the two. Thus they are different.

Against this the Sāṁkhya holds that the production of an already existent effect is just its manifestation through the operation of other causes. According to Sāṁkhya production and destruction is manifestation of the existing effect and restoration of the same to its original form respectively.

The Nyāya-Vaiśeṣika closely scrutinises the Sāṁkhya postulation of manifestation of the pre-existent effect and questions its logical validity. After all, what is their manifestation? Is it a product or not? Since it comes into being, it is a product and, therefore, is as good as an effect. Now, is the manifestation pre-existent or not? If the manifestation pre-exists, the operation of the causes for the manifestation will not be required. If it is not, there will be ad-infinitum. The argument on this point is carried on to a great length.

To all these the Sāṁkhya replies in the same vein and says that the postulation of the 'origination' also involves the same objection. The Nyāya-Vaiśeṣika, however, does not concede and points out the nature of origination. According to him the origination is a product and no sooner it is produced it stands inhered in the pre-non-existent effect. Origination having the character of inherence does not seed another relation for inherence and hence, the question of ad-infinitum does not arise.

The Sāṁkhya raises an objection to the postulation of distinctness of effect. The effect or the whole being different from the cause or the part should have separate weight. Similarly, the two entities should also occupy two different spaces. This question is discussed in the chapter "whole and part".

This Sāṁkhya asks: If the essence of the effect is different from that of the cause where from does it come? The reply would be-the essence or the quality of the effect is produced along with the production of the effect. Or, in the alternative, it may be stated that the effect being related to its cause through *samavāya* relation appears inseparable and that makes the quality of the cause (though different) to appear as that of the effect.

The Nyāya-Vaiśeṣika persistently maintains a difference in his doctrine of causation from that of the Sāṁkhya. It is for this reason the yarns are also considered somewhat extraneous for the production of the cloth.

Uddyotakara says: "The yarn is an entity quite different from the cloth, because it is the cause of the latter like the shuttle etc. The shuttle etc. the cause of the cloth, is different from the cloth, in the same way, the yarn, which is a cause of the cloth, different from it".[29] According to him both the yarn and the shuttle being the cause of the cloth are equally extraneous to the cloth: the position is implicit, though not explicit.

The Sāṁkhya asserts that a cause changes into the state of effect while the essence stuff remains the same. This raises the question— if the essence stuff of the cause and the effect remains the same where the change occurs or what the change means? Apparently the change must be in the form only, or it is unreal. This objection is anticipated and a solution is offered in the *Vyāsa-bhāṣya* on the *Yogasūtra*. It says:

"The change is in the form only (*bhāvānyathātvam*) and not in the essence stuff (*na dravyānyathātvam*)".[30] The meaning is, while the essence stuff of a thing remains unchanged its visible form is changed. When the ring, the necklace etc. are made from a piece of gold bar the essence stuff of the gold remains the same everywhere, while its utility and form change. This position is intelligible from the commonsense. But does it stand logical scrutiny?

How there can be a real change without any change of the essence stuff? Either the change is unreal or there is some change in the essence stuff also. The Vedāntin takes the clue from Sāṁkhya and says that the change is unreal. The Buddhist also criticises the view of Sāṁkhya, which we discuss below:

3.12. *The Vedāntin's (Śaṅkara) View of Causation*

The Advaita school of Vedānta holds that if there is no change in the essence, there cannot be a change in the form also. Hence the change is only apparent and unreal. Thus the process of change is not *vikāra* or *pariṇāma* but *vivartta*.[31] The difference lies in the fact that while the Sāṁkhya holds the change in the cause as the real one the Vedāntin takes it to be unreal. The Vedāntin's view may be stated like this:

If a pair of earrings are held to be the changed form of a piece of gold without any change whatsoever in the essence stuff of the gold, the change is unreal and as a consequence the earrings are also bound to be unreal. This leads to the conclusion that only Brahma is real which is the cause; the effect, the world, is unreal. In other words, from an existent one something is manifested, which is not real.[32] It leads to the *satkāryavāda* which is not consistent with the realism of the Nyāya-Vaiśeṣika. Hence, to maintain the realism of the system it holds that the effect originates afresh with new quality or essence and functions as a separate entity. It is why the Naiyāyika is known as upholder of the doctrine of *asatkāryavāda* (origination of the non-existent effect).

3.13. *The Buddhist Theory of Causation*

The Buddhist theory of causation is known as *pratītysamutpāda* or dependent origination. This causation theory, says Kamalaśīla, "among all the jewels of Buddhist philosophy the theory of causation is the chief jewel".[33] The dependent origination means that every point instants of reality arises in dependence upon a combination of point instants and it succeeds to them. In other words, it arises in functional dependence upon a totality of causes and condition which are antecedent to it. According to the Buddhist view the ultimate reality is nothing but point instants of efficiency. For the emergence of the point instants they depend on the functional efficiency of other. Thus the point instant is both cause and existence. And the existence which has no duration is described as efficiency.

This theory of causation is conceived as a consequence of the doctrine of *kṣaṇabhaṅga* (universal flux) of everything. The effect being a contingent event has its origination but the antecedents which are regarded as cause have no causality. A thing cannot be produced by another thing because that thing has no time for the motion, it has no duration. A thing completely vanishes in the next moment it was born and hence can produce nothing. But it is succeeded by another thing and, therefore, the former is called antecedent without causality. The succession takes place because something is to be succeeded. The consequent thing originates because there is the antecedent. In other words, "when this is present, this originates" (*asmin sati idaṁ jātam*).

Like the Nyāya-Vaiśeṣika the Buddhist admits the effect is non-existent and originates anew, which does not possess the quality of the cause. The Buddhist maintains that the cause does not exist for a moment, no sooner the succeeding thing comes into existence, the antecedent disappears. The question arises then what is the cause of a thing, the thing being a contingent event must have a cause. The Buddhist says—it is the non-existence. Surely a second production is not needed. Moreover, when two things are static then only they can exist simultaneously, the dynamic things cannot. According to the Buddhist, the reality is dynamic, there are no static things at all. "What we call existence they are never tried to repeat, is always an action"[34] (*sattaivavyāpṛtiḥ*).

According to the Buddhist, existence is nothing but efficiency (*arthakriyākāritvam*)[35] and what is non-efficient is a non-cause and non-existent. Kamalaśīla explains that to the Buddhist logicians (*nyāyavādino Bauddāḥ*) non-cause is nothing but non-reality (*akāraṇam asad eva*).[36] In other words, nothing but a cause can be real and whatever is cause is existent. The Buddhist for his convenience accepts two different realities—one is ultimate and pure, and the other is artificially imposed on a thing by our imagination. The reality of the point instant is the pure and ultimate reality while the imposed reality is the reality of the empirical objects. Thus one has to admit two different causality, the causality of the point instant and that of the empirical one. This means one is the efficiency of the point instant and the other is the efficiency of empirical objects. Now there seems to be a contradiction that every point of reality is efficient, and no efficiency by the point-instant is possible. The solution is this that there is no separate efficiency in addition to existence, itself is the causal efficiency. To put the lengthy and the detail argument of the Buddhist in brief is like this:

That a contingent and its origin can only be understood with reference to some other antecedent, but that antecedent does not produce as has been stated above. The effect is produced by the non-existence only. It is a pre-negation or non-entity which is responsible for the production of the contingent event.[37]

The Buddhist, by non-existence, does not mean that the effect emerges from the void and not regulated. He opposes the theory of irregulated nature of the cause as propounded by the sceptist. There is a point of similarity between the Buddhist and the Nyāya-Vaiśeṣika, because the latter also admits the effect is non-existent and is produced *de-novo* and this appears to be similar with the doctrine of production *ex-nihilo*. However, this similarity does not prove to be identical on the scrutiny of logic. Though the non-existence implies that the effect comes into being by negative its pre-non-existence, the association and operation of other causes determine its character and the precise moment of its production. In the absence of such a determining factor, the effect, as per Buddhist theory, should occur at all the times, because pre-non-existence is a phenomena without a beginning, and as such does not cease to exist. The pre-non-existence ceases to exist when its counterpositive (*pratiyogin*), the effect is produced. For example, when the pot is produced the pre-non-existence of the pot ceases to exist i.e. the pot is the counterpositive of the non-existence.[38]

The Buddhist rejoins the issue and says that the Nyāya-Vaiśeṣika also has to admit the non-existence as the cause. According to him the seed is not alone responsible for the production of the sprout, it requires soil, moisture etc. i.e. a group of causes. When the sprout is produced does the entire complex of causes exist? If it exists, it will produce again, it must do so.[39] But that is not the experience of ours. The real cause (the constituent cause) must have ceased to exist at the time of production then only the effect comes into existence. To be precise, so long the seed is there, there is no sprout, when the sprout is produced, the seed is destroyed, it is no more. Thus, it means, immediately before the effect comes into being there is the non-existence, which occupies the position of the cause to that effect. Therefore, it is logical to presume that the non-existence is there before causal group is formed.

The Nyāya-Vaiśeṣika says that at a particular moment when the inherent cause ceases to exist the effect originates i.e. the non-existence qualified by a particular moment is the determinant of the production. Following this the Buddhist may say that the pre-non-existence qualified by the moment immediately preceding the occurrence of the effect, is responsible for the occurrence of the effect, which also determines its character and pin-points the time of occurrence. Thus the apprehension that the effect may occur at all the times is not justified.

But Buddhist points out that even according to Nyāya-Vaiśeṣika also there is a non-existence before the effect is produced and hence only unreal can be the cause which is the immediate antecedent to the effect. It has been stated in the case of the sprout and the complex of causes that a state of non-existence intervenes between the production and the group of causes. Thus it is more logical to admit the non-existence as the cause of production.

WHOLE AND PART

4. *The Concept of Whole as Distinct from the Part*

4.1. The Nyāya-Vaiśeṣika holds that the objective reality is one integrated whole, because it is at the bottom of the knowledge of whole. It is one and comprises of parts, but quite distinct from the parts. This principle makes the Nyāya-Vaiśeṣika position different from other realists and idealists. Therefore, the theory of whole (*avayavin*) as conceived by the Nyāya-Vaiśeṣika is one of the two main pillars of the system on which the entire edifice of the objective realism of the system rests. This principle also envisages a relation between part and whole. The relation of *samavāya*, which relates the part with the whole and make the two appear as one to the commonsense.

The Nyāya-Vaiśeṣika holds that the material body as produced as the result of conjoining of parts is neither a conglomeration of constituents nor a mere aggregate of the parts. This means the effect, which is produced in the parts, the 'whole' (*avayavin*), is different from the constituent parts, and it exists simultaneously side by side with the parts. Acceptance of this position that 'a whole is different from its parts" enables the Nyāya-Vaiśeṣika school to explain the theory that the sensible material order is produced from the infra-sensible atoms.

Beginning from the *Nyāya-sūtra*[40] to the latest treatises of the Nyāya-Vaiśeṣika school there are lengthy arguments to prove separate entity of the whole and also to refute the criticism of the opponents. The whole gamut of argument to prove the separate entity of the whole is boiled down to the causation theory of the school. Without accepting the whole as a distinct entity and separate from its constituents it is not possible to resolve the difficulties involved in the causation theory, as propounded by the Nyāya-Vaiśeṣika.

The Nyāya-Vaiśeṣika theory of whole has been criticised, on one hand by the realist Sāṁkhya and Mīmāṁsaka, and on the other, by the idealist and nihilist Bauddhas. The Nyāya-Vaiśeṣika had to wage a long drawn war against them to defend his own fortress from the attack of those schools.

4.2. Sāṁkhya opposes the theory of 'whole' since it goes against the causation theory of Sāṁkhya, which says that the effect is not different from the cause, it is simply a change.

The Buddhist opposition is aimed at to do away with the concept of objective reality of the external world. The Buddhist holds that the external object is conceptual. The concept of whole makes the external object absolutely real. Hence there is the strongest opposition from the Buddhist.

The Sāṁkhya and Mīmāṁsaka being realist agree in admitting objectivity of the whole. However, they differ from the Nyāya-Vaiśeṣika position that the whole is quite distinct and different from the parts.[41] The Sāṁkhya raises a number of objections to the Nyāya-Vaiśeṣika stand and says that the effect is produced from the cause and there is no qualitative difference between the two. He further says that the Nyāya-Vaiśeṣika concept of whole invites many logical absurdities.

The Sāṁkhya argues that the yarns as closely conjoined in a specific relation (*saṁsthāna-viśeṣa*) and not the isolated facts, are called cloth.[42] What the argument means is that the whole is nothing but a combination of parts joined in a given order.

The Sāṁkhya raises the question that the parts which are different from a particular whole, are not parts of that whole. As the branches of a tree are not the parts of the cloth.

To this Uddyotakara replies that the above assumption is not warranted by the logic of identity. For instance, it is not necessary to establish identity of 'A' with 'B' in order to prove that 'A' is not a part of anything other than 'B'. 'A' is identical with its own self and since one thing cannot be the part and the whole, the part and whole must be different.

4.3. *The Problem of Same Weight*

The Sāṁkhya says that part and whole are to be taken as identical, or in other words, one is not different from the other on the ground that both have the same weight. This argument seems to go against the principle of qualitative causation. According to Nyāya-Vaiśeṣika theory of causation the quality of the cause produces a corresponding quality in the effect and since effect is qualitatively different from its cause, the quality of effect must be different from that of the cause. Otherwise the theory of qualitative causation (known as *ārambhavāda*) would succumb to the theory of *pariṇāmavāda* of Śāṁkhya). The whole, therefore, should have its own weight, different from the weight of the parts. Thus the weight of the whole is not the weight of the parts. On the other hand the whole resides in the parts as a distinct entity.

The logical conclusion of the above presumption would be that with the production of the effect (whole) the weight of the object, which stands inseparable from its cause (material), should get increased, because, while the weight of the cause, for that matter of the parts, remains as before; the weight of the effect i.e. of the emerging whole, is added to it. This question has been discussed by Uddyotakara, Vācaspati, Śrīdhara and many others and have offered solution.

In *Avayavaparīkṣā*[43] the question has been raised, if the whole were an entity different from the parts, the whole and the parts must have separate weight—each being different from the other.

While trying to find out a convincing reply to this objection Uddyotakara puts the views of others which, it is clear, are not acceptable to him. One of the views is that the weight of the cause (parts) after the emergence of the effect (whole) is obstructed by the weight of the whole (*pratibaddha*)[44] and according to other,[45] the weight of the cause is destroyed by the weight of the effect. Both these views seem to be illogical and, therefore, rejected by Uddyotakara. According to first view, the weight of the parts is obstructed (*pratibaddha*) by the weight of the whole. This means, the weight of the whole makes the weight of the parts and the result is, there will be no difference in the sum total of the weight. This is illogical because, when the whole ceases to exist parts do not exist.

The same objection is levelled against the second view. Moreover, if it be presumed that the weight of the whole destroys or neutralise the weight of the parts, when the whole is destroyed, the parts would be weightless, and as such they would be incapable of falling, because their weightlessness will make them float.

Finding the above two views unacceptable Uddyotakara gives his own views on the problem. That the weight of an effect and the weight of its cause is not manifested separately, and hence, it is impossible to ascertain, in the total weight, what is the share of the cause and what is that of the effect. He says: "The weight of a substance means the weight of the total collection of substances—beginning from the atom to the last effect".[46]

The underlying meaning of the observation of Uddyotakara is this that when a piece of cloth is being weighed, the weight is not of the last effect (cloth) alone, it is the total weight of the all the intervening particles between the atom and the cloth, such as *dvyaṇuka, aṁśu* (fibre), etc.

Uddyotakara makes another point in explaining the above proposition. He says: "The human being with his inadequate knowledge is not able to say that this much is the weight of the cause and this much is that of the effect".[47]

In his commentary on the *Nyāyavārttika* Vācaspati Miśra makes the point clear by another illustration. He says that the collection of substance (*dravya-samāhāra*) is to be understood as both effect substance and the cause-substance (cause-effect-substance also). He further says that the weight of a pot includes the weight of the particles of earth, power of earth, the pebbles of earth, the halves of the pot (*kapāla*) and the pot itself.[48]

Śrīdhara offers another answer. He says that the difference between the weight of the cause and effect is so little that it evades cognition. When a heavy substance (*mahati dravya unmīyamānc*) is being weighed the weight of the minute things clinging to it is not experienced.[49]

4.4. *The Problem of Variegated Colour (Citrarūpa)*

The Sāṁkhya being supported by the Mīmāṁsaka and the Buddhist assails the Nyāya-Vaiśeṣika position on the question of the colour of the whole. The Buddhist ridicules the notion of *citrarūpa*: "What can be more strange (*citra*) than to call variegated colour (*citrarūpa*) as one colour."[50]

The entire question of whole revolves round the theory of visual perception of the whole and its cognition as a distinct entity. If the whole be a distinct entity it must have its own colour (without which it will not be an object of visual perception) and that must be distinct from the colour of the parts. But where do we perceive such colour which pertains to the whole? What we perceive is the colour of the parts. At least on this ground the Nyāya-Vaiśeṣika should give up its theory that the whole is a distinct from the parts.[51]

To this the Nyāya-Vaiśeṣika replies that there is no denying the fact that whole is perceived and where it is perceived on the strength of its perception the colour that is associated with the whole, should be regarded as its own colour. In accordance with the accepted principle, the colour of the whole is to be taken as the product of the colour of the parts, but our faculty of vision fails to distinguish between the two colours. That the colour of the whole is a product, is proved by the emergence of a colour in an object produced from parts. For instance, a coloured cloth is produced from the yarns of divergent colour and the cloth has a variegated variegated colour. Now it is to be noted that the variegated colour (*citrarūpa*) and the varieties of colours are not the same thing. The word *'citra'* (variegated) is used both singular and plural.[52] Therefore the variegated colour means a particular type of colour. The underlying meaning of this statement is this that when one speaks about a piece of cloth of variegated colour one means that the particular piece of cloth has one colour known as variegated colour; it does not convey the sense of the presence of many colours.[53] In short, the whole has its own colour which is responsible for the perception of the whole. The whole cannot become perceptible by the virtue of the colour of its parts, because the colour of one substance, by association, cannot produce perceptibility in another object. Had it been so, the air would have been also perceived by the visual organ because air remains in close contact with colour, say, the colour of a tree.

4.5. In the *Nyāya-sūtra* in course of discussion of 'whole and part' an epistemological theory, which asserts that all perception of external objects are at their bottom nothing but inference, has been brought in.[54] That the perception has inference as its basis can better be illustrated by a reference to the perception of a physical object, say, perception of a tree.

An external object, in order to be perceived by the sense organ, must possess magnitude (*mahattva*) and extension (*pārimāṇḍalya*) without which nothing becomes perceptible. Therefore, the tree must be composed of parts. Now the question arises—whether the tree is an aggregate of the parts (*avayava-samūha*) or a complex whole (*avayavin*) and a distinct entity from the parts. The Nyāya-Vaiśeṣika school accepts the second alternative, and hence, criticises the epistemological theory of perception based on inference.

The question of inference arises like this:

When we see a tree, but we do not see the entire tree or all parts of the tree, of which the tree is composed. When we perceive a tree, we perceive only some front parts of the tree and on the basis of perception of those parts, the tree as a whole is comprehended. It is the comprehension of the tree by inference, as the fire is comprehend on perception of smoke. On perceiving some front parts of the tree we may infer that there are some other parts of the tree and the whole tree is perceived through inference, and hence, the perception is nothing but inference.

However, such inference does not prove that the tree is a composed whole of parts, it simply suggests that there are some other parts which are not exposed to our sense organ.

What is inferred? The unperceived parts or the tree as a whole which is different from the parts? If the concept of the tree is an aggregation of parts only and not a complex whole (*avayavin*) then the comprehension of the tree will not be possible even taking recourses to inference. Because, the front parts of the tree are perceived and the back parts are inferred. Neither the perceived parts nor the unperceived parts is the tree. If the tree can neither be perceived nor inferred, then how can we have the cognition of a tree? How is it possible to have knowledge of a tree?

The Nyāya-Vaiśeṣika would reply by the process of synthesism of experience, which in its turn implies the unitive principle.[55] But the unitive principle is not acceptable to the opponents, hence he goes on arguing his case [acceptance of unitive principle will negate the whole theory of instant particular (*kṣaṇa*)].

Vācaspati Miśra says that perception of an object as a whole (*avayavin*) be taken on the perception of a few parts, not of all parts, because nobody can perceive all the parts at one and the same time. If it is insisted upon that all parts are to be perceived, the perception of a whole will never be possible. If, the object is a whole, the perception of few parts of a whole is sufficient to generate the perception of the whole object.[56] If you ask in order to perceive a whole how many parts of the whole are to be perceived, the answer is experience. It is our experience when only a little part of the whole is perceived the whole is not perceived, when some more parts are perceived the whole is perceived.[57]

4.6. The conclusion of this discussion is that acceptance of whole will simplify the problem of perception which means that when we see a whole it will imply the cognition of the unperceived parts also, because we cognise it as a whole entity and not as an aggregate of parts. The reason is, whole is one, and if one part of the whole be perceived, the whole is perceived, in its entirety.[58]

Another objection to the perception of the whole is raised. When the whole is perceived, it is to be perceived in its entirety, and the whole must be present in all its parts. This is simply impossible because no one can see all the parts at one and the same time. When the front part is seen the back is not seen, i.e. only one part of the whole is seen not the entire whole. However, the whole can be perceived in its entirety, if the whole resides in its entirety in the perceived parts and nothing of the whole is left. This again is an absurd proposition, because, in such a position the other parts would cease to be called parts because they would be redundant.

He asks:

Does the whole resides in the perceived parts partially (*ekadeśena*) or wholly (*kṛtsnena*)? If it be partially, the whole will not be perceived in its entirety, and, if the answer is wholly, the other parts would lose their utility.

To this Uddyotakāra retorts:

"It is a unfair question, to ask whether the whole tree resides in the perceived parts partially or wholly. The tree is one whole, which stands in its own right. It should not be conceived as a cluster of parts. A cluster of parts is comparable to a heap of apples. It is in order when we say that the heap of apples exists partially on the floor and partially on the carpet, because we only mean there by that some of these apples (forming the heap) are on the floor while some other are on the adjoining carpet. And it is again in order when we say that the heap of apples exists wholly in the basket. But with respect to the whole tree and its so called parts, such dialectical question will be pointless because the supposed answer will be humorously tautologous or simply meaningless. For are we to construct the answer as: (1) Some of the parts forming the whole occurs in some parts of the whole; or (2) Some of the one whole occurs in some parts?"

The Buddhist may again ask:

"If the whole body exists neither partially nor even wholly in the perceived parts, why and how else then will the whole be said to be present in the perceived parts?"

To this Uddyotakara replies:

"This is again a unfair question since it arises from a misconception of what may be called the grammar of the verb to occur in (*vṛtti or vṛttatā* in Sanskrit). There is nothing unusual in our saying that the whole tree as one object occurs in many parts and this will imply that it occurs in perceived parts too. But error creeps in when we ask, "do the perceived parts present the whole tree completely or incompletely?" The question of completeness or incompleteness in this connection presupposes wrongly the divisibility of one whole tree. A tree as whole body can be destroyed or torn apart, but it is not divisible in a way a group of students can be divided into several sections. We may say that the stuff of the tree is divisible, but not the tree itself. Therefore, the proper answer to the above question will be: "the perceived parts may present the whole tree".

Uddyotakara compares the notion of the whole body with the notion of numbers. The number two, for example, is present in two apples. From this we may say that the number two is presented by either of the two apples when accompanied by the other. But it is senseless to ask whether either or each of them presents the number two completely or incompletely.[59]

4.7. The Buddhist further argues that the necessity of accepting the whole arises from the presumption that the atom being minute is not perceptible but the gross element formed by the atoms has magnitude and perceptibility. There is a similarity, that though a piece of hair is not perceived by a person of defective vision (*taimirika*) but a mass of hair is perceived by him; in the same way one single atom is not perceived but a number of them would be perceptible.[60] Therefore Vācaspati Miśra replies:

"Whether knowledge is generated from the cognition that particular knowledge has an object, the cause of the cognition (there must be an object 'whole' for generating the knowledge of whole).[61] The cognition cannot have the detached and discrete atoms as its object and for such cognition of a gross element is to be accepted, in absence of which we cannot have the cognition a gross element. The Nyāya-Vaiśeṣika further points out the difference between the two and says that a piece of hair is an object which can be perceived by eyes, but not the atom. A person of weak vision does not perceive a piece of hair but he perceives a mass of hairs. Both a piece of hair and a mass of hair are perceived by a healthy person, and thus the hair is perceptible, but the atom is beyond perception of the sense organs.

There is the apparent contradiction. The atoms being together give up their characteristic of imperceptibility, and being disunited reach the non-perception stage by the sense organ, and, therefore, not perceived—this a great contradiction.[62]

4.8. *Uddyotakara poses this question*

"May we ask them those who hold that the atoms themselves are the object of comprehension like a pot, whether this difference in respect of perceptibility in atoms (one atom is imperceptible but a number of them when combined is perceptible) is due to something special that occurs there, or, without anything? If you say something special is produced and that makes the atoms perceptible, we say that the said special thing is the whole (*avayavin*), and if you prefer the second alternative, then you are contradicting yourself by describing atom both as perceptible and imperceptible."[63]

The opponents may say that it is the connection (*saṁyoga*) which is perceived. The atoms being in close proximity become perceptible because they stand connected. The author of *Vārttika* does not agree on this premise and asserts that the objects which are not perceptible their connection is also not perceptible.

Dharmakīrtti retorts:

"What contradiction would be there, if many atoms being together acquires excellence which the atom lacks when it is single, cause comprehension, like the sense organs and others."[64] (The sense organ, *manas* (intellect) and the object operating jointly cause the cognition of the object, none of them can do it singly).

The Buddhist Critique

In the course of discussion of the Nyāya theory of 'whole' the Buddhist views on the subject have been referred to or mentioned in the foregoing paragraphs. Some of their arguments against the theory of 'whole', as conceived by the Nyāya-Vaiśeṣika, are mentioned below to make the Buddhist stand more clear.

4.9. Where from comes the grossness? It cannot be said that there is another element distinct from all those atoms which is the cause for the formation of the gross element. There is nothing, and nothing is accepted which is different from the atoms. Moreover, the two atoms also cannot combine; the contact of atom has neither been proved by perception, nor by inference (the two means of valid knowledge). The contact exists neither in every substance separately nor in one substance for the reason that there cannot be "many", which is different from every individual.

We do not see that the whole resides in the part in its entirety, hence it cannot be said that the whole resides entirely in a part. Because the whole cannot be perceived in every single part. If it is conceded that the whole resides in every single part, we shall be faced with the absurd proposition that when a part of the whole is effected with a shiver or a colour the whole is to be taken effected by those activity and attribute.[65] This is not a fact in reality. Moreover, when only one part is effected by the activity such as shivering etc. the other parts where those activities are absent shall have to be taken as possessed of those activities. And thus you will find yourself in a very ambiguous state of affairs as to whether or not by the shivering of a part whole is shivering, with the colouring of a part the whole is coloured.

In the alternative it may be said that the whole does reside in its part partly. But this stand cannot be taken because there is no separate part other than the whole. Then again the following position will arise: If the whole is suppose to be related partly to its parts, then the whole which consists of its parts will be regarded as related somewhere to certain part and somewhere to another part—such relaisation is inevitable.

Again the proposition will arise that if the whole does not pervade certain parts, it is bound not to pervade the parts at all, because there cannot be plurality of parts different from the individual parts.

4.10. That the whole subsists in its parts by some other way, that is, by a way which is different from the above mentioned two, namely, subsistence by partly and wholly, is absurd. Nothing of the sort is realised and there is none.

Now another question arises:

Whether or not the whole is different from its parts? Neither can be supported by reasons. If the reply to the above question is, the whole is different from its parts then when the whole is not perceived, sometime it may appear that the parts are perceived. When there are two jars, one is different from the other, and since the two jars are different they cannot be perceived together. There is no rule that two different things should be perceived at the same point of time. Similarly the whole being different from its parts is not perceived along with the parts at the same point of time. When this position is accepted, that the whole and the parts are two distinct entities and as such cannot be perceived at the same point of time, it may so happen that the whole might be perceived without the perception of the parts. Nobody on this earth can perceive the whole without perceiving the parts.

If, on the other hand, it is stated that the whole does not exceed the parts, or, it is not a different entity from its parts, then there is no 'whole'. By saying that the whole is not different from its parts you have asserted the non-existence of the whole in your own style of speech.

4.11. The Vaiśeṣika accepts *samavāya* as a relation of complete occurrence (*vyāpyavṛtti-sambandha*). Hence to accept *avyavin* partially exist in *avayava* would amount to self contradiction. And the relation of *samavāya* would turn out to be a relation of incomplete occurrence (*avyāpyavṛtti*) which the Vaiśeṣika cannot accept.

If, on the other hand, the Vaiśeṣika admits that the *avyavin* exists in *avayava* in its entirety, in that case *avayavin* would be identical with *avayava* and the relata being identical, the concept of relation existing between them would be impossible, for the reason that the two relata of a relation must be different from each other. Hence, the Buddhist asserts that it is better to accept the *avayavin* as nothing but the systematic adjustment of *avayava* in the same way as the row of ants (*pipīlikā paṅkti*) is nothing more than the individual ants proceeding in a particular order.

Moreover, if a particular cloth is distinct from its parts, the yarns, where it inheres, then on seeing a particular yarn of a piece of cloth we should have seen simultaneously the entire cloth also, through the relation of contact-inherence between sense organ and the cloth. The eyes come into contact with the yarns wherein the cloth inheres. But in fact, when a particular part is perceived, the entire cloth is not perceived, hence the whole is not distinct from the particular parts.

The existence of whole as distinct from the part is further nullified by the fact that a distinct whole is never perceived. Had it existed it would have been perceived as the parts are perceived. When we perceive a particular pot, we see only one part of it, but not all the parts simultaneously and also not the whole as distinct from the parts.

4.12. The upholder of the theory of 'whole' must admit that before *avayavin* is perceived *avayava* must have been perceived. In that case, however, the perception of *avayavi* is conditioned by the perception of *avayava*. The Buddhist thinks that if it is said that 'X' is perceived only when 'Y' is perceived, then 'X's perception of circle of fast moving fire ball in a circle (*alātacakra*) is conditioned by the perception of the fast movement of the fire ball. Hence like *alātacakra avayavi* is bound to be turn out to be a produce of imagination due to erroneous perception.

When we search for the thing, you call 'whole' (*avayavin*), and try to prove it by reasonings, the very thing 'whole' completely disappears. In other words, the whole, separate from its parts is not proved and cannot be proved.

If it is so, how one can have the knowledge of the grossness of a thing one cognises? Wherefrom such cognition does appear? The reply is:

For the cognition of grossness of a thing the so called subtle elements need not combine to produce a gross element. The instant particulars being born in every moment without interruption arrange themselves in up and low, become fit for perceiving by the sense organs, and when they reach that stage at a particular point of time they are perceived by the eyes as a gross one. When one realises that it is gross element (though the constituents of that gross element do not continue to exist and they do not produce a separate entity) one's mind is influenced by the grossness of the element, and in such a mind the grossness and its alternative alternately appear.

The simple meaning of this statement is this that though in reality there is no separate entity of a gross element in the external world, which are only instant particulars, do appear as gross element in one's mind. For instance, when we see rows of trees from a distance they appear to us as forest. In order to make a forest the trees do not combine to produce an entity separate from then, but it appears to our mind as gross element and notionally separate from the rows of the trees. Such cognition is due to one's mental make up. Hence, it is established that instant particulars do not produce the gross elements, and there is no entity to be termed as the "whole".

The Mīmāṃsaka View

The Mīmāṃsaka says: When we see a cow we cognise her as an entity and from that cognition the conception which arises is the conception of a gross element. There is no dispute about this conception and this has also been proved by reasonings. Moreover, we have the same recollection when we see a cow i.e. after seeing a cow we have the concept about the caw and when we see a cow again somewhere else the same concept of the cow comes to our mind. Such a consistent concept is only possible if the cow is a gross element, separate from the instant particulars.

It may be argued that it is just a recollection, a mental process, by which one realises that—"this is that". In fact, the whole (*avayavin*) has not at all been proved by reasonings. What we see there is nothing which leads to the realisation of the whole.

There again arises the question that in order to become a separate entity the whole requires to undergo through the process of beginning. That is, the discrete particulars at a given point of time should undergo the process of combination, but there is no beginning of such process and hence the concept of whole is not realised (*anupapattiḥ*).

The reply to this is like this: This non-realisation is itself not realised. The accepted rule is—when an action is perceived that action becomes the proof for the inference for the cause of the action. For instance, when there is rain, the rain presupposes the existence of the cloud. In other words, rain itself proves the existence of the cloud.

Though *saṁyoga* is one it is present in many objects, because separately in each single individual object the concept of *saṁyoga* cannot be realised. On the other hand, though there cannot be plural without the single, the single is the second substrata of *samyoga*, thus, there s no incongruity.

The intended meaning of this statement is this, that *samyoga* is one, and it is comprehended when it resides in more than one substrata. When we say "many" it means more than one, which includes one also. If contact does not subsist in one, how it can subsist in many, which includes one. In order to avoid this riddle it is stated that contact being one subsists in one, and, it subsists in a second one also, which is its second substrata. Hence, it is proved and to be accepted that though *samyoga* a is one it subsists in many.

4.13. Another question may arise that the two substances in the which the contact subsists, they themselves are produced as conjuncted and create the notion of conjunct and disjunct, hence there does not exist contact as a separate quality distinct from the substances. Such a supposition has no basis. Because the two substances can be cognised when they become the object of knowledge. Sometime the two substances in which the contact subsists assume such a stage which is different from them and, therefore, it is different from its substrata.

Again *pratyabhijñā* (consequent knowledge) has been explained and proved in the *Mīmāṃsājīvarakṣā*. Parts which are endowed with the common qualities of contact and not possessed of by a constituent cause, they themselves do create constituent cause in the whole.

Generic Property or Universal: Sāmānya

The Nyāya-Vaiśeṣika theory of universal (*sāmānya*) is as important aṣ the theory of "whole" (*avayavi*) for the concept of objective reality of the school. It is intimately connected with the concept of *samavāya*. The relation between the universal and the individuals presupposes the existence of *samavāya* without which the theory of *sāmānya* falls flat.

The Nyāya-Vaiśeṣika theory of generic property has been contested by the other schools of Indian philosophy. While the Buddhist does not recognise it at all the Mīmāṁsaka accepts *sāmānya*, which they call *jāti* with substantial modification,[66] i.e. as a quality. The Jaina, so also the Rāmānuja vedāntin does not accept *sāmānya* as a separate category, neither they consider it as an eternal one. However, they do not fall in the line of the Buddhist in repudiating *sāmānya*. According to the Buddhist *sāmānya* is a conceptual and not real, the Jaina and the Rāmānuja do not admit the said position. The latter Jaina philosophers, however, have taken a somewhat more radical views against the conception of *sāmānya*.[67] The Jaina has advanced the conception of similarity (*sādṛśya*) to replace universal and with the acceptance of similarity he explains the cognition of "cowness" in the cow. This change of approach by the Jainas to the concept of *sāmānya*, according to Satkari Mukherjee, is due to the Buddhist influence.

The concept of the whole is ontological but the concept of universal is both ontological and epistemological. The epistemological character of universal is so important that the Buddhist, who does not admit universal, has got to coin a new term *apoha* (exclusion) which in a negative way, performs the function of universal.

Stcherbatsky says: "The Indian theory of universals can be divided into two main groups, the realistic one and idealistic one. The Realists assume that every universal exists in the external world as a separate unit invariably connected with all the individuals in which it is present. The idealist, who can be characterised as conceptualists and as nominalists, maintain that only individuals are real Ens-es, the individuals are mere images, mere concept, or names (*saṁjñā-mātra-vastuvikalpa-śūnya*)".[68]

Jāti, Vyakti and Ākṛti

It has been mentioned that one of the instances of occurrence of inherence is that which holds between the universal and the individuals. The Nyāya-Vaiśeṣika and the Bhāṭṭa admit that there is a class character (*sāmānya*) inherent in all the individuals belonging to a particular class. This class-character (*sāmānya*) is a distinct category from individuals.[69] It is an eternal unitary attribute inhering in all individuals of the class past, present and future. The main argument behind postulating such class character is as follows:

To the Nyāya-Vaiśeṣika every instance of cognition has an object behind it. A cognition without a cognizable objective is an impossibility, because the external object is real. Moreover, the character of a cognition is determined by that of the object of cognition. Now, when we see a number of cows in the field possessing different colours and forms we at once cognise them as cow and also differentiate them from all other individuals—each cow is different from the other.[70] Now this cognition in the form of "this is a cow", "this is a cow" is what is called continuous similar notion (*anuvṛtyākārā buddhiḥ*).[71]

This similar notion must be due to some similar objects behind it and this is what is called cowness (*gotva*). This class-character had to be admitted to explain universal concomitance (*vyāpti*) as well as the notion of causality. For, in the case of a universal concomitance between the fire and the smoke, the relation holds good not between two particular individuals, but between all fires and all smokes, irrespective of time and space. The pervasion of the fire-universal (*vahnitva*) by the smoke-universal (*dhūmatva*) is at the root of the inference. This is why whenever and wherever we cognise the smoke, the existence of the fire is at once inferred. This has led the Nyaiyāyika and the Bhāṭṭa to postulate an universal distinct from the individuals. The universal may be defined as that they are real, independent, timeless ubiquitous entities, and according to Nyāya-Vaiśeṣika such entities inhere in individual substance, quality and motion. Such entities may again inhere in several distinct individuals of the same class at one or at different times and places.

While in the Vaiśeṣika system of philosophy the term used for such an entity is *sāmānya*, Gautama uses the word *jāti*[72] to mean the same thing which is termed as *sāmānya* by Kaṇāda and the followers of the school. However, Vātsyāyana makes a distinction between the two terms and defines them. His definition is like this:

That *sāmānya* is a pure universal like "Being" which assimilates without differentiating.[73]

But *jāti* is a common property (*sāmānya-viśeṣa*) like 'potness' and 'cowness' differentiates and assimilates as well.[74] In this context the real import of the term *sāmānya* and *viśeṣa* may be illustrated.[75] Both the terms *sāmānya* and *viśeṣa* figure in the *Kaṇāda-sūtra* and are usually taken as mutually contradictory.

Gautama has posed a question: "What does the word cow mean?"

(a) Does it mean an individual cow? or,
(b) the characteristic shape and other qualities associated with the cow?
(c) the property of cowness which is common to several individuals to which the word cow is customarily applied?[76]

After examining all the three *jāti, ākṛti* and *vyakti* the conclusion reached at is that all the three are involved *vyaktyākṛti-jātayastu padārthāḥ.*[77]

Śivāditya has poses this question and answers that *sāmānya* includes both *jāti* and *upādhi,* and he makes a distinction between the two.[78] While *jāti* is considered as natural universal, *upādhi* is accepted as an imposed or acquired property.

Existence, substancehood and qualityhood are *jāti,* while cookness (*pācakatva*) is *upādhi,* that is an acquired property. Similarity (*sādṛśya*) is a universal belongs to *upādhi* class. He further classifies universal into three—viz. (a) the highest (*parā*), (b) the lowest (*aparā*), and (c) the intermediate (*parāparā*).

The Sāṁkhya does not admit eternality of universal and says that except *Puruṣa* and *Prakṛti* all other things of existence are products and hence non-eternal. All products being non-eternal any quality or property of a non-eternal thing is bound to be non-eternal. In view of this how there can be a cognition of property like universal (*sāmānya*) which is not destroyed with the destruction of the objects where it resides. In other words, the universal resides in individuals and the individuals are empirical. For instance, the universal cowness resides in the individual cow. The individual cow borns and dies. How there can be eternal universal which is a property of the individual cow?

The reply of the Nyāya-Vaiśeṣika to this objection by Sāṁkhya is this:

It is true that the individuals are momentary, but though they are momentary yet the cognition, "this is that pot" is permanent and this cognition is the basis for the cognition of the universal.

Without universal there cannot be such lasting cognition. The underlying meaning of the statement is that since there is a lasting cognition pertaining to the individual, which is momentary, proves that there is something common among all individuals of that species and that is universal (*vyaktīnām anityatve'pi sa evāyaṁ ghaṭaḥ iti sthiratvayogena yat pratyabhijñānaṁ tat sāmānyasya*).

The school of Pūrva-Mīmāṁsā have admitted *sāmānya* without taking recourses to *samavāya* for its relation with the individual.

When we cognise a thing we cognise it as the possessor of the universal i.e. both the universal and the individual are cognised. For instance, when we cognise a cow the cognition is "this is a cow". The cow individual and the universal cow are object of our cognition. In other words, there are two aspects in every cognition of an object—one aspect is that of the particular object and the other of its class-character. The individual aspect is cognised by the operation of the differentiating function of knowledge (*vyāvṛttyākārā buddhi*) and the class-character of the object by the operation of continued course of knowledge (*anuvṛttyākārā buddhiḥ*).

In the instance of the cognition "this is a cow" the knowledge of "this" distinguishes the particular cow from all other cows. This cognition is due to the function of the differentiating process of knowledge and that is by the word "this" (*ayaṁ*). Again, the cognition of the "cow" is the cognition of all individuals of that particular species of the animal i.e. the class itself.

Moreover, Kumārila says that the knowledge caused by inference is also based on the class-character of an object. For instance, when on seeing the smoke coming out from the mountain we infer the existence of the fire on the mountain, this knowledge by inference is caused by the knowledge of the class i.e. the universal. Had it been between two individuals nobody would have cognised them as pervador and pervaded in all cases. The very basis of inference is dependent on the class-character of the entities and not on individual entity. Therefore, the class-character of the entities cannot be denied. Thus on the basis of the knowledge caused by both perception and inference the existence of *sāmānya* has been established.

Unlike the Nyāya-Vaiśeṣika the Bhāṭṭa holds that the universal is not entirely different entity from the individual where it resides, and against the Buddhist view he maintains that universal is not identical with the individual. The universal is different from and identical with the individual. The universal is different from and identical with the individual—the Bhāṭṭa asserts, Had universal been completely different from the individual like the horse and the cow the both would have not been cognised as one. We do not cognise the horse and the cow as one entity, because the horse differs from the cow and vice versa. Like the cognition of horse and the cow, the "cow" and "cowness" would have been cognised separately. But in the case of the cognition of "this is a cow" we do not cognise the cow individual (*gau*) and the cow universal (*gotva*) separately. Hence, the two may be considered as identical, and since the two have different connotation and function they may be taken as two different entities. The Bhāṭṭa finds it more logical to accept the class as identical with, as well as different from the individuals. The relation holding between the two is identity-cum-difference (*tādātmya*) but not *samavāya*, because *samavāya* presupposes complete difference of the two relata.

Thus there is nothing inconsistency, according to the Bhāṭṭa, in admitting universal, and at the same time rejecting inherence, which the Nyāya-Vaiśeṣika considers indispensable.

The Nyāya-Vaiśeṣika says that the generic property *sāmānya* is entirely different from the individual where it resides, but the manifestation of the universal is strictly confined to the individual. Though the universal is eternal and all pervasive one it can be cognised only in the individual. And that manifestation is by the power of a relation which holds between the two. The said relation is *samavāya* (inherence) which is eternal. It is the power of the relation of inherence which makes two different entities to appear as one.

The Nyāya-Vaiśeṣika, however, may raise an objection to the conclusion of the Mīmāṁsaka that the generic property is responsible for the continued process of knowledge and the particular (individual) for the differentiating process of knowledge, and if both the universal and the individual are taken as identical the result would be that one universal, identified with one individual, will be different from the other universal, or, all individuals being identified with the universal will appear as one. This is totally absurd.[79] Hence, universal cannot be accepted as identical with the individual.

This objection of the Nyāya-Vaiśeṣika has been brushed aside by the Bhāṭṭa. He says that if the universal is entirely different from the individual as the Nyāya-Vaiśeṣika has made, how the perception of the cow individual as the possessor of cowness will be possible? Had they been two completely different entities in the cognition of "this is a cow" the perception would have been of "this" and "cow" separately. The perception of "this" would be completely different from that of the "cow". Again if they are taken as identical, "this" and "cow" will stand "this" "this" or "cow" "cow", and "this" will be the synonym of "cow", which is totally absurd.

Now a question may arise, how two contradictory attributes (identity and difference) can reside together? The Bhāṭṭa says that though difference and identity are contradictory there is nothing wrong in their being together in the same locus. It is not as contradictory as "this is silver" and "this is non-silver", therefore both can take place together. Moreover, in a relative sense such contradictory attributes may reside in the same universal. Yajñadatta is taller than Viṣṇudatta and smaller than Devadatta. In this case both tallness and smallness reside in Yajñadatta at the same time. In the same way "difference" and "identity" can remain as the attribute of the universal.

The Nyāya-Vaiśeṣika maintains that the universal is omnipresent (*sarva-sarvagata*) which is manifested through an individual. Kumārila does not agree on this assertion and says that the universal is always confined to the individual. It cannot be an omnipresent entity. He says that the universal is cognised in an individual and no where else, hence there is no entity of the name universal like the other.[80]

The Nyāya-Vaiśeṣika may raise another objection to the Bhāṭṭa view by saying that if the universal is confined to the individual only where did it reside when there was no individual? Where does it go when the individual is destroyed? When an individual is born wherefrom it comes? The universal is eternal, hence it cannot be born. The universal is devoid of shape (*amūrtta*) hence it does not possess action and without action it cannot join an individual. To this objection the Bhāṭṭa replies in a circuitous way. He says that when an individual is born the universal of its own unites with it. The function of union is by the power of self-linking relation (*tādātmya sambandha*). This relation, unlike *saṁyoga*, is not caused by any other agency or action. It is self-caused and, therefore, the question of coming from somewhere or going away from it does not arise.

Pārthasārathi Miśra seems to have affected a compromise when he says that whether the universal be accepted as an omnipresent one or as an entity entirely dependent on the individual—it is manifested through the individual.

In fact what is called *tādātmya* by the Bhāṭṭa and *samavāya* by the Prābhākara is a relation which is caused by itself and that is responsible for the universal being invariably identified with the individual.

If it is omnipresent its manifestation in the individual is through the relation of *samavāya* (inherence) or *tādātmya* relation, and if it is confined to the individual only, it is manifested in the individual where it resides.[81]

The Prābhākara Views

The Prābhākara admits universal and holds that it is an entity of existential nature. The universal (*jāti*) is different from where it resides and is perceptible. Like the Nyāya-Vaiśeṣika he also maintains that *jāti* is eternal. Unlike Nyāya-Vaiśeṣika he does not accept *samavāya* (inherence) as an eternal relation.[82] The relation between the universal and the individual emerges as soon as the individual is born and the relation disappears when the individual perishes. While the Bhāṭṭa calls that relation *tādātmya* the Prābhākara calls it *samavāya* (inherence), but the Prābhākara's conception of *samavāya* differs from that of the Nyāya-Vaiśeṣika. There is also difference between the Prābhākara and the Nyāya-Vaiśeṣika in the question of admitting *sattā jāti* (beingness universal).

The Nyāya-Vaiśeṣika admits a *sattā jāti* in the first three categories (*dravya, guṇa* and *karma*) and he calls the rest three categories (*sāmānya, viśeṣa* and *samavāya*) simply *sat* (existent). The intention is that there is a common character in the substancehood, qualityhood and activityhood which makes them a class. But there is no such common class-character pervading *sāmānya, viśeṣa* and *samavāya. Sāmānya* itself is a *jāti*, acceptance of another *jāti* of it will lead to regressus ad infinitum.

The Prābhākara does not admit *sattā sāmānya* as the common character in those three categories. He says, we cognise substancehood in a substance but nothing common is cognised among substancehood, qualityhood and activityhood. The substance, quality etc. are different categories, they do not present common characteristics for our perception. (The Prābhākara holds that *jāti* is *pratyakṣa*). For instance, we cognise a common property in one and all pots, but we never cognise such common property in the pot (substance) and in the potness (quality).[83]

From the above discussion it becomes clear that the Mīmāṁsaka's concept of *sāmānya* is different from that of the Nyāya-Vaiśeṣika.

The Perception of Sāmānya

How *sāmānya* is perceived? There are different views as to the perception of *sāmānya.* Praśastapāda maintains that a universal being resident of a perceptible locus is perceived by that sense organ by which the locus is comprehended. Candramati introduces a new idea and holds that one can perceive the universal with one's internal organ only. This observation means that the perception of substance, quality etc. is different from the perception of universal. The reason for this distinction lies in the fact that for the perception of universal contact between self and the internal organ is required, whereas for the perception of substance, quality etc. contact of the sense organ with the external object is necessary.

Vyomaśiva holds that universal is perceived only by that type of perception which is termed as non-prepositional (*nirvikalpa*).

Śālikanātha says that the universal is perceptible and different from its locus, and he quotes the views of Prabhākara.[84]

Both the Prābhākara and the Vaiśeṣika admit that *jāti* is different from its locus (*āśraya*) but according to the Prābhākara *jāti* is perceptible (*pratyakṣa*) while Vaiśeṣika holds that it can be known by inference only.

"After all the universals are the features by which recognise, re-identify and thus are able to classify individuals, so that surely we must be able to perceive them."[85]

It has been stated that the Buddhist holds that universal is imaginative construct (*vikalpa-vilasitam*). Dharmakīrtti states that it is not different from the knowledge and it cannot stand for different entity.[86]

The Diṅnāga school holds that universal is a fiction and its purpose is served through double negation; that cowness only means—what is 'not a non-cow'.

Bhāsarvajña rejects the Buddhist theory and argues in support of the universal property as distinct from the individual. There are likely to be two alternatives in this regard:

(i) That the universal property, such as the 'cowness' may be taken as all-pervasive, that is, it exists anywhere and everywhere.

In the alternative, it may be postulated, as

(ii) That the 'cowness' exists in an individual cow. Both these alternatives may be examined. Let us take the second one first.

In the premise that the 'cowness' exists in an individual cow, then when a new cow is born, the cowness shall have to move from its previous locus to a new locus in order to reside in the new-born cow, then only it can be cognised there. If the first alternative is accepted, i.e. cowness is universal and it exists everywhere, then everything would be called cow, because as per presumption cowness will be present everywhere. To the above two objections the reply would be as follows:

It is true that universal, such as cowness exists in the individual cow and not everywhere, but such is the special nature of a universal property, that it can be associated with any new cow without "physically" moving from its former location.[87]

However what is that special nature and how it operates has not been explained. In this context Dharmakīrtti's view on the meaning of a word that it cannot be the individual object, because meaning is a social or conventional (*vyavahāra*) fact, has been criticised by Bhāsaravajña. He states that there are two types of meanings:

(a) express meaning or denotation (*vācya*), and
(b) implied meaning or connotation (*gamya*).

"The express meaning of the word cow is an individual cow qualified by cowness, while its implied meaning is the exclusion of what is not a non-cow. The express meaning of "not a non-cow" is the individual qualified by the exclusion of what is a non-cow, and its implied meaning is cowness."

In his view without the universal properties like cowness it would be impossible to introduce a natural classification of empirical subjects.

Notes and References

1. *NKP.* Pt. 1, p. 33.
2. Śatakṛtvo' pi taddṛṣṭau vyabhicārasya sambhavāt. —*NM.* pt.1. p, 108.
3. bhūyodarśanatastāvad udeti matiridṛśī /
niyato'yamaneneti sakalaprāṇisākṣikā // —Ibid, p.111
4. An Enquiry Concerning Human Understanding, Sec. VII, pt. 2.
5. *NK,* pt.1, pp. 42-43.
6. nityaṁ sattvaṁ asattvaṁ vā hetorasyā napekṣaṇāt /
apekṣāto hi bhāvānāṁ kādacitkatvasambhavaḥ //
quoted in *Nyāya-Vārttika-Tātparya* as Dharma kīrtti's verse.
7. kāryotpādakatvam kāraṇatvam —*SP.* p. 85
8. ananyathā siddha-niyatapūrvabhāvitvaṁ kāraṇatvam —*TBh.* p. 2.

9. ananyathāsiddha-niyata-paścādbhāvitvaṃ kāryatvam. —Ibid. p. 2
anyathāsiddhi-śūnyasya-niyatā pūrvavarttitā /
kāraṇatvaṃ bhavet tasya traividhyaṃ parikīrttitam // —*Bh. p.k.*16
10. *Samavāyikāraṇa* is usually rendered into English as the material cause. According to the Sāṁkhya doctrine the effect is nothing but the cause itself in different form and hence to Sāṁkhya the material cause is *upādāna-kāraṇa.*
11. While Gaṅgeśa enumerates three kinds of *anyathāsiddha,* Vardhamāna in *Nyāya-kusumāñjali-prakāśa* and Viśvanātha in *Bhāṣāparicheda* enlist five types of *anyathāsiddha.*
See *Tattvacintāmaṇi, Īśvarānumāna,* p. 154.
NKP, pp.149-154; Bh.p.SM. pp.19-22.
12. yathā rūpādyasambaddho na vyaktirupalabhyate /
tathaiva jātyayukteti kā te vyasana-santatiḥ // —*NM*.pt.1.28 b.
13. yat samavetaṁ kāryamutpadyate tat samavāyikāraṇam. —*TBh.*
14. SM. on kārika 17.
15. yat samavāyikāraṇa-pratyāsannam avadhṛtasāmarthyaṁ tadasamavāyi-kāraṇam. —*TBh.*
kāryaikārtha-kāraṇaikārthānyatara-pratyāsattyā samavāyikāraṇe pratyāsannaṁ kāraṇaṁ jñānādibhinnaṁ samavāyikāraṇam. —*SM*.k.17.
16. D.N. Shastri describes this as "the magic of *samavāya.*
—*Critique of Indian Realism,* p. 376
17. na tad asattvam na kriyate kintu kāraṇābhāvāt, na ca asattvam utpattau hetur apitu sataḥ anutpatteḥ asad utpadyate. —*NV.* iv.i.50
18. tantusaṁyogasya guṇasya paṭasamavāya-kāraṇeṣu tantuṣu guṇiṣu sama-vetatvena samavāyikāraṇa pratyāsannatvād ananyathāsiddha-niyatapūrva-bhāvitvena paṭam prati kāraṇatvācca. —*TBh*.p. 3
19. kāraṇasya jātiniyamābhāve kāryajātiniyamo hetvabhāvena vyāhanyate. —*NKB.*,p. 12
20. sarvabhāvānāṁ śaktiradṛṣṭalakṣaṇāpi kāryeṇānumīyate. —*PP*.p. 218
21. agner yathā bhūtādeva dāho dṛṣṭaḥ, tathābhūtādeva agner mantrauṣadhi-praṇidhānena kāryaṁ dṛśyate. —Ibid.p. 218
22. yacca khalu ajanaka-daśāto niratiśayaṁ, tataḥ kāryaṁ notpadyate, kuṇṭhādiva kuṭhārāt. —Ibid, p.218
23. The Prābhākara school of Mīmāṃsaka does not accept *abhāva* as the cause of any effect. The Naiyāyika admits absence as a cause and the Bhāṭṭa Mīmāṁsaka indirectly does so. The Bhāṭṭa admits non-cognition (*anupa-labdhi*) as a means of valid proof which amounts to acceptance of *abhāva* as a cause.
Bhavanātha elucidating the Prābhākara concept says: "bhāvabhed-ādeva sarvatra kāryaṁ, abhāvasya kāraṇa tānupagamāt.—commentary on *PP*, p. 219
24. *NKP.*, p. 14

25. *NV.* IV. i. p. 50
26. *STK.*, p. 65; Gauḍapāda bhāṣya on S.K.
27. Ibid. p.66.
28. *STK.*, pp. 65-66.
29. arthāntaraṁ paṭāt tantavaḥ tadhetutvāt turyādivad iti tūryādi paṭakāraṇam iti dṛṣṭam, tathā ca tantavaḥ tasmādarthāntaram iti. —*NV.* 11.i. 36
30. bhāvānyathātvaṁ bhavati na dravyānyathātvaṁ yathā suvarṇabhājanasya bhittau anyathā kriyamāṇasya anyathātvaṁ bhavati na suvarṇānyathātvamiti. —*YS. VBh.* III. 13
31. sattvato'nyathā prathā vikāra ityudāhṛthaḥ / asattvato' nyathā prathā vivartta ityudāhṛtḥ // —Quoted in *Vedāntasāra.*
32. tadananyatvam ārambhaṇa-śabdādibyaḥ. —*VS.* 13-32
    Śaṁkara says: kāryam ākāśādikaṁ bahuprapañcaṁ jagat, kāraṇam paraṁ brahma tasmāt kāraṇāt paramātharto' ananyatvaṁ vyatirekeṇa abhāvaḥ kāryasyāvagamyate.—Śaṁ. Bh. on the above. See Vācaspati's elucidation.
33. *TSP.*, p.10, 19.
34. *TS.*, p. 19.
35. *NV.*, 1. 14-15.
36. *TSP.*, p. 21.
37. *KKKH.*, p. 50.
38. *NK.Pt.* I, p. 43.
39. *KKKh.* Com., p. 51.
40. *Nyāya-bhāṣya, Nyāya-vārttika, Nyāya-vārttika-tātparya-ṭīkā, Nyāya-kandalī* and *Kiraṇāvalī* have dealt with it in some details.
41. na avayavinamapahnumahe dravyāntarotpattiṁ tu na icchāmaḥ, pratipattyabhāvāt. —Sh. D. p. 245.
42. tantava eva tena tena saṁsthānabhedena pariṇataḥ paṭaḥ, na tantubhya arthāntaraṁ paṭaḥ. —*STK.* p.
43. *AP.*
44. apareṇa tu kāryagurutvena kāraṇagurutvaṁ pratibaddhaṁ bruvate. —*NV.*II.i.33
45. etena kāryagurutvena kāraṇa-gurutva-vināśo' pi vyākhyātaḥ. —*NV.* II.i.33
46. ācaramād āca paramāṇor dravya-samāhāra anumīyate. —*NV.* II.i.33
47. tatra manuṣyadharmāṇo na yuktaṁ vaktum iyat kāraṇa-gurutvam iti. —*NV.*II.i.33
48. dravya-samāhara iti kārya-kāraṇa-dravya samāhāro mṛtkaṇā-mṛccūrṇa-śarkarā-kapāla-kumbha-samāhāra iti arthaḥ. —*NV. TT.*, II.i.33
49. yat punaravayavi-gurutvasya kāryātireko na gṛhyate tad avayavāvayavi-gurutvabhedasyā lpāntaratvāt, yathā mahati dravye' numīyamāne tatpatita-sūkṣmadravyāntara-gurutva-kāryagrahaṇam. —*N.K.*, p. 264
50. citram tad ekam iti ced idam citram mahat. —Quoted in *NVT*, p. 1051

51. S.D., p. 287.
52. citraśabdasya anekaviṣayatvāt; citraśabdena ekambhi dhīyate' nekañca; citraṁ rūpam, citrāṇi rūpāṇi. —*NVT*. iv.ii.12
53. na ca nīlapītādaya eva bhāvā avyāpya-vṛttayaścitra-padāspadamiti sāmpratam, rūpādīnām vyāpyavṛttitvāt. —*NVTT*. iv.11-12
54. *Nyāya-sūtra* II.i.31 and Nyāya-bhāṣya and Vārttika there on.
55. *NV*. p. 1051.
56. kiṁ sarvāvayava-darśana-dvāreṇāvayavinaḥ pratipattir uta katipayāvayava-draśana-dvāreṇa? pūrvasmin kalpe nāvayavi kadācid api dṛśyeta. na hi asarvavit sarvāvayavopalambha-kṣamaḥ, arvāgbhāgena-madhyāparabhāgayor vyavadhānāt. —*NVTT*., p.1052
57. Regarding the parts that are to be perceived for the perception of the whole Śrīdhara in his *Nyāya-kandalī* gives an example: When a person is immersed in the water and only his head is visible the whole, the man, is not perceived (yathā jala-nimagnasya śiromātradarśanāt.) —*NK*. p. 42
58. na hi indriyeṇa sannikṛṣyamāṇaikadeśe tat saha caritāvayavinā sannikṛṣṭaḥ tena yathā ekadeśaḥ sannikarṣād upalabhyata evam avayavi api sannikarṣād upalabhyate. —*NV*. II.1.32
59. *NV*. on *Nyāya-bhāṣya;* sūtra II.i.32, 42-47.
60. keśa-samūhe taimirikopalabdhivat tadupalabdhiḥ yathā ekaikaḥ keśaḥ taimirikeṇa nopalabhyate keśasamūhastūpalabhyate, tathā ekaikāṇur nopalabhyate aṇusañcaystūpalabhyate.
—*NV*. on the *Nyāyabhāṣya*, 4.ii.13, p.1042-47
61. yadāvabhāsā hi buddhis-tadasyā ālambana-pratyaḥ. —*NV*. on the above *sūtra*.
62. te khalvime paramāṇavaḥ sannihitā gṛhyamāṇā atīndriyatvaṁ jahati, viyuktāścā-gṛhyamāṇā indriya-viṣayatvaṁ na labhante iti. so 'yaṁ dravyāntarānutpattau ati mahān vyāghātaḥ. —*NBh*. on *N.S*. IV.ii.14
saṁhatā aindriyakā asaṁhatā atīndriyā iti mahān vyāghātaḥ.—*NV*. Ibid.
63. yasya paramāṇavaḥ ghaṭādi-buddhi-hetavo bhavanti sa sedaṁ praṣṭavyaḥ kiṁ paramāṇava eva upajāta-viśeṣa-buddhibhedaṁ kurvanti uta anupajāta-viśeṣa iti? kiṁ cātaha? yadyupajāta-viśeṣa yo' sau viśeṣaḥ, sa avayavīti prāptam, atha anupajāta-viśeṣaḥ ta eva atīndriyā aindriyakāśceti mahān virodhaḥ. —Ibid.
64. ko vā virdho bahavaḥ samjātātiśayaḥ pṛthak /
bhaveyuḥ kāraṇaṁ buddher yadi nāmendriyādivat //
—Quoted in *Sambandha-parīkṣā*.
65. pāṇyādi kampe sarvasya kampa-prāpter virodhinaḥ /
ekatra karmaṇo' yogāt syāt pṛthak siddhiranyathā.
—*Avayavinirākaraṇam*.
66. The Mīmāṁsaka considers *sāmānya* or *jāti* as a quality hence it comes under *guṇa*.

67. Samantabhadra of the Jaina school in his work *Āptamīmāṁsā* describes universal as not one and without parts. But the latter scholars like Akalaṅka, Vidyānandi and others differ from him.
68. *Buddhist Logic*, Vol. 1. p. 444.
69. samānānāṁ bhāvaḥ svābhāviko nāgantuko bahūnāṁ dharmaḥ sāmānyam.
—*Kiraṇāvalī*, p.117
samavetatva-rahita-sarvānyonya-bhāva-samānādhikaraṇa-samavetaṃ sāmānyam. —*Lakṣaṇāvali*, p. 39.
70. This position has been explained by the Buddhist as "*apoha*", which means double negation i.e. "this is not a non-cow".
71. bhinneṣu yadabhinnā jātirupayate, tatra anuvṛttākārāvabhāsinī budhireva nibandhanam. —*PP.*, p.531
72. vyaktyākṛtijātayastu padārthāḥ. —*NS.* 2.2.66
73. yā samānāṁ buddhim prasūte bhinneṣu adhikaraṇeṣu yayā bahūnītaretarato na vyavartante, yo'rtho' nekatra pratyayānuvṛttinimittaṁ tat sāmanyam.
—*NB.* on *sūtra* 2.2.69.
74. yacca keṣāñcidabhedaṁ kutaścid bhedaṁ karoti tat sāmānya-viśeṣo jātiḥ.
—*NB.* on *sūtra* 2.2.69
75. In English translation *sāmānya* is rendered as universal and *viśeṣa* as particular. It is suggested by others that 'genus' and 'species' will be more appropriate rendering of the terms *sāmānya* and *viśeṣa* respectively. It is maintained that such rendering "will explain the puzzle of the statement that *sāmānya* (other than being) may also be viewed as *viśeṣa*." For instance, the term "potness" may refer to a particular pot or a series of pots. Potness is invariably there in a particular pot or in a number of clay objects known as pot. It may be noted that Candramati accepts the term "potness" both as *sāmānya* and *viśeṣa*.
76. vyaktyākṛti-jāti-sannidhau upacārāt saṁśayaḥ. —*NS.* 2.2.59
77. *NS.* 2.2.68.
78. sāmānyaṁ jatirūpam upādhirupañca jātirūpaṁ sattaguṇa-karmatvādi, upādhirūpaṁ pācakatvādi. —*SP.* p. 28
bhavati ca vināpi jātyā pācaka-mīmāṁsakādi-śabda-pravṛttiḥ. —*SP.*, p. 28
79. In order to avoid this absurdity Pārthasārthi Miśra has re-defined *samavāya* as follows:
yena sambandhenādheyam ādhāre svānurūpāṁ buddhiṁ janayati,
svākāreṇa bodhayatītyarthaḥ sa sambandhaḥ samavāyaḥ. —*SD.*, p. 297
80. piṇḍeṣveva sāmānyaṁ nāntarā gṛhyate yataḥ /
nahyākāśavad icchanti sāmānyaṁ nāma kiñcana //—*SV ākṛtivāda*, V.25
81. tatra yat yāvat pṛṣṭaṁ sāmānyaṁ sarvagataṁ vyktigataṁ veti tatra pakṣa-dvayam pi vayaṁ kukṣīkurmaḥ. —*MM*, p. 231
82. samavāyaṁ tu na vayaṁ kāśyapīya iva nityamupahnumaḥ.—*PP.*, p. 206

83. tasmāt svarūpa-sattopādhika eva sacchabdo na punar ekahārtha sattānāṁ dravya-guṇa-karmaṇām. —*PP.*, p. 29
84. jātirāśrayato bhinnā pratykṣajñānagocarā /
pūrvākārāvamarśena prabhākaragurormatā // —*PP.*, p.130
85. *Encyclopedia of Indian Philosophy*, V.II, p. 17.
86. śaktayo nānayantyanyadanuyayi na bhāsate /
jñānādavyatiriktaṁ ced kathamarthāntaraṁ vrajet // —*PV.*
satīm api jātim āśrayebhyo' bhinnam anumanyante. —Comm. on *PV*
87. ekavyakti-samanvita-grahaṇe' pi tadaiva paścād vyāpitva-grahaṇasyoktatvāt. —*NB.*, p. 237

Chapter 4

The Concept and the Definition of Samavāya

4.1. In the Vaiśeṣika philosophy *samavāya* is conceived as synthetic principle—the principle which is evolved for providing a logical explanation of the emergence of the universe, objective and real, from the desecrate atoms. *Sāmānya* (generic property) is also another synthetic principle conceived in the system. Both *sāmānya* and *samavāya* are the two of the six categories enumerated by Kaṇāda. Both these two principles are unique to this system, hence, they have been defined and defended from the attack of the other schools of philosophy.

The origin of the concept of *samavāya* can be traced to the *Kaṇāda-sūtra* but the concept has developed in later works and the definition also has undergone modifications.

Samavāya etymologically means the act of coming together closely. It conveys the senses such as to meet, combine and flock together. Amarasiṁha gives different synonyms of the word *samavāya* such as *samūha, samudaya, samudāya,* etc.[1] Rāyamukuṭa in his *Padārthacandrikā*, a commentary on the *Amarakośa* derives the word *samavāya* by adding the suffix *ghañ* to the root in instrumental case and locative case.[2] It denotes a kind of intimate relation between two things. The two things are so related that they cannot be separated without one of them being destroyed. *Samavāya*, keeping in view its nature and function, has been rendered variously into English, such as 'inheresion'[3], 'inseparable relation'[4] 'intimate union'[5], 'co-inherence'[6], 'inherence'[7], [7a], etc. We prefer the term 'inherence' which seems to be more appropriate and is also widely used.

Samavāya is a relation like *saṁyoga*, but *samavāya* is defined in contrast to *saṁyoga*, and *samavāya* can be understood when this difference is clearly brought out. *Saṁyoga* being a relation is a *guṇa* (quality) but *samavāya* is a separate category (*padārtha*) by itself. In the following passages we shall try to show why *samavāya* has been considered as a separate category and how the concept developed.

In the *Kaṇāda-sūtra samavāya* is conceived as a relation based on causality.[8] It is a relation holding between the cause and the effect. The notion that the product subsists in the cause is generated by the relation, called *samavāya*. Kaṇāda in the definition of *samavāya* lays emphasis on cause and effect (*yataḥ kāryakāraṇayoḥ*) and considers the notion "this is here" (*inhedam*) as the basis of *samavāya*. Thus, in the early Vaiśeṣika system *samavāya* is conceived as the relation between cause and effect with the notion 'this is here'.[9]

The idea germinated in the *Vaiśeṣika-sūtra* developed by Praśastapāda in his *Padārtha-dharma-saṁgraha*. Prasaśtapāda has explained the notion of "this is here" as the state of container (*ādhāra*) and contained (*ādheya*), and also introduced a new concept, the concept of *ayutasiddha* (inseparably connected). Therefore, he defines *samavāya* as a relation that holds between two entities which do not exist without being related to the other, and which is based on the container-contained notion.[10]

Like Kaṇāda Praśastapāda also considers *samavāya* as a relation by which two entities are related as things container and contained. But this new concept of *ayutasiddha*, introduced in the definition of *samavāya*, is given more importance by him. In fact, the concept of *ayutasiddha* has been the criteria for distinguishing *samavāya* from *saṁyoga*.

While Kaṇāda has laid stress on *samavāya* as the relation on cause and effect Praśastapāda does not consider it as an exclusive reason for recognition of *samavāya*, and hence, he is silent on this aspect of *samavāya* in its definition. Of course, while explaining the nature of *samavāya* he says that the notion of cause and effect (*kāryakāraṇa-bhāva*) is just an adventitious qualifier (*upalakṣaṇa*), because things which do not stand as cause and effect are also included in the fold of *samavāya*.[11]

Following Praśastapāda Śrīdhara[12] and Śaṅkara[13] also consider this portion of the definition of *samavāya* as adventitious qualifier. Prior to them Vyomaśiva, the earliest known commentator of the *Praśastapāda-bhāṣya* while examining and explaining the definition of *samavāya,* as given by Praśastapāda refers to the definition of *samavāya* in the *Kaṇādasūtra* and points out the difference between the two. He states clearly that the new concept of *ayuta-siddha* has been introduced by Praśastapāda.

Vyomaśiva points out that the condition of *kāryakāraṇa-bhāva* (the state of cause and effect) is not exclusive for holding *samavāya.* It is neither regulatory nor mandatory. It simply suggests that *samavāya* holds between two entities which stand as cause and effect. This means that *samavāya* also holds between two entities which do not stand as cause and effect.

It is to be noted that Praśastapāda in his commentary has neither mentioned nor referred to any criticism that might have been offered to the Kaṇāda's definition of Samavāya by any school of philosophy. But he has modified the definition and enlarged its scope by introducing the concept of *ayutasiddha* (inseparably connected). He has also left out from his definition the phrase *kāryakāraṇabhāva.* It is not known to us what prompted Praśastapāda for introducing this new concept of *ayutasiddha.*[14] All writers of the Nyāya-Vaiśeṣika system after Prasaśtapāda have laid stress on the concept of *ayutasiddha* for cognising *samavāya.* Therefore, the term *ayutasiddha* is defined and discussed by them and as already this has been made the ground for differentiating *samavāya* from *saṁyoga.*

4.2. *Concept of Ayutasiddha*

The term *ayutasiddha,* for the first time, perhaps, is used by Praśastapāda to convey the sense of inseparable existence of the objects related by the relation of *samavāya.* He has introduced this new concept to explain the occurrence of *samavāya* as distinct from *saṁyoga.* According to him the term *ayutasiddha* means—"things become when stand related". The term *ayutasiddha* is opposite to *yutasiddha.*

Let us examine the derivative meaning of the word*yutasiddha* first. *Yutasiddha* may be taken to mean either "prove to be joined" proved to be separated", because, the root *'yu'* from which the word *yuta* is derived, means "to join" and "to separate".[15] In either case the meaning of *yutasiddha* is the same. "In the first sense, *yutasiddha* means things which are proved to have been actually joined and therefore which must have once existed in a state of separation, while in the latter sense *yutasiddha* simply denotes things which are proved once have been separated."[16] With the negative *nañ* the term *ayutasiddha,* therefore, stands for those objects which have never existed in a separate state.

Ayutasiddha has been defined by Udayanācārya as those objects not separate and related, which exist being only related and not otherwise.[17] In other words, those objects which are in such state that being related they come into existence.

Vardhamāna further explains this while discussing the occurrence of *samavāya.* He says that there may be three alternatives in the denotation by *ayutasiddha.* First, the term *ayutasiddha* cannot be taken as *apṛthak-siddha,* which means the objects do not have their separate existence, because for holding a relation two distinct entities are required.[18]

Secondly, those objects which exist without being separated, i.e. their existence is cognised when they stand related; the same objection in a different form will be there.[19] It also cannot be said that the term *apṛthaksiddha* means existence in identity, because the identity of the two entities does not leave scope for operation of a relation. Thus *ayutasiddha* does not mean either "non-existent separately" or "existent being related". There the meaning of *ayutasiddha* may be taken as—although the two objects have their separate existence ontologically, one cannot exist without being associated with the other, or, in other words, one is dependent on the other for its manifestation.[20]

Śrīdhara while discussing the question of *samavāya* defines *ayutasiddha* in clear terms. According to him *samavāya* is a dependent relation (*asvātantryaṁ samavāyaḥ),* because the concept of *ayutasiddha* presupposes interdependence, or, to be precise, it means the dependence of one of the two objects, locked in *ayuta-*

siddha, on the other. For example, the cloth and the yarns—the cloth is dependent on the yarns for its emergence and existence, too.

Śrīdhara says: the objects which are known to be mutually different and whose state of separation is also cognised, but one being dependent on the other, the two do not exist separately.[21]

Śrīdhara further explains *ayutasiddha* as a relation between the two, both of them do not exist on separate locus, as for example, the cloth and the yarns. Here Śrīdhara anticipates an objection that though the cloth exists in the yarns, the yarns do not exist in the same locus as the cloth—but in the parts of the yarns (*aṁśu)*, which are different from the locus of the cloth. Then how they can be regarded as *ayutasiddha* ?

To this Śrīdhara replies: that although the yarns exist in a locus different from the locus of the cloth, the cloth exists in the yarns. To be precise, although the yarns do exist in their own parts (*aṁśu)* still the yarns never remain separated from the cloth.[22]

Two entities will be considered *yutasiddha* only when both of them exist separately quite independent of the other. If 'X' and 'Y' are related through 'R', for example, *samavāya*, the locus of 'X' and the locus of 'Y' cannot be unrelated and independent of other. In the case of *yutasiddha* the 'X' and 'Y' have two different locus, say, 'A' and 'B', which are in no way related to each other.[23]

To make his point clear Śrīdhara cites an example when the two are not so related through *samavāya*. For example, the relation between the body and the tactual sense-organs is *saṁyoga* and not *samavāya*, because the body exists in its parts and while being so related it is absolutely independent of the tactual sense-organ. For instance, a man being paralised cannot experience the touch but the body is still there.

In case of eternal substances *yutasiddha* means separated existence of entities having capacities to move separately, when this is absent, they are *ayutasiddha*. For example, the relation between other (*ākāśa*) and substancehood (*dravyatva*) would be the case of *samavāya*.[24]

Śaṅkara Miśra defines *ayutasiddha* in a very simple way. According to him the state of non-existence of the objects without being related is *ayutasiddha*.[25] Those entities which do exist without being related, are not the entities of inseparable existence. While there are some other entities which do not exist without being related—the state of inseparable existence is there.

Annaṁbhaṭṭa gives a similar explanation to the one given by Śrīdhara. He has also laid stress on dependence of one of the objects on the other. He says that *ayutasiddha* denotes things, one of which is always dependent on the other, as the pot on its components, the quality on the substance etc.[26] According to Jagadīśa *ayuta* means always related, i.e. the entities that stand persistently related to each other and cognised as such are *ayutasiddha.*[27] What is really meant by the term *ayutasiddha* may be understood by one or two illustrations. Let us take the example of the red pot, i.e. the redness in the pot or cowness in the cow. The redness is never seen apart from the pot, and for that matter from any substance. No one can visualise redness without at the same time finding its correlate. Similarly, nobody can perceive cowness without perceiving the cow. The redness and the pot are distinct entities ontologically, so also the cowness and the cow. But while one of them, the pot can exist by itself, the other, redness cannot; it has to depend on the pot (substance) for its subsistence. It lacks independence.[28] In other words, one of the entities, those are termed *ayutasiddha,* is independent, and the other is dependent on it. Thus so long the former exists the latter also exists. This state of existence presents the two as *ayutasiddha.* This point has been stressed by Annaṁbhaṭṭa and Vardhamāna.[29]

Consequent to it, it appears that *samavāya* which holds between two entities stand in the tie of *ayutasiddha,* is a relation of necessity—the necessity of the entity which is dependent on the other. The entity which is not dependent does not stand in the necessity of this relation, at least, at that point of time when it is born.[30]

4.3. *Emergence and Being Related Simultaneously*

Now the question arises if the two entities are mutually so dependent (*ekamavinaśyad aparāśritamevāvatiṣṭhate*) then why the two be not taken as one. Dependence (*āśritatva*) is not a disproof of distinctness. It is stated that such objects are ontologically distinct, then why the distinct objects are not visualised as separate? The reason for not being seen separately by itself is that there is no time gap between its emergence and it becoming related, or, in other words, no sooner it "comes to be", it becomes related. Hence it cannot be said that it is related after its emergence, nor it can also be said that it emerges after being related. In fact, both—"becomes related" and "comes to be"—take place simultaneously at the same point of time.[31] It is why the two are not perceived separately. Jayanta says that the two are different due to the different cognition, in reality they do not exist in two separate places.[32]

This theory seems to go against the maxim that at the moment a substance is born, is devoid of quality etc. It is true, there is apparent contradiction, but the intention is that the substance which is stated to be devoid of quality cannot be an object of the determinant knowledge (*savikalpa pratyakṣa*), hence there is no contradiction.

That the origination of the object and its relation to its corelata both are simultaneous and there is no sequence of time between them. Uddyotakara says that the moment the whole is emerged it is related to its parts (*jātaṁ ca sambaddhaṁ ca iti ekaḥ kālah*).[33] In the same way the relation between the whole and the part is *samavāya* and the two are *ayutasiddha.*

Jayanta while defining *samavāya* refers to the concept of *ayutasiddha* and also to the objection (against *samavāya*). "When two entities are non-existent there cannot be any relation between the two and when they exist (separately) then the relation would be of *yutasiddha,* and that is *saṁyoga."*[34] This objection, says Jayanta, has been refuted by *Ācārya* (Uddyotakara), who stated that the emergence and the relation occur at the same moment. This principle is equally applicable, says he, to the whole and the part, quality and quality-possessor.[35] That in *ayutasiddha* the two entities are different but they are cognised as one for the reason that the effect stands related no sooner than it is produced.

Śrīdhara further explains this position with an illustration by pointing out the difference of *samavāya* from *saṁyoga.* In the case of *saṁyoga,* says he, the process of two things being related occurs after their emergence, whereas in the case of *samavāya* the process of being related and their emergence occurs simultaneously.[36] That is to say, that the condition of the cause of something being related through inherence is the cause of its production—the two processes occur simultaneously. For example, in the act of felling a tree by an axe, the act of felling (*chidi kriyā*) emerges simultaneously with its relation with the tree. The cause of felling is also the cause of the relation between the act of cutting and the tree which is being felled.[37]

The term *ayutasiddha* is not used by other Indian philosophical schools in the sense the Nyāya-Vaiśeṣika has used it. The term is occasionally mentioned with reference to *samavāya* which they do not admit.The reason for this lies in the fact that the notion of *ayutasiddha* is linked to the causation theory of the Nyāya-Vaiśeṣika, which is rather unique and which differs from that of the others. Therefore, the notion of *ayutasiddha* is foreign to them and the concept of *samavāya*, which being based on *ayutasiddha* presents the discrete particles as the gross element, is not acceptable to them.

The Mīmāṁsaka admits universality which he calls *jāti* and which is manifested through *vyakti.* The two may be treated as having without difference. Kumārila says that *viśeṣaṇa* is not entirely different from *viśeṣya*,[38] otherwise there would not have been the same cognition, and hence, there is no need to conceive a relation between *vyakti* and *jāti*. *Samavāya* is conceived for nothing and *samavāya* does not hold between two such entities.

4.4. *Container Contained*

Ayutasiddha or inseparableness alone does not qualify a relation to be called *samavāya*, because of the relation between merit (*dharma*) and happiness (*sukha*) which are related as cause and effect should have also been regarded as *samavāya*, because both of them have the same locus, namely, *ātman* (self) and both of them cannot exist separately from each other.[39]

In order to avoid this over-pervasion (*ativyāpti*) Praśastapāda and Śrīdhara introduced the condition of the things container and contained in the definition of *samavāya*. Although merit and happiness have the same locus, namely, self, both of them do not stand as entities container and contained (*ādhāryādhāra*).

When we say a star is in the sky, the relation between the star and the sky is *saṁyoga,* and such cases are excluded by the stipulation of the condition of inseparability in the definition of *samavāya.* But still the possibility of the defect of over-pervasion is not ruled out. Let us take an example. In Vaiśeṣika theory the sound (*śabda*) exists in the ether (*ākāśa*).[40] Now the meaning of the word *ākāśa* (ether) is related to its corresponding object (*ākāśa)* through the relation of *vācya-vācaka* (denotor denoting). So every word is related to its meaning by *vācya-vācaka* through which we have such cognition that this particular meaning is expressed by this word, or, this meaning (object) is to be understood from this word. Now this *vācya-vācaka* relation, particularly the word *ākāśa* and the substance *ākāśa* are things container and contained, because the sound of the word, for that matter the word itself, is a quality of *ākāśa.*[41] But such case according to Śrīdhara are not *samavāya,* because we do not have the word and its meaning as "this is in this". To be precise, we do not say that the word is in the meaning, but a word denotes a meaning. Hence in such cases there is not the notion of "this is in this" (*ihedaṁ-pratyayaḥ*) and, therefore, are not *samavāya* .

In this context Śrīdhara further clarifies the term *ayutasiddha.* The negative particle of *nañ* is either to be construed with *siddha* or *yuta.* But it cannot be construed with *siddha,* that means it cannot be a negation of existence, because without the existence of the relata (*dharmiṇorabhāvāt*) the relation is impossible. And if on the other hand, it is a negation of separability (*apṛthak-siddhatva*) how they can be related? Because to be related the relata must exist separately before they are related, as in the case of the book and the table. Śrīdhara thinks both these alternatives and the corresponding objection do not carry any weight, since none would postulate a relation between two non-existent entities. Nor does the Vaiśeṣika says that the two relata of *samavāya* should be identical, or of the same nature. Had they been of the same nature, there would not have been two things, but one.

When we say 'A' and 'B' both, the bothness implies that both of them have the absence of the nature of the other (*parasparātmakābhāva-lakṣaṇatvād ubhaya-rūpatāyāḥ*). Or, in other words, the nature of 'A' is different from 'B' and the nature of 'B' is different from 'A', and, hence we call them 'A' and 'B', both. So the relation between two things implies that by nature the two are different. The later Nyāya school terms them as *pratiyogin* (adjunct) and *anuyogin* (subjunct) of the relation.

Śrīdhara categorically says that two things will be different only when they generate two different cognitions of two different forms (*vilakṣaṇākāra-buddhi-vedyatvasya eva bheda-lakṣaṇatvāt*). Hence, *samavāya* is not a relation of identity, but on the other hand presupposes implicit difference between the two relata. But the fact is, although in *samavāya* they are different, they are so related that without this relation they cannot exist without the other. The only difference between *saṁyoga* and *samavāya*, is this that although the postulation presupposes difference between the relata, in the case of *saṁyoga* the difference is explicit while in the case of *samavāya* it is implicit.

4.5. *Samavāya between Non-causally Related Things*

We have stated that in early Vaiśeṣika literature *samavāya* is cognised between two things which are causally related, i.e. the cause and the effect. Unlike Kaṇāda Praśastapāda does not think that inherence should hold only between two things which are causally related. According to him it may hold between two things which are not causally related. His concept of *ayutasiddha* has enlarged the scope of *samavāya*, which we have discussed.

Let us point out some of the examples where *samavāya* holds between two non-casually related things. By pointing out the contact between the two sets of entities the position may be explained.

For example in the case of relation between the part (*avayava*) and the whole (*avayavin*) the same is the causal relation, so also in the case of non-eternal substances (*anitya dravya*) and their qualities, in case of activities and their locus which is a substance, inherence is the relation between the two, which are causally related entities. But in the case of universal and individuals, and between *antyaviśeṣa* (ultimate particular) and the eternal substance, for example, *ākāśa* etc. which is in no way causally related, and between whom *samavāya* relation holds. Neither of them is an effect.

The next is the condition of *ādhāra-ādheya* (container-contained), which has already been stated in some details. The two other points about the nature of *samavāya* which have been stressed by Praśastapāda and Śrīdhara are that the whole (*avayavin*) and the universal (*sāmānya* or *jāti*) have definite locus, i.e. the whole resides in parts so also the universal in the individual. This nature of existence in a definite locus can only be explained if we admit some kind of intimate relation between the two.[42]

The other point stressed by Praśastapāda is that a relation presupposes the notion of distinction. Hence *samavāya* also being a relation its relata must naturally be different. But although by nature they are different, they do not have independent existence. When two different things are held together it presupposes that there is a relation between the two. This is supported by our practical experience—when we say that there is yoghurt (*dadhi*) in the pot so also we have such notion, the cloth is in the yarns, the quality and the activity are in the substance (*dravya*), the class character (*sāmānya*) exists in substance, quality and activity. That is the substancehood in the substance, qualityhood in quality, and the activityhood in activity, the ultimate particular in the eternal substance, and the relation which is responsible for the emergence of such type of notion is *samavāya*. Vyomaśiva also lays stress on this aspect of *samavāya* and says that it holds between the universal and substratum (*ādhāra*).

Whatever may be the condition, i.e. whether there is the state of cause and effect or not, the existence of substratum-superstratum relation between the two entities is absolutely necessary. Without the cognition of "this is the substratum and this is the superstratum" the knowledge of "this is here" is not possible. Vyomaśiva further says that *samavāya* exists between entities which are *sarvagata* (all-pervading) and *asarvagata* (non-all-pervading). For instance, the ether is an entity which is *sarvagata* and it stands in *samavāya* relation with its quality. There is no cause and effect relation between the two, but quality of ether reside in the ether, and hence there is the substratum-superstratum relation between the two.

Samavāya holds between two *asarvagata* (non-all-pervading) entities (*tathā ca sarvagatānāmeva samavāya ityayaṁ niyamo na ghaṭate yataś cāsarvagatānāmapi samavāyo dṛśyate).*

4.6. *The Notion of Qualified Cognition*

Śaṅkara seeks to establish *samavāya* on the ground of the qualified cognition of the substratum and superstratum and says that the usage, such as, "the cloth is in these yarns", "the quality and action are in this substance", "cowness is in this cow", "knowledge is in this soul", "the sounds are in this ether"—we have the cognition of "this is here" between two sets of entities which are of inseparable existence in their nature. Such a qualified cognition cannot occur without a relation obtaining between the two entities, because the qualified cognition must have a qualified entity as the object of such cognition. Therefore, a relation between the two is to be admitted. The relation, which is assumed here, cannot be the contact, and, hence it is to be regarded as inherence.

He further raises the question of confusion of substratum and superstratum on account of *samavāya* being one and speaks about the manifesting power and the power of being manifested (*vyaṅgya-vyañjaka-śakti*) of the substratum and the superstratum respectively. This principle is there in case of contact also. The contact that holds between the curd and the can is the same in respect of the both, hence the curd could have appeared as the substratum and the can as superstratum but it is due to the governing principle of the cognition that the curd and the can are cognised as superstratum and substratum (*ādheya-ādhāra*) respectively. In the case of qualified cognition of the two relata one is cognised as *ādhāra* and the other as *ādheya.*

Further evolution in the concept and for that matter in the modification of the definition of *samavāya* can be traced in the persistent attempt made by the writers belonging to the Nyāya-Vaiśeṣika school to point out the difference of *samavāya* from *saṁyoga* and *tādātmya* (self-linking) relations. Udayana and Śrīdhara, two renowned authorities of the Nyāya system had taken much trouble to point out the difference and thus established *samavāya.*

Vāgīśvara and Vallabha have made an all out endeavour to establish *samavāya* and refute the objections raised against it, by logical argument coached in the terminology of Navya-Nyāya and they are more concerned with defending the position rather than importing new notion to the concept of *samavāya.*

Gaṅgeśa Upādhyāya has dealt with the subject in great detail and refuted all the objections by the opponents. These will be presented separately as they are class by themselves.

The later writers have paid their attention to the accuracy of the definition of *samavāya* and formulated the definition with such wordings so that the definition neither suffers the defects of over-pervasion nor non-pervasion. The difference of *samavāya* from *saṁyoga* and *tādātmya* has been pointed out in the course of discussion of the various definition of *samavāya* . However, we reserve the full discussion of this aspect of *samavāya* to a subsequent chapter, *samavāya* differs from *saṁyoga.* It will be seen that *samavāya* can be understood only in relation to *saṁyoga* and such other relations.

4.7. *The Definition*

The definition of *samavāya* by Kaṇāda[43] provides, as has been stated above, only cause and effect state of the entities which are related and the basis for the relation is the notion of "this is here". The said definition seems to be defective as it suffers from non-pervasion (*avyāpti*), because the definition is not applicable to such entities which do not stand as the cause and the effect but related through *samavāya.* Therefore Praśastapāda modified the definition[44] by providing the concept of *ayutasiddha.* The modified definition does not cover *saṁyoga* and it is strictly restricted to *samavāya* only. That the definition of *samavāya* by Praśastapāda does not over-pervade (*ativyāpti*) *saṁyoga* relation may be analysed by an example of *saṁyoga,* such as, "the book is on the table". The table and the book exist without being related, i.e. the table does exist before and after it is connected with the book, so also the book. Again, the book exists elsewhere other than the table, and the table in its space. In other words, both the adjunct and the subjunct[45] of a *saṁyoga* exist separately in respect of time and space. But the adjunct and the subjunct of *samavāya*, as in the case of "cowness in the cow", cowness and cow cannot be cognised separately in respect of time and space. Since cowness and cow fulfil both the conditions—inseparability and container-contained-hood, the relation subsists between the two is *samavāya*. But neither cowness nor cow is the cause or effect of the either. To overcome this difficulty Praśastapāda laid stress on container-containerhood. What Kaṇāda intended by the cause and effect principle *(kāryakāraṇayoḥ)* is explained by Praśastapāda as to include those which do not stand as cause and effect and he understands both cause-effect and non-cause-non-effect (*kāryakāraṇabhūtānām akārya-kāraṇa-bhūtānāṃ vā*)[46] by the expression of *kārya-kāraṇa* of Kaṇāda. The commentators of the *Praśastapāda-bhāṣya* while elaborating the concept of *ayutasiddha* have explained the cause-effect principle differently. Śrīdhara is inclined to accept the expression to mean non-cause-non-effect (*kāryakāraṇa-bhūtānām akārya-kāraṇa-bhūtānām*). Śaṅkara considers the expression, as has been pointed out above, just as an adventitious property (*kāryakāraṇayor ity upalakṣaṇam).*[47]

This suggests the difference in approach by the two writers of the system to the original concept of *samavāya*. In order to exclude *tādātmya* (self-linking) relation from the scope of the definition of *samavāya*, the qualifying clause container-contained is introduced. The underlying meaning is this that in the case of self-linking relation also there is inseparability, but self-linking relation is not intended to be identified with *samavāya* (the difference between the two is discussed separately).

Udayana in the *Kiraṇāvalī* mentions inseparability as a primary condition of *samavāya* and he defines *samavāya* as the eternal relation of the existence,[48] i.e. both the relata exist so long as they are related. He also lays stress on the inseparableness of the two relata—the relata which never exist without being related.[49] The underlying meaning of this statement is this that those two things which never exist unrelated leads to the conclusion that the relation holding between the two is eternal, because those which never exist without being related the relation between them cannot be produced. The things those exist, before being related separately can be related after and the relation in such case is a product. That is not the character of *samavāya* and thus *saṁyoga* is excluded.[50] Moreover, the things which are *sat* (of positive character) and are not produced, are termed eternal. *Samavāya* is also *sat* and non-product, hence it is eternal.

Prāpti (relation) means direct relation, i.e. where there is nothing in between the two relata. Thus *prāpti* includes both *saṁyoga* and *samavāya* but excludes other relations such as *janya-janaka* (producer-product) relation, etc. because in such relations there is the intervention of time or space.[51]

The portion *"ādhāryādharabhūtānām"* has been included in the definition of *samavāya* to exclude indirect relation.

A question has been raised as to the working of the definition of *samavāya*, i.e. *"nitya-sambandhaḥ samavāyaḥ"* and *"nityaprāptiḥ samavāyaḥ"*. It has been mentioned before that the term *sambandha* and *prāpti* are synonymous, that being so why *samavāya* has been defined as *"nitya-prāpti"* instead of *"nitya-sambandha?"*

Vardhamāna Upādhyāya makes a distinction between the two terms and says that if *samavāya* be defined as *"nitya-sambandha"* it will over-pervade the denotor-denoted relation which exists between the word and the meaning. In the Nyāya-Vaiśeṣika philosophy the relation between word and object denoted by word is God-ordained; it is the Will of God, which is known as power of the word. This Will of God is eternal and, therefore, the relation based on that eternal Will is to be taken as eternal. To exclude this from the scope of the definition of *samavāya* the term *"prāpti"* is used instead of *"sambandha"* for the reason that *prāpti* means only the direct relation, while *sambandha* embraces all relations, direct and indirect. According to Nyāya-Vaiśeṣika there is no direct relation between the word and the object. Had there been a direct relation one would have tasted sweet when one uttered the word 'honey'. This implies even though there is relation between the two, which we call power, is not direct, because the two relata are intervened by time and space.

Accordingly there is another objection to the definition of *samavāya*. It may be alleged that the contact between eternal omnipresent entities is eternal and hence the definition of *samavāya* will over-pervade this. The time and ether both are omnipresent entities, therefore, one must admit that contact occurs between the two. The rule of logic is:

> If an entity is in contact with many objects at the same time and space, those objects are to be taken as mutually in contact. For instance, the rays of the moon are seen coming through the branches of a tree and at the same time the branches are seen tossing in the air. It means the rays of the moon and the air are in contact with the branches of the tree, thus the rays of the moon and the air are to be taken as in mutual contact.

The time and ether, by the same logic, are in contact. Again the contact of two eternal entities is to be regarded as eternal for the following reason.

The contact is caused by the action of either of two relata or by that of both or by the contact itself.

In the case of contact of two eternal entities the contact is neither caused by either of the relata or by both or by the contact itself.[52] Therefore the contact is not caused. An entity of existential nature, if not caused by any other object is eternal. By this logic the contact of the two eternal entities has got to be regarded as eternal.

The argument that has been advanced regarding the contact of two eternal entities does not actually prove the contact, because such a contact is neither perceived nor inferred. The argument simply suggests the probability of such a contact. Therefore, the above definition of *samavāya* is perfectly in order.

However, an inference may be cited in support of the contact of ether with some other eternal entity. The ether has contact with an omnipresent entity, because it has a contact with an object which is lesser than the omnipresent one, like the body.[53]

The body has the contact with the air (which is lesser than the soul) and also with the soul which is *vibhu* (omnipresent). Similarly, the ether has the contact of earth, air (which are lesser than the soul, time, etc.) and it implies that the ether has the contact of soul, time, etc. which are omnipresent. Thus the contact of two eternal objects (*vibhu dravya*) has been proved.

The inference suggested above suffers from the defect of having counter reason. The ether has not the contact of an eternal entity, because the relata are not entities of separate existence.[54]

Objections are raised to the effect that if the definition of *samavāya* be the eternal relation then it may over-pervade the self-linking relation, because some of the self-linking relations are to be regarded as eternal, such as the relation of *abhāva*.

Again, the ether is devoid of action. Here the relation between ether and absence of action (*kriyābhāva*) is to be regarded as eternal. Because the question arises—if the relation of ether with the absence of action is an entity; to which entity it belongs? It is not a *saṁyoga* like the *saṁyoga* of a bird with a tree, and hence, does not come under quality (*guṇa*). The contact (*saṁyoga*) can occur between two entities which exist separately (*yutasiddha*). But ether and absence of action are not *yutasiddha*, i.e. separate existence is not seen, because absence of action always existed in the ether. At no point of time the ether is cognised without the absence of action, hence, the two entities are not *yutasiddha*. In other words, though the absence of action may reside in some other objects, the ether is always without action, i.e. there is absence of action.

On the other hand the relation between absence of action and the ether cannot be termed as *samavāya* also. The ground for not accepting the above relation as *samavāya* is this:

That while the absence of action always exists in ether it may also exist in some other object, say, in a motionless pot—through temporal relation. But when the motion is seen on the pot due to some action, say by a push, then nobody will cognise the pot as motionless. If the relation between them is accepted as *samavāya* it will lead us to the absurd situation that the pot having the motion also shall have to be regarded as motionless, because the relation assumed between the two is eternal.

It also cannot be said that with the commencement of the action, the absence of action (*kriyābhāva*) moves away from the pot, because absence (*abhāva*) has no action. The only manifested entity possesses action. The absence is of non-existential nature and unmanifested one.

Neither it can be said that the particular absence, with the advent of the action, has been destroyed, because the absence of action is seen in some other places even after the pot is charged with motion. The absence of action is one, and therefore, it cannot be said that the absence of action is destroyed. If the assumption is that it is destroyed, then the absence of action will not be experienced anywhere. At the same time nobody can cognise a moving pot as motionless.

In order to avoid this difficulty the Nyāya-Vaiśeṣika would say that the absence of action neither moves away from the pot nor it is destroyed, only the relation that exists between the two is destroyed. The rule of the logic is this if an entity be related to another entity by a relation then only the entity which is related is cognised. In a moving pot the relation of *kriyābhāva* with the pot is destroyed, it is no more there, hence *kriyābhāva* will not be cognised in the moving pot. However, in order to make this solution appear logical the relation between absence and its locus should be regarded as something else other than *saṁyoga* and *samavāya*. It has been discussed that the said relation cannot be a *saṁyoga*. *Samavāya* being an eternal relation cannot be destroyed and, hence it is not *samavāya*. The relation between absence and its locus is *svarūpa* (self-linking).

The self-linking relation is to be regarded as identical either with the *ādhāra* (substratum or locus) or with *ādheya* (superstratum), i.e. the absence itself. If it be taken as identical with absence, the relation of absence of action will be the same as the absence of action itself, and absence being eternal cannot be destroyed. The result is, the objection raised in this regard remains as before.

With a view to riggling out from this riddle another solution is suggested so as to make the relation of the pot with the absence limited by space and time. The underlying meaning of this suggestion is this that the pot being non-eternal a particular pot is to be taken to be existent in a particular point of time and space, and the relation of absence subsists in that pot, i.e. that pot itself is the *svarūpa sambandha*. In other words, whenever *kriyābhāva* is cognised in a stationery pot, existing in a particular point of time, that particular pot is the relation of *kariyābhāva*. Thus the moving pot has no scope to cause the cognition of *kriyābhāva* in it. It further implies that the cognition of *kriyābhava* is generated by a particular pot existing at a particular point of time, when it possesses action, the pot will no longer be the same pot, it will be a different pot from the previous one.

This suggestion, though saves the situation, places the Nyāya-Vaiśeṣika in an unenviable position of admitting momentariness of the external objects. This is neither anticipated nor replied.[55] This, however, is not the universal flux of Buddhism.

On the other hand when the self-linking relation is taken as identical with the locus, the ether, the locus of absence of action, will be the nature of the relation. The ether being eternal the relation, which is in the nature of ether itself, will also be eternal. Thus the self-linking relation, in the shape of absential relation, will come within the purview of the definition of *samavāya,* i.e. eternal relation.

Let us take another example to make the point clear. "There is no book on the table"—the absence of the book is a constant absence and hence, eternal according to the Nyāya-Vaiśeṣika. An absence subsists in its locus through self-linking relation, and the locus itself is not different from the relation. Therefore, if *samavāya* be defined as an eternal relation it will be difficult to differentiate it from the *svarūpa* relation, since the constant absence (*atyantābhāva*) resides in its locus through *svarūpa* relation. Therefore, an attempt has been made to modify and redefine *samavāya* relation by Ramarudra.[56] That the relation is to be accepted as something different from its relata[57] states Dinakara. This means that the so-called *svarūpa* relation is not a relation at all.

Since relation is different from its two relata, the adjunct and subjunct, the self-linking relation being constituted of the relata only, i.e. being identical with the relata the definition of *samavāya* will not over-pervade the self-linking relation.[58]

In the case of self-linking relation of absence, as illustrated above, the relation is not different from its relata i.e. the counter-positive of absence and the locus of absence. But what is required in case of *samavāya* is that the relation must be different from its relata and this characteristic of *samavāya* differentiates it from the self-linking relation.

The self-linking relation sometimes is of the nature of counter-positive of absence and sometimes is identical with the locus of absence. As in the case of 'there is no book on the table', the relation of absence of the book subsisting in its locus is nothing but the absence of the book itself. That the self-linking relation is identical with the locus of absence may be stated as follows:

According to Nyāya-Vaiśeṣika the eternal time (*mahākāla*) is all-pervading and as such is the locus of all products through temporal relation of self-linking. To be precise, when we say that "the book is on the table"—it means at present the book is related to a table and there is absence of the same in another place at the same time, because both exist in the same *mahākāla* (time eternal). Hence temporal relation is nothing but the eternal time itself, which is the locus of all products. It thus stands that in such case self-linking relation is identical with its locus and not with the superstratum.

As the substratum and the superstratum are distinct entities and the self-linking relation is identical with either of them, we shall have to admit two kinds of self-linking relation.[59]

But *samavāya* being an absolutely different identity from its relata, remains as the unchanged same, in spite of the fact that one relatum differs from the other. Moreover, the effect and quality subsist in substance, hence subsistence will be of the nature of their loci (the substances). In the event the substances being endless, the *svarūpa* relation is bound to be endless. As we have discussed *samavāya* remains unchanged, it is better to admit a simple *samavāya*, which is one, than the complex and manifold *svarūpa* relation. *Samavāya* presupposes simplicity (*lāghava*) and *svarūpa* involves multiplication of assumption (*kalpanāgaurava*).[60]

The criticism by D.N. Shastri of advancing simplicity (*lāghava*) as the ground for the assumption of *samavāya* by the Naiyāyikas seems to be rather lop-sided.[61] He accuses Viśvanātha and others attributing total ignorance of Nyāya-Vaiśeṣika metaphysic, for advancing argument of brevity. The ground of brevity (*lāghava*) is just a logical argument. It is not due to the ignorance that Viśvanātha and other writers of the Navya-Nyāya have advanced *lāghava* as one of the causes for assuming *samavāya.* In this context they are concerned with the logical soundness of the concept and not that of metaphysics. At the same time he himself takes his stand on *lāghava* (brevity).

Let us take up again the examples of the ether and the pot and their relation to the absence of action (*kriyābhāva*).

One may hold that it is true that the relation between the motionless pot and the absence of action cannot be the case of *samavāya* relation as you have stated, but what is the harm if *samavāya* is assumed between ether and absence of action?

To this the reply would be—*samavāya* cannot be assumed between the ether and the absence of action, for the reason that the relation that exists between the ether and the absence of action is the same with that which exists between the motionless pot and the absence of action. The sameness of the relation is determined by the same cognition in both the cases. And the same nature of cognition implies the same nature of relationship.

4.8. *The Object of the Cognition*

When we cognise—'the mountain is with fire'—the object of cognition is *saṁyoga*, and such cognition will be irresistible, where there is the contact of fire, say, in the kitchen. Again, where there is the cognition of 'fire-possessing' (*agnimān*) in the parts of the fire, the object of the cognition is *samavāya,* which causes the knowledge of fire residing in its parts through *samavāya* relation. It is thus evident that the same cannot have both *saṁyoga* and *samavāya* as its object. From this it follows that in order to have the same nature of cognition of the relation that exists between the motionless pot and the absence of action, and also between the ether and the absence of action—the relation must be of the same nature. Otherwise, the cognition will differ.

4.9. *Over-pervasion in Svarūpa Relation*

On the basis of the admission of this principle it is apprehended that the definition of *samavāya* will over-pervade the domain of the self-linking relation, whether it is identical with the substratum or locus or the superstratum. For instance, let us take the absence of substancehood in quality. The relation of absence of substancehood in quality is nothing but the absence of substancehood itself. The absence of substancehood in quality being an eternal one applies to the definition of *samavāya*. To avoid all these complicacies *samavāya* may be redefined so as to make it perfect. Accordingly the definition of *samavāya* is laid down as follows:

"That is *samavāya* relation, which is different from the adjunct and subjunct of the relation, which is eternal and the direct relation."[62]

The above mentioned definition again, says the critic, is not free from the defect of over-pervasion, *'prāpti'* (relation) has been interpreted as to mean the direct relation only, while the term *'prāpti'* may mean both direct and indirect relation. The criteria for treating a relation as direct relation are, as stated before, when the two relata of a relation are not intervened either by time or space. However, the above interpretation is not found adequate to determine the nature of direct relation. There are such instances wherein the two relata are not intervened by time or space, but the relation between them cannot be considered as direct relation. For example, the colour of the fire and the heat of the fire are not directly related, because the colour of the fire is related to heat through an intermediary, the fire, and hence no one will call the relation between the said two a direct one. On the other hand, these two, the colour and the heat of the fire are not intervened either by time or space, because both exist in the same time and in the same space.

However, one may hold that both *saṁyoga* and *samavāya* are intended by the term *'prāpti'*. In that case the definition of *samavāya* shall have to be modified to include both. To put it accordingly

"That relation is *samavāya*, which is different from the adjunct and subjunct (of the relation), which is eternal, and either a *saṁyoga* or a *samavāya*."[63]

This definition is defective on the ground that it involves self-dependence (*ātmāśrayatva*) because the knowledge of *samavāya* invariably precedes the knowledge of *samavāya* relation. Again, when one knows the definition of *samavāya* then only he would be able to know *samavāya.* Thus this definition leads us nowhere. Moreover, *saṁyoga* being different from *samavāya,* how *samavāya* can be identified with *saṁyoga*?

Vardhamāna finding fault with the above definitions defines *samavāya* in his own way:

"That is *samavāya,* which does not possess universality, is other than universal, and particular, and is of positive nature."[64]

The intention of this definition is just to exclude all the six categories (long before Vardhamāna the Nyāya-Vaiśeṣika admitted *abhāva* as an independent category and thus made the number of categories seven) from the scope of the definition of *samavāya* and by this process of elimination to find out *samavāya.* By the expression that this relation "is of positive nature" absence is excluded. Of the six positive categories, the first three are termed as *'sattā-sāmānyavat'* (of existential nature) and, as such, they are possessed of universality. By the expression "does not possess universality" the aforesaid three categories are excluded. Both universal and particulars are excluded specifically and hence *samavāya* remains in the field as the object of the definition. It means, in other words:

"That category is *samavāya* which is of positive character, which being one cannot be the locus of universality, and is neither universal itself nor particular."

This definition seems to be perfect since it does not over-pervade the relation of the word and meaning, known as the relation of power, because, power of denoting an object flows from the "Will" of God. This "Will" is a quality and, therefore, it comes under the category of quality (*guṇa*) and leaves *samavāya* alone.

Moreover, even if the contact (*saṁyoga*) of two all pervading entities (*vibhu*) is admitted, that being a quality will not apply to the definition of *samavāya.*

However, Rucidatta does not consider this definition as fool-proof. In his opinion this definition suffers from the defect of mutual dependence (*anyonyāśraya*).[65] He correctly puts his finger in the weakest point of the definition and says that *sāmānya* (universal) and *viśeṣa* (particular) can be understood only with the knowledge of *samavāya*, because both universal and particular involve *samavāya*.[66]

In the definition of *samavāya* quoted above, both universal and particular form a part of the above definition. Thus the definition lands us in a cyclic order, such as—without the knowledge of *samavāya* universal and particular cannot be understood, and again without knowing universal and particular *samavāya* cannot be known. (Universal resides in many through the relation of *samavāya*, while particular resides only in one through *samavāya*). Thus without knowing *samavāya* how could one know the definition of *samavāya*? Therefore Rucidatta would define *samavāya* anew as follows:

"That relation is *samavāya*, which, even though its relata differ, itself does not differ and is always one."[67]

The underlying meaning of this definition is that both *saṁyoga* and *samavāya* occur between two relata and these relata vary from occasion to occasion, and the relation of *saṁyoga* vary with the variation of the relata, *samavāya* does not, but it always remains as one, even though either of the relata or both vary.

For instance, in such usages—"the pot is on the ground", "the book is on the ground", the contact of the pot and the book with the ground is specified. Here the pot and the book are the adjunct and the ground is the subjunct of the contact. The contact of the pot with the ground is different from the contact of the book with the ground. This means the relation (contact) varies with the variation of the adjunct of the relation. Again when we say "the pot is on the table", "the pot is on the carpet"—though the adjunct of the relation is the same, the subjunct differs. With the difference of one subjunct from the other, the relation also differs, i.e. the contact of the pot with the table is different from that of the pot with the carpet. Since with the variation of either of the adjunct or the subjunct the relation differs, it is more than evident that when one set of relata differs from the other set of relata, the relation differs.

It states that *samavāya* does not vary with the variation of either of the adjunct or the subjunct or both.

For instance, in the usages such as, "the colour inheres in the earth", "the touch inheres in the air"—both adjunct and subjunct of inherence in the former sentence differ from that of the latter, but in spite of the difference in the relata *samavāya* is the same in both the cases.

This definition lays emphasis on oneness of *samavāya*, and that has been made the main point for defining *samavāya*.

4.10. *Objection to the Oneness*

On the point of oneness of the relation, which *samavāya* is sought to be made out, an objection is raised as to its over-pervading the *vācya-vācaka-bhāva sambandha* (denotor-denotehood relation) which exists between the word and its meaning. The relation is regarded as the power of the word to denote an object and this power, associated with the word is nothing but the "Will" of God. The "Will" of God being one and unitary does not vary with the variation of the words and their objects. In other words, though one word differs from the other and so also the object, the relation holding between the word and its meaning is always one. And thus the above definition of *samavāya* will include word-meaning relation also.

The reply to this objection is like this: Of course, the probability of over-pervasion is there, but in fact it does not occur. Though the "Will" of God is one, which is manifested as the power of the word, it is limited by a particular word, the meaning of which is restricted to a particular object. For instance, "the object pot is to be understood from the word pot"—means that the power of denoting an object by the word pot is limited by that word and its relation is restricted to the object pot, and it does not mean anything else than the pot. In the terminology of Navya-Nyāya the above position is expressed like this:

"The 'Will' of which the pot is the substantive, is limited by the qualifierness *(prakāratā)* of the cognition about the object pot, caused by the word pot." [68]

By introducing the concept of *prakāratā* (qualifierness) and *avacchedakatā* (limitorship) the school of Navya-Nyāya admits an artificial division of indivisible entity, such as, time, ether, etc. The ether is one, but the ether which is limited by a pot is supposed to be different from the ether limited by one's earhole. In the same way, though the "Will" of God is one it is to be admitted as different on account of limitorship.

Another aspect of *samavāya* is that it is a *nitya sambandha.* While defining *samavāya* as an eternal relation some scholars would like to define *'nitya'* (eternal) in a different way. According to this interpretation the definition of *samavāya* as an eternal relation does not over-pervade the relation of word and its meaning. It is argued that the term *'nitya'* does not qualify the relation but it qualifies the relationship. The underlying meaning of this interpretation is this—that while all other relations, except *samavāya,* need some other relation for their subsistence in the relata, and as such, these relations themselves become the relata of the relation by which they subsist. As against this, *samavāya* does not require another relation for its subsistence, and, hence it is always a relation, never a relatum.

For instance, "the pot is on the ground"—the relation of the pot with the ground is *saṁyoga,* both pot and the ground are the relata of the relation, called *saṁyoga.* Again this *saṁyoga* relation subsists in its relatum, the ground through *samavāya;* thus *saṁyoga* itself turns into a relatum so far its subsistence in the ground through *samavāya* is concerned. But nothing of this sort is required for the subsistence of *samavāya* and, hence it is always strictly a relation, nothing else. Therefore it stands—"that is *samavāya,* which is only other than relata".

However, the critic finds fault even with this definition also and points out that the object *samavāya* which is a category itself, and the word *samavāya*—both stand in the denotor denoterhood relationship and as such *samavāya* is to be regarded as the relatum of the aforesaid relation. The result is that the definition of *samavāya* will be inoperative.

To this objection the reply would be—what is meant by other than relata is to be understood "other than the superstratum" (*ādheya*).[69] After acceptance of this interpretation of the definition all the probable objections being cleared the definition stands in order. Though there is a relation between the word and its meaning, neither of them is either substratum or superstratum of the relation.

In other words, the word does not reside in the meaning through the relation that exists between the two, again the meaning also is not the substratum *(ādhāra)* of the word.

One may, however, raise an objection to this by citing the example of ether. The ether being a non-occurrent *(avṛtti)* entity cannot be a superstratum *(ādheya)* of any relation and as such the definition of *samavāya* as given above will over-pervade the ether. To avoid this possible objection the above definition of *samavāya* is to be further modified by a qualifying clause, and be redefined as:

"That is *samavāya*, which is other than the existent *(sadbhinna)* and other than the superstratum."[70]

The qualifying clause *'sadbhinna'* in the definition will exclude substance, quality and action—these three categories being existential nature, i.e. qualified by the universal existence. The ether being a substance comes under substance and the objection of inclusion of ether is removed.

Again looking into the definition from a different angle the above definition has been brought in for criticism on the ground that *samavāya* cannot be other than the superstratum, hence that portion of the definition, such as:

"Which is other than the superstratum" *(ādheyabhinnatva)* leads to an absurdity.

How *samavāya* becomes a superstratum? It can be established by the following logic. That without the occurrence of substance of the relation, a relatum which is related to another relatum, cannot reside there through that relation.

'A' is related to 'B' and if the relation of 'A' does not subsists in 'B', 'A' cannot reside in 'B'.

Let us take the example of two different objects, say, water and fire. No contact exists between water and fire, which means fire does not exist in water through the relation of contact. From this it follows that if inherence of quality *(guṇa-samavāya)* does not subsist in the substance, the quality cannot subsist in the substance. In other words, quality resides in substance through the relation of *samavāya*, which presupposes existence of *samavāya* of quality *(guṇa-samavāya)* in the substance. It is thus evident *samavāya* must subsist in substance through some relation. If this position be conceded, it is to be admitted that *samavāya* constitutes the relatum of that relation through which it is supposed to exist.

In reply to this, the position may be clarified like this:

If the subsistence of *samavāya* be construed like this, of course, *samavāya* can be regarded as the superstratum. But superstratum of what and for the operation of which relation? It is an admitted fact that *samavāya* does not require any other relation or another *samavāya* for its subsistence. Presumption of any other relaton for the former's subsistence requires another *samavāya*, that *samavāya* will need another *smavāya*. Thus in both the cases it will go on adinfinitum. Therefore, *samavāya* is regarded as subsisting by itself without the assistance of another relation. Thus the logical conclusion is this, that *samavāya* may be stated as to serve as the superstratum of its own, and not of others.

The expression "other than the superstratum" in the definition may, if you would, be modified as "other than that which is not the superstratum of any other relation except the *samavāya*, which is a relation". In other words, that *samavāya* is other than the superstratum of all other relations except *samavāya* which is in operation. This explanation saves the definition from being absurd.

In order to keep the absence out from the purview of the definition of *samavāya* the qualifying term 'positiveness' *(bhāvatva)* is to be inserted in the definition. Without this it will over-pervade absence as indicated below:

All eternal entities are possessed of absence of producthood *(janyatvābhāva)*. This absence resides in the eternal entities through self-linking relation. It is stated before that the self-linking relation is either of the nature of the substratum or of the superstratum. In the case of absence that resides in an eternal entity, the self-linking relation is to be regarded as to be in the nature of superstratum for the sake of simplicity. If the self-linking relation of absence be taken as to be in the nature of substratum, there will be assumption of many, whereas the superstratum is one in the form of absence of the producthood. Thus, this kind of absence is regarded as the superstratum of the self-linking relation, it cannot serve in that capacity in respect of any other relation. Thus, this kind of absence in its relation to an eternal entity through the self-linking relation satisfies the condition of the definition of *samavāya*[71] and the question of over-pervasion arises. Therefore, if the term 'positiveness' *(bhāvatva)* is added to the above definition it will debar absence coming under *samavāya* and the definition will be in order as amended.

"That is *samavāya*, which is other than *sat* (i.e. the existential categories—substance, quality and action), other than the superstratum of all other relations except self, and is of positive character."[72]

"That is *samavāya* relation, which is other than *sat (dravya-guṇa* and *karma)*, which does not constitute the superstratum of any relation other than self, i.e. *samavāya* relation"[73] —says Śeṣānata.

Although absence of something subsists in its locus through the self-linking *(svarūpa)* relation and this relation also does not turn out to be the relata of any other relation, as in the case of "there is absence of pot on the ground" *(ghaṭābhavavad-bhūtalam)* the absence is not a positive category. Hence in order to exclude the absential self-linking relation from the scope of the definition of *samavāya* the term positiveness *(bhāvatva)* has been added.[74]

An objection may be raised that according to the Nyāya-Vaiśeṣika theory of creation and destruction during the period of absolute dissolution of the world *(pralaya)*, the universal, etc. which are eternal categories subsists in *kāla* through *svarūpa* relation, and the universal is also a positive category *(bhāvapadārtha)*,[75] hence the above definition of *samavāya* would be applicable to such of *svarūpa* relation involving the defect of over-pervasion (*ativyāpti)*.[76]

This objection may be met in this way that here the *svarūpa* relation is in the nature of the universal and different from it, hence the question of over-pervasion does not arise.

Notes and References

1. samudayaḥ samudāyaḥ samavāyaśca yo gaṇaḥ. —*Amarakośa*, 2.41
   paścād avasthāyibalaṁ samavāyaśca sannayau. —Ibid., *Nānārtha*, 151
2. samavayanti anena, bāhulakād ghañ, samavetā bhavanti atra vā, adhikaraṇe-ghañ (Pāṇini 3.3.19)

samavāyah aṁ pūrvo dṛśyate, samavāyaḥ iti *madhumādhavī.*

–*PC.*, p. 329.

3. Gough, Translation of Vaiśeṣika sūtras, p. 4 (Benaras).
4. Dasgupta, S., *History of Indian Philosophy*, Vol. I. p. 332.
5. Bodas, *Tarkasaṁgraha*, English notes, p. 96.
6. Ballantyne, Ibid. p. 96.
7. Keith, *Indian Logic and Atomism*, p. 196.

7a. Faddegon, *Vaiśeṣika System*, p. 105.

8. *Vaiśeṣika System*, p. 105.
9. *ihedam iti yataḥ kārya-kāraṇayoḥ sa samavāyaḥ.* —*VS* .,7.2.26.
10. *ayuta-siddhānām ādhāryādhāra-bhūtānāṁ yaḥ sambandha iha pratyayahetuḥ sa samavāyaḥ* —*PP Bh.* on the above *sūtra.*
11. kārya-kāraṇa-bhūtānāmakārya-kāraṇa-bhūtānāṁ vā

    —*PP Bh.* on *samavāya.*
12. ayutasiddhānām-ādhārya-ādhāra bhūtānāṁ kārya-kāraṇa bhūtānām-akārya-kāraṇa-bhūtānāṁ yaḥ sambhandha iha pratyaya hetuḥ sa samavāyah.

    —*NK.*
13. kārya-kāraṇayorityupalakṣaṇam, akārya-kāraṇayor ityapi draṣṭavyam.

    —*Upaskāra*, p. 193.
14. It is presumed that the concept and the definition of *samavāya* had been attacked by the Buddhist before and after Nāgārjuna. Unfortunately, no work either of the Vaiśeṣika school or the Buddhist schools has come to our knowledge to trace the development in the concept of *samavāya* between the intervening period from Kaṇāda to Praśastapāda. There might have been some criticism against the definition of *samavāya* given by Kaṇāda, and in order to defend it from the said attack Praśastapāda might have introduced the new concept of *ayutasiddha* in the definition, and thus he made the definition up to date (of his time).
15. *'yu' miśraṇāmiśraṇayoḥ. —Dhātupāṭha.*
16. Bodas, *Note on samavāya, —TS.*, p. 96.

    Gaurinath Shastri in his explanatory note on *ayutasiddha* (*Kiraṇāvalī*, Bengali, pp. 149-50) says that *'yuta'* means things which exist separately, those which do not exist separately is called *'ayuta'.*
17. *ayutaḥ prāptaśca siddha iti ayutasiddhaḥ. prāptā eva santi na apraptā iti yāvat teṣāṁ sambandhaḥ prāptilakṣaṇaḥ samavāyah.—Kiraṇāvalī*, p. 249.
18. nanu cāyutasiddhau yadi yutau na siddhau tadā kayoḥ sambandho dharmiṇor-abhāvāt. —*KP.*, p. 133.
19. atha ayutau siddhau tathāpi kayoḥ sambandhaḥ sambandhinor-apṛthag-bhūtatvāt, pṛthagbhūtayoreva *sambandhatvāt.* —Ibid., p. 133.
20. anyonyāpariharena pṛthagāśray anāśrita ityarthaḥ. —*KP.*, p.134.
21. yataśca asarvagatānāṁ niyatadeśāvasthitānām adhigatānyatvānām adhigatasvarūpa-bhedānām avisvagbhāva apṛthagbhavāḥ. —*NK.*, p. 37

On the point of *asvātantrya* of *samavāya*, the Mīmāṁsaka views may be compared. —SV., 4.146 See also, *PSPM*., p. 88.

22. yadyapi tantavaḥ paṭavyatiriktāśraye samavayanti tathāpi ubhayoḥ parasparāparihāreṇa pṛthagāśrayāś rayitvaṃ nāsti paṭasya tantuṣvevāśrayitvāt. —*NK*., p. 37.
23. tatra yutasiddhir yathā tvagindriya-śarīrayoḥ, śarīraṁ hi tvagindriya-parihāreṇāpi pṛthagāśrayasvabhāve samāśritam, tena anayoḥ saṁyogaḥ, na samavāyaḥ. —*NK*., p. 38.
24. nityānāṁ tu pṛthagavasthitiḥ, pṛthag gamanayogyatā, sa ca yayor nāsti, tau ayutasiddhau, tayor yaḥ sambandhaḥ sa samavāyaḥ, yathā ākāśa-dravyatvayoriti. —*NK*., p. 38.
25. asambaddhayor avidyamānatvaṁ ayutasiddhiḥ. —*Upaskāra* on *samavāya.*
26. yayor drvayor madhya akamavinaśyad aparāśritameva, avatiṣṭhate, tāvayutasiddhau, yathā avayavāvayavinau, guṇaguṇinau . . . . —*TS*., p. 61.
27. ayutasiddhānām apṛthgbhūtānāṁ sarvadā mithaḥ sambaddhānām iti yāvat. —*JS*., p. 35.
yutasiddhiḥ pṛthaksiddhiḥ pṛthagavasthitiḥ, ubhayorapi sambandhinoḥ paraspara-parihāreṇa pṛthagāśryāśrayitvaṁ, sa yeṣām nāsti teṣām. —*JSD*., p. 36.
28. See, Mind, Vol. I. p. 207.
29. *TS*., p. 61; *KP*., p. 133.
30. utpannamātraṁ dravyaṁ kṣaṇam aguṇam akriyakaṁ ca tiṣṭhati. —*NM*., p. 167.
31. *TSD*., pp. 4,7.
The substance at the time of emergence and destruction is stated to be devoid of guṇa ādyakṣaṇe utpanna-vinaṣṭa-dravye etc.
32. pratītibhedād bhedo'sti deśabhedastu neṣyate. —*NM*., p. 165.
33. *NV*., 2.1.33.
34. This objection is raised by Kumārila.
nāniṣpannasya sambandhaḥ
niṣpattau yutasiddhatā // —*SV*., 1.1.5.
35. avayavāvayavinor guṇa-guṇinośca iyameva vṛttiḥ, tayorarthāntaratvaṁ upariṣṭād darśayiṣyate. —*NM*., p. 167.
36. saṁyogo hi yutasiddhānāmeva bhavati, ayam tu ayutasiddhānām iti ... saṁyogaḥ svatantrayorapi bhavati yathorddhvāasthitāṅgulyoḥ, ayaṁ tu adhikaraṇādhi-karttavyoreva bhavati. —*NK*., p. 168.
37. iyāṁstu viśeṣaḥ—vahnirutpatteḥ paścād ayaḥpiṇḍena saha sambaddhyate; iha tu svakāraṇa-sāmarthyād upajāyamanam eva tatra sambaddhyate, yathā chidi kriyā chedaneti alam. —Ibid., p. 167.
38. yadi hyekāntato bhinnaṁ viśeṣyāt syad viśeṣaṇam /
svānurūpāṁ sadā buddhiṁ viśeṣye janayet katham //
—*SV*., 4.142.

39. dharmasya sukhasya ca yaḥ kārya-kāraṇabhāva-lakṣaṇa-sambandhaḥ so'pi samavāyaḥ prāpnoti, tayor ātmaikaśritayor a yutasiddhyabhāvāt. —*NO.*, p. 38.
40. śabdaguṇam ākaśam. —*SP.*, p. 21.
ākāśasya viśeṣa-guṇah śabdaḥ. —*S.M.*, p. 97.
41. evamapi ākāśasya ākāśapadasya ca vācya-vācaka-bhāvaḥ samavayāḥ syāt. —*NK.*, p. 38.
42. ihedam iti buddhir yataḥ kāraṇād bhavati yataśca asarvagatānāṁ niyata-deśāvasthitānām adhigatānyatvānām adhigata-svarūpabhedānām aviṣvagbhāvo' pṛthagbhāvo' svātantryaṁ sa samavāyaḥ, bhinnayoḥ parasparopaśleṣasya sambandha-kṛtatvopalambhāt. —*NK.*, p. 774.
43. ihedam iti yataḥ kārya-kāraṇayoḥ sa samavāyaḥ. —*VS.*, 7.2.26.
44. ayutasiddhānām ādhāryādhārabhūtānāṁ yaḥ sambandhaḥ ihapratyayahetuḥ sa samavāyah. -*PPBh.* on the above *sūtra.*
45. The thing which is related is adjunct *(pratiyogin)* and to which or where it is related is subjunct *(anuyogin).* For instance, "cowness is in the cow"—here "cowness" is the adjunct and the "cow" is the subjunct of the relation that exists between the two.
46. *PPBh.*
47. *Upaskāra,* p. 292.
48. nitya-prāptiḥ samavāyaḥ. —*Kiraṇāvalī,* p. 249.
49. Ibid., p. 249.
50. tena saṁyogavyavacchinnastasya prāpti-purvakatvāt. —Ibid., p. 249.
51. Relation means getting into contact, and this implies direct relation. In other words, the two relata of which are not intervened by any other entity except the relation, that is the direct relation. Both *saṁyoga* and *samavāya* are direct relations, because nothing intervenes between the relata of the above two relations. In contrast to this the relation between the son and the father may be cited. The two are related by the relation of *janya-janaka-bhava* (the son is off-spring and the father is progenitor) but this relation is not the direct relation—time and space intervening between the two.
52. *saṁyogaja-saṁyoga* means a contact arising out of another contact. For instance, when there is a contact between the hand and the tree, the body comes into contact with the tree. The contact of the body with the tree is caused by the contact of the hand with the tree, hence it is a *saṁyogaja-saṁyoga.*
53. ākāśa aparicchinna-dravya-saṁyogī, paricchinna-dravya-saṁyogitvāt, śarīravat paricchinnatvam apakṛṣṭa-parimāṇavatvam.
The entity which has lesser magnitude in comparison to another entity is termed as *paricchinna,* hence all entities except *vibhu dravya* (omnipresent) are *paricchinna,* because they all possess smaller magnitude than *vibhudravya.*
54. ākāśo na aparicchinna-dravya-saṁyogī yutasiddhatvābhāvāt.

55. This aspect deserves detailed consideration for establishing the fact that this does not smack the universal flux of the Buddhist.
56. sambandha-pratiyogy-anuyogi-bhinnatve sati nityatve sati sambandhatvam. —*Rāmarudrī*, p. 87.
57. sambandhaśca sambandhibhinno grāhyastena nityabhāvādi svarūpa-sambandho nativyāptiḥ. —*Dinakarī*, p.87.
58. For cognition of a relation there must be two relata and a relation between the two, and in *svarūpa* relation nothing more is cognised except the two relata.
59. svarūpa sambandhasya kvacit pratiyogirūpatā kvacidanuyogi-rūpatā iti vibhāgo bodhyaḥ. —*Rāmarudrī*, p. 87.
60. ananta-svarūpāṇāṁ sambandhatva-kalpane gauravāt lāghavadeka-samavāya-siddhiḥ. —*SM.*, p. 87.
61. It is clear that the significance of the intricate structure of the Nyāya-Vaiśeṣika metaphysics was not realised by the latter Nyāya-Vaiśeṣika writers. Viśvanātha declares that *samavāya* is assumed as a separate category for the sake of brevity *(lāghava)* ... Little did these later writers realise that the theory of *samavāya* was not conceived for the sake of brevity, but that it was the very basis of the entire Nyāya-Vaiśeṣika metaphysical structure." —*Critique of Indian Realism*, pp. 377-78.
62. It is, however, doubtful if the assumption of *samavāya* actually leads to brevity. As a matter of fact, acceptance of a new category involves more assumptions *(gaurava)* then the acceptance of the relation in the form of substrata which, although endless, do not involve the assumption of a new category. —Ibid., p. 378.
63. pratiyogy-anuyogi-bhinnatve sati nityatve sati prāptitvaṁ samavāyatvam. —*KP.*, p. 133.
64. pratiyogy-anuyogi-bhinnatve sati nityatve sati saṁyoga-samavāyānyataratvaṁ samavāyatvam. —Ibid., p. 133.
65. sāmānya-śūnyatve sati sāmānyatva-viśeṣatva-śūnyābhāvatvam samavāyatvam. —*KP.*, p. 133.
66. *KPV.*, p. 134.
67. sāmānya is defined as "nityatve sati anekasamavetatvam sāmānyatvam." while Viśeṣa's definition is "niḥ-sāmānyatve sati ekamātra-samavetatvaṁ viśeṣatvam. —*SM.*, p. 75; —*KPV.*, p. 134.
68. sambandhibhede'pi abhinnasambandhatvam. —*KPV.*, p. 134.
69. ghaṭapadajanya-bodha-viṣayatva-prakāratā-nirūpitaghaṭa-viśeṣyatāśālīcchā.

    In the case of a cloth the expression would be—paṭapadajanya... paṭaviśeṣyatāśālī icchā.
70. ādheyabhinnatvaṁ samavāyatvam. —*KPV.*, p. 136.
71. sadbhinnatve sati ādheya-bhinnatvaṁ samavāyatvam. —Ibid., p. 136.
72. "svabhinna-saṁbandhādheya-bhinnatva" and "sadhinnatva".

73. "sadbhinnatve sati svabhinna-sambhandhādheya-bhinna-bhāvatvam samavāyatvam."
74. sadbhinna-svabhinna-sambandhā-dheyabhinnatvam. —*PC.*, pp. 118-19.
75. abhāve ativyāptivāraṇāya bhāvatvam. —Ibid. pp. 118-19.
76. jāti śūnyatve sati asamavetabhāvatvam. —Ibid.
77. abhāvo' pi jātisśūnyaḥ asamavetaḥ na samavāya-sambandhena tiṣṭhati paraṁ tu svarūpeṇa. —Ibid., p. 120.

Chapter 5

Some Characteristics of Samavāya

5.1. *Samavāya Differs from other Relations*

The authors of Nyāya-Vaiśeṣika system down from Kaṇāda seek to establish *samavāya* by showing its difference from other relations, such as *saṁyoga* (contact), *svarūpa* (self-linking), *tādātmya* (essential identity), *abhāva sambandha* (absential relation), *vācya-vācaka* (denoting-denotor-hood), *paryāpti* (the relation of completion), etc.

That a question may be asked as to what is the necessity of assuming a separate relation such as *samavāya?* The function of *samavāya* can well be served by *saṁyoga,* it being a relation between two entities. The reply would be that by nature *samavāya* is different from *saṁyoga.*

5.2. *Samavāya Differs from Saṁyoga*

The distinction between *samvāya* and *saṁyoga* lies, according to Kaṇāda, in the fact that the former is a relation, which holds between cause and effect while the latter holds between two entities without such condition. The ground advanced by Praśastapāda for holding *samavāya* is that the two relata of it should be inseparable connected entities, whereas this is not a requirement for holding *saṁyoga* and here lies the distinction between the two.

Commentators on Praśastapāda *bhāṣya,* in addition to the above, have adduced more grounds to establish the difference of *samavāya* from *saṁyoga.*

Jayanta, Śaṅkara, Śrīdhara, Annaṁbhaṭṭa and many others have pointed out the difference of *samavāya* from *saṁyoga* on the grounds that both have separate characteristics and function. The difference between the two as stated by those writers may be summarised as follows:

(1) *Saṁyoga* relation unites two exclusively separate entities, which are absolutely independent of each other and can exist without the other. Two things are related in *saṁyoga* either due to the activity of one of the two or of both of the relata, or, one *saṁyoga* may cause another *saṁyoga*.

But in case of *samavāya*, neither independent existence of the two is possible, nor *samavāya* is the result of the activity of either or both or of another *samavāya*. Rather *samavāya* is cognised along with the emergence of the *samavāyin*, the entity to be related by *samavāya*. For instance, the relation between cowness and the cow, which is *samavāya*, is not caused by the action of either cowness or the cow. The adjunct, of the relation, cowness cannot have any action, although the subjunct, the cow, possesses action; in relation to cowness the cow cannot serve as the cause of cowness. If the relation between cowness and the cow be admitted as caused by the cow it will have to be conceded that the cow was without cowness when it was born. Because the cause must precede the action, hence for any action of cow, cow itself being the inherent cause (*samavāyikāraṇa*) must precede the action, and the action is caused after the cow was born. Now, if this action is regarded as the cause of the relation between 'cowness' and the cow, then it is to be admitted that the said relation holds between the two, after the effect was generated in the cow. This makes the position absurd, because the assumption would be that the cow at the moment it was born, and immediately thereafter was without 'cowness'.

(2) The second point is—the action which is generated in the cow must subsist through some relation. What is this relation? If it is said to be through *saṁyoga* relation, then for that *saṁyoga* another action will be required (because *saṁyoga* is caused by the action of the relata) and thus it will lead to the fallacy of ad infinitum. On the other hand, the subsistence of an action in the substance (action of the cow in the present case) is considered through some relation, and thus it will not involve infinite regress. This means the same, that is admittance of *samavāya* in other name.

(3) *Samavāya* is an eternal *(nitya)* relation but *saṁyoga* is a non-eternal *(anitya)* or transient relation, because it is caused. *Saṁyoga* ceases to exist with the emergence of the new quality, namely, *vibhāga* (separation)[1] whereas *samavāya* being an eternal relation never ceases to exist.[2] It is not caused by the relata or by their action or cannot be destroyed so long the relata exist.

(4) Further more, *saṁyoga* does not always unite two objects as the things container and contained. As for example, when two fingers made erect perpendicularly *(yathordhvāvasthitayor aṅgulyoḥ)*[3] one being in the contact with the other, nobody can say that one finger is on the other. But in the case of *samavāya* there must always be a relation of container and contained of the two relata. Hence *samavāya* is a relation different from *saṁyoga* and is to be admitted as such.

(5) *Samavāya* is one while *saṁyoga* is many. *Saṁyoga* varies when the adjunct and the subjunct of the relation vary, but that is not the case with *samavāya*. For instance, the contact of the book with the table is different from the contact of the man with the staff. But the relation (viz. *samavāya*) of the potness with the pot is not different from the relation of cowness with the cow. In other words, cowness subsists in cow through the same *samavāya*, through which potness subsists in the pot.

Now one may ask—both *saṁyoga* and *samavāya* being the relation why one *saṁyoga* differs from the other while *samavāya* does not? The reply is: the reason is consistent cognition and usage of oneness in the case of *samavāya*, which are absent in *saṁyoga*. Moreover, there is nothing to distinguish one *samavāya* from the other. For instance, cowness is the same in all cows, nobody can say this cowness is different from that cowness, because cowness is one. Similarly the constant absence of the pot *(ghaṭātyantābhāva)* is one, because, the constant absence of the pot on the ground and on the table is the same; the absence does not differ with the differnce in the locus. No proof can be adduced to prove that the absence differs from locus to locus. The same way the cognition of inherence is one and the inherence is also used as one. For instance, the inherence of potness, the inherence of substancehood, the inherence of qualityhood, etc. in all cases, the inherence is cognised as one. There is nothing by which one inherence can be differentiated from the other inherence.

(6) One may say that the contact of pot (in any locus) is the same with the contact of cloth (in any locus), both being the same and one contact. Hence, *saṁyoga* is also one. Of course, apparently we may have such cognition, but the difference of contact is perceptible by the sense-organ. One can perceive the emergence and the destruction of the contact, such as, the contact of the pot with the ground emerges, while the contact of the cloth with the basket is destroyed. Thus, the difference of contact in different loci being perceptible gives support to the conclusion of manifoldness of contact. Such characteristics are absent in *samavāya* and, therefore, *samavāya* is one. Herein lies the difference between *saṁyoga* and *samavāya*. Praśastapāda clearly states that *samavāya* is to be inferred[4] from the cognition "this is here" *(iha-pratyaya-buddhi)*. When it is stated the apples are in the basket the relation between the apples and the basket is a temporary phase and an extraneous one.

When we say a red pot, the redness resides in the pot and the relation between the two, i.e substance and quality is that of *samavāya*. These two are so intimately related that they are not cognised existing separately. Therefore the relation of *samavāya* is held to be the internal relation.

(Whether *samavāya* is an exclusively internal relation has been discussed in the following chapter).

(7) In *samavāya* the two relata do not occupy two different spaces. The two objects which are related through *saṁyoga* relation are in juxtaposition and the two occupy two different and distinct spaces; for instance, the staff and the man; while two entities when related by *samavāya* relation, they are experienced in one position. Jayanta Bhaṭṭa states that since we have the cognition of two, hence they are two; but they do not occupy two distinct spaces.[5]

(8) *Saṁyoga* is transient *(anitya)* and manifold *(aneka)* while *samavāya* is eternal *(nitya)* and one *(eka)*.

The two objects related through *saṁyoga* exist independently before *saṁyoga* connects them, and they also can be separated without causing any harm to them, after they conjoined. We have stated that the relata of *saṁyoga* are not effected by the relation. They are not effected even after the separation, and remain as before, only the relation of *saṁyoga* is destroyed. As a matter of fact a new quality, *vibhāga* (separation) emerges and with its emergence, contact disappears; and this is regarded as one of the factors which differentiates *saṁyoga* from *samavāya*. Since the objects are innumerable, *saṁyoga*, that takes place between the objects, is also innumerable.

On the other hand objects related by *samavāya* cannot always be sundered, as in the case of redness and the pot; and where it can be effected, at least one of the two relata is destroyed as the result of such sundering, as in the case of the cloth and the yarns. This is the criteria of *ayutasiddha* for the occurrence of *samavāya*.[6]

(9) The relation of *samavāya* in such cases is not destroyed; what happens, it ceases to be revealed through that particular entity, which is destroyed, but continues to exist and manifested through some other objects, which stand related. For instance, cowness resides in a cow through *samavāya*, after a particular cow is dead cowness does not die along with that cow, but subsists in other cows through *samavāya*. Thus both *sāmānya* or *jāti* (universal) and *samavāya* (inherence) being intimately related remain as all pervading of the same class, hence *samavāya* is an eternal relation and one.[7]

(10) *Saṁyoga* exists while *samavāya* subsists. The difference between existence and subsistence can be explained by tracing the nature of the two categories to which they belong. *Saṁyoga* is a quality like *pṛthaktva* etc. and as such it comes under the category of *guṇa*, while *samavāya* is a category by itself.

Of the six categories of Vaiśeṣika the first three, are called *sattāsamānyavat* or of existential nature and the latter three as *svātmasat* or intrinsically real. These latter three are neither in time nor in space and hence independent of both. Contact being a quality is of existential nature and, therefore, exists, while inherence is only intrinsically real, hence it subsists.

(11) That *saṁyoga* connects two substances, the connection may be termed as physical contact though the two substances need not come to the close proximity in all cases, as in the case of contact

of sense organ with colour. *Samavāya* like *saṁyoga* holds between two substances, but there is a big difference between the two because *samavāya* cannot relate any two substances, if they do not belong to the prescribed ones.

(12) Another distinction between *saṁyoga* and *samavāya* may be pointed out as mediate and immediate relation. *Saṁyoga* or its dependence on another relation for relating to the relata is a mediate relation while *samavāya* is an immediate relation.

That *samavāya* relation holds between inherent cause[8] *(samavāyi-kāraṇa)* and the effect. The Nyāya-Vaiśeṣika in conformity with his doctrine of realism postulate absolute distinction *(atyantābheda)* between inherent cause and the effect by the notion of 'this is here' *(iha idam)* and conceived the unique functional relation *(vṛtti)* of *samavāya* for linking the two *(tenātra kalpyate vṛttiḥ samavāyaḥ sa ucyate)*.[9] *Saṁyoga* which is contrasted against *samavāya* has also a reference to the causation theory, that is, *saṁyoga* being a product is produced by the cause. Since all effects, which are of positive nature are to abide in their material cause and *saṁyoga* being a product, must abide in, as it comes to be, in a substance, its material cause. *Saṁyoga* cannot be a substance or an action. On the other hand substance, quality and action—only these three categories can be produced, not the rest three. Thus *saṁyoga* being a product differs from *samavāya*.

On the other hand, *samavāya* is a category by itself– which only relates, but is not caused and cannot be caused. For this reason it has been repeatedly stressed that *samavāya* does not need any other relation to be related with its relata—it is related of its own.[10]

Saṁyoga, as against this, being a quality needs another relation, *samavāya*, to be related with its relata. Thus, *saṁyoga* being related through an intermediate is a mediate relation, while *samavāya* being directly related is an immediate relation.

(13) The difference between *saṁyoga* and *samavāya* may be stated in some more ways. We may conclude by saying that *samavāya* holds between two such objects which by nature presupposes a relation between them, and one of them is dependent on the other for its existence, hence, it is intimate. The inherent cause, is as extraneous to the effect as the other causes are. For instance, in

the case of the cloth and the yarns, the yarns are considered to be as extraneous as the loom, shuttle and the weavers are to the cloth.[11] It suggests that *samavāya* has the characteristic of external relation also, because it relates external objects. Again *samavāya* holds between substance and quality etc. which are intimate. Therefore, *samavāya* may be termed as internal or quasi-internal relation, while *saṁyoga* is entirely an external relation.

5.15. *Can Saṁyoga be a Superimposition?*

The opponent further raises an objection—if in the case of *samavāya* the notion of *samavāya* existing through some relation is explained as a case of superimposition, why not then the notion of *saṁyoga* existing in the two relata of *saṁyoga* can be explained as a case of superimposition?

To this the reply would be that the very nature of the two relations, *samavāya* and *saṁyoga* bars out such possibility. In the case of *samavāya* the two relata are apprehended to be inseparably related *(ayutasiddha)* and when the two relata are distinctly perceived to be so related the notion of their being so related cannot be explained away as a case of superimposition *(āropa)*, and moreover, in that case the two relata would have been perceived as being related through conjunction and not inherence.

The opponent further asks that if the relation between *samavāya* on the one hand and the two *samavāyins* (the two relata of *samavāya*) on the other is not the case of a relation but a case of super-imposition, then how is it that such super-imposition has a reference only to definite entity? Or in other words, how is it that *samavāya* exists in substance and quality, universal and individual etc.? Such an objection does not hold good in view of the fact that we often experience one unitary experience as two, and by that we super-impose difference *(bheda)* between the two, as in the case of one moon appearing as many.[12] Likewise, although *samavāya* is not related through another *samavāya* with its relata because that leads to regressus adinfinitum. But a logical difference between *samavāya* and its relata and consequently a relation between the two, although such relation is superimposed, has to be admitted because they appear to be related.

The opponent taking clue from this solution of the Vaiśeṣika further argues that in that case, when I say, "the pot is known" *(jñāto' yaṁ ghaṭaḥ)* the co-existence between the pot and its cognition is no doubt cognised and in that case also on the basis of having a common locus *(sāmānādhikaraṇya)* the Vaiśeṣika would be forced to admit some relation between the pot and its cognition.

To this the Vaiśeṣika replies that the cognition has reference not only to the present entity but also to the past and further, and obviously which are not present to our sense, can in no way be said to be related to the corresponding cognition.

It cannot, however, be said that although the past and the future object cannot be related to their cognition there should be no bar to the present object being related to its cognition in view of the fact that there is no difference in the character of cognition irrespective of the objects known, whether it belongs to the past, present and future. But the difficulty will arise in such cognitions as this is the cognition of a pot, for here no doubt some sort of relation between the object and its cognition must have to be postulated, otherwise it will be difficult to explain the generic case-ending associated with the word pot *(ghaṭasya jñānam).*

To this the reply would be that such usages are not real but super-imposed. In the case of *samavāya* relation we have an uncontradictory experience such as of two entities mutually related as co-existing. The same way as we postulate the relation of conjunction *(saṁyoga)* when we have such uncontradicted experience such as the staff and the earring are related to Yajñadatta. If it is asked that how is it in the case of the pot and its colour we postulate a *samavāya* relation on the basis of their co-existence, but we do not feel any necessity of postulating any such relation in the case of *samavāya* existing in the *samavāyins* although in such cases we experience uncontradicted cognition of their co-existence. Such an objection has been removed by Vallabha saying that the generic attribute etc. *(jātyādi)* are related to its own locus through *samavāya;* but in case of *samavāya* existing in *samavāyin* no such additional relation is cognised excepting the self-linking relation. We have such cognition as 'X' is related to cowness *(gotva),* but X is not related to the relation which is related to cowness. It cannot, however, be argued that the admission of the self-linking relation leads to the logical complexity because such a relation would differ in each relata, because the Nyāya-Vaiśeṣika will be least concerned even if one has to admit innumerable relations since one has no preference for restricting the number of categories *(aniyata-padārthavādinaḥ).*

The opponent may, however, again retort that in such cognition that "this is a cow" we cognise "this" as identical with "*gotva*" and "this" and as co-existing, so that they would try to find out a case of perception of *samavāya* through sharing the common locus *(sāmānādhikaraṇya),* because the individual instances of cow differ in each case, which cannot be collated together so as to bring them under one class and prove them to be co-existent with cowness. In any case when the Nyāya-Vaiśeṣika admits the generic character and the individual as co-existent he will have to admit that there is a mutual difference between the two, whereas such cognition as "this is a cow" proves no doubt that the two are identical. The result would be that one would be compelled to admit a relation of identity-cum-difference *(bhedābheda)* and hence the Naiyāyika's attempt to prove the perceptibility of *samavāya* through co-existence would fall flat, because identity and difference are mutually contradictory.

To this the Naiyāyika argues that such a difficulty would not arise in view of the fact that the universal and the individual (*jāti* and *vyakti*) are never cognised as identical. Such a postulation is barred by experience. To cognise 'A' and 'B' as co-existent does not mean that they are identical.

What is after all co-existence *(sāmānādhikaraṇya)*? Does it mean that two mutually different attributes are related to one unitary locus, or, is it the identity of attributes and the attribute possessors? The first alternative does not hold good in view of the fact that this will prove only identity of two attributes with the locus. The second alternative will also meet the same fate, since we do not cognise attribute *(dharma)* and attribute possessor *(dharmin)* as identical. Then how do you explain the cognition "this is a cow?" Could it said that in such cognition what are revealed are cowness, the cow individual, and their relation of inherence. If, however, these three were cognised descretely the cognition would have taken the form of "cowness" "cowness", "individual" "individual" and "inherence" "inherence" (*gotvaṁ gotvaṁ; vyaktiḥ vyaktiḥ; samavāyaḥ, samavāyaḥ*) and not as "this is a cow", because the relation of *samavāya* would be cognised directly, on the Nyāya supposition, not as a *vyakti* and *jāti*. If, however, it is said that such cognition as "this is a cow" refers to the ground there also the cognition "this is a cow" should have occurred.

5.16. *Vaiśiṣṭya*

It will not serve any purpose if the Naiyāyika wants to say that the cow individual has a determining character (*vaiśiṣṭya*) generated by the relation with cowness, because the question will necessarily arise what is after all this *vaiśiṣṭya* by which the cow individual is qualified? If it is another relation over and above the original *samavāya* it will lead to the assumption of unending number of relations involving the defect of regressus-ad-infinitum. If, however, it is said that *vaiśiṣṭya* is nothing but determination *(nirūpaṇam)* of inherence with cowness on the one hand, and the cow individual on the other, then the question will arise that in the colour white etc., which resides in cows, which also occurs through *samavāya* relation. The determining character "cowness" will occur, or, in other words, to be explicit, since the Naiyāyika holds *samavāya* as one, so inherence of cowness *(gotva samavāya)* shall occur in the cow individual's colour red, white, etc. The result would be, as we have the cognition with regard to the cow individual that "this is a cow" we should also have the same cognition "this is a cow" in the colour of the cow. If you say, in the colour of the cow no such determination is possible then how is it that the inherence is determined with the cow individual. Therefore the happy solution of the entire discourse will be as follows:

That there is no difference in the inherence of cowness in different cow individuals. We do not cognise any difference in the relation of cowness in each individual instances of cow. It is unitary and common to all individuals although it appears to be many individuals in relation to different time and space. Although it is one, its appearance is manifold and this appearance is due to some extraneous accident *(upādhi)* which in the present instance is time and space. To conclude *samavāya* is per-se related to its *samavāyins* (relata) and requires no other relation to be so related and finally its existence is proved through perception.

To this Vallabha rejoins: The Naiyāyika makes capital out of the introduction of the concept of *vaiśiṣṭya,* but *vaiśiṣṭya* is nothing but the nature of the cow. Although *samavāya* is one but it is the nature of the locus, cowness that is the cow which determines the emergence of the cognition that "this is a cow", but where there is constant absence of cowness, such cognition as "this is a cow", will not occur. This is the nature of *samavāya* relation, hence the unitary character of *samavāya* will in no way contradict the emergence of the cognition of a cow in the locus of cowness.

The opponent may raise a further question: the Vaiśeṣika says that generic character 'cowness', which is said to be inherent in all individual cow, but the question will arise do we at the time of cognising the first individual cognise the generic character, 'cowness' as a consecutive attribute or a differentiating character? The first alternative is not possible, because a consecutive character *(anugata-dharma)* is that which occurs in an individual as well as in other individuals consecutively, unless the other individual is also known, the consecutive character of the generic attribute, nor example, cowness cannot be known. The second alternative is equally unsound, because the individual is unitary in character is responsible for differentiating notion *(vyāvṛtta-buddhi)* whereas a generic character generates a consecutive notion *(anugata-buddhi).* If the generic character is supposed to be responsible for generating the differentiating notion then there would have been no difference between *jāti* and *vyakti* and they would have been identical. It is, therefore, safe to admit that the cognition "this is a cow" refers to something unitary and consecutive in character.

The Vaiśeṣika, however, cannot maintain that *jāti* is cognised neither as a consecutive nor as a differentiating character but it is perceived per se, because it is nature of *jāti.* That it appears as consecutive character, so *svarūpa* is equal to the consecutive character. If it is held that *jāti* is responsible for the cognition of difference, then the very character of *jāti* would be violated.

To this Vallabha replies that the consecutive character of *jāti* is nothing but existing through inherence in many individuals. And this generic nature of *samavāya* is cognised where the first individual is cognised. It cannot be argued that if *Jāti* is different from *vyakti*, then it would have been the case that sometimes *jāti* without being related to *vyakti* would have been cognised, because the relation between the two is held to be eternal.

5.3. *Samavāya Differs from Tādātmya (Relation of Essential Identity)*

Vyomaśiva in order to establish *samavāya* has elaborated the difference of *samavāya* from *tādātmya* as follows:

In the relation of essential identity *(tādātmya)* the relation is identified with its relata in *samavāya* the relation is different from its relata. In *samavāya* though the relata are many, *samavāya* is one *(adhigatānanyatvaṁ nānātvaṁ yeṣāṁ te tathoktāḥ, teṣāmiti tādātmya-vyudāsaḥ).*

The entities which are completely different one from the other do not constitute the relata of a *samavāya.* The horse is different from the cow and *samavāya* does not hold between a horse and a cow. In order to exclude entities such as horse and cow from the scope of *samavāya* Vyomaśiva has inserted a qualifying clause in the definition of *samavāya.* That is there must not be identity of the things but they must exist in the same space *(aviṣvag-bhāvenāvasthitānām).* He sums up the definition of *samavāya* thus:

"That relation which generates the cognition of "this is here", whose relata are proved to be different but do not exist in different spaces is called inherence."[13]

The opponent may, however, argue, says Vyomaśiva, that there is no proof for existence or acceptance of *samavāya.* The cognition that "this is here" cannot be cited as a proof of *samavāya,* because that i.e. such cognition cannot be the basis of *samavāya.* The cognition of "this is here" leads only to the generation of the knowledge of a locus of an entity, therefore, by that cognition *samavāya* cannot be proved.[14]

If the cognition of "this is here" is interpreted as the cognition of a relation, that would be the relation of *tādātmya* (identity). Moreover, this hurddle is there:

When the two relata do not exist separately they cannot be related and no relation holds, because a relation needs the existence of two relata for holding on, and when the two relata exist separately and are related by a relation, the position would be that of *yutasiddha* (contact).[15]

If, however, it is argued that *samavāya* does not need the assistance of any other relation for its subsistence in the relata, then everything would be related to everything. There is no counter rule which would prevent everything being related to everything.

Such objection is not valid, says Vyomaśiva. *Samavāya* relates two entities by subsisting in them without the assistance of other relation, hence the question of everything related to everything does not arise. Śaṅkara has also raised the question of subsistence of *samavāya* in its relata. He puts the views of the opponents like this:

If there is no relation between inherence and the object of inherence, how one can have the cognition of inherence of cloth in the yarns, of the colour in the cloth? Without a relation between them there cannot be a qualified cognition of inherence.

The reply given by Śaṅkara is, through the self-linking relation.[16]

It is to be noted here that Śaṅkara differs from others for his stressing the need of self-linking relation for the subsistence of inherence in the locus. All other writers of the Nyāya-Vaiśeṣika system are of opinion that inherence does not require any other relation of its subsistence. Inherence itself operates between the self and the locus.

Śaṅkara does not pose the question through which the relation self-linking relation does subsist? However, the self-linking relation being the nature of the relata does not require any other relation for its subsistence.

If inherence exists through self-linking relation then the cognition of "this is here" such as, "the colour is in the cloth" could also be regarded as to be caused by the self-linking relation and what is the use of assuming inherence in such cases?

The reply to this question is : There is nothing against assuming another relation in the form of inherence for the cognition of "this is here" in the usage such as "the colour is in the cloth".

5.4. *Is Samavāya Identical with Apṛthaksiddhi?*

Apṛthaksiddhi, a relation of inseparable existence has been admitted by Rāmānuja school of Viśiṣṭādvaita philosophy. The sense conveyed by *apṛthaksiddhi* seems to be the same what is conveyed by *samavāya.* However, the two relations as conceived in two systems is neither one nor inter-changeable for the simple reason that the two schools—the school of Nyāya-Vaiśeṣika and that of Viśiṣṭādvaita differ on fundamental issues; the former being pluralist while the latter is monistic, qualified monistic.

It is seen that the term *apṛthaksiddha* has been used as the synonym of *ayutasiddha* in certain works of the Nyāya-Vaiśeṣika school. By *pṛthaksiddha* Praśastapāda means those entities which have their independent existence before they are joined by a relation. Rāmānuja uses the term *apṛthaksthiti* (non-existence separately) and *apṛthakpratīti* (non-cognition separately) but in the Nyāya-Vaiśeṣika system the term is used in the former sense only. It means that the Nyāya-Vaiśeṣika has laid emphasis on ontological aspect only while the Rāmānuja school is more concerned with epistemology.

In what respect *apṛthaksiddhi* corresponds to *samavāya*? If both the conceptions are identical then where lies the difference? What is the reason for refuting *samavāya* by the Rāmānuja school of Viśiṣṭādvaita? Is the difference in name only?

Let us try to answer these questions one by one. *Samavāya* is a relation which holds between two entities which exists only being related, though the two are quite distinct entities, one depends on the other *(svātantrya-pratirodhakaḥ). Apṛthaksiddhi* also conveys the same sense, i.e. the two entities are distinct but they exist being associated, one being dependent on the other for its existence.

The operation of *samavāya* is restricted to five pairs of entities, which include *nitya dravya* and *viśeṣa* (the ultimate substance and the particular) as its relata, in other words, *samavāya* holds between the ultimate substance and the particular. The relation of *apṛthaksiddhi* is not admitted to occur between the above mentioned two entities by the Viśiṣṭādvaita school, because the school does not admit *viśeṣa* as a category.

On the other hand, the Viśiṣṭādvaita school maintains that *apṛthaksiddhi* holds between the body and the soul. The relation which exists between the body and the soul, according to the Nyāya-Vaiśeṣika, is not *samavāya.*

The points or similarity between the two concepts are like this. *Apṛthaksiddhi* like *samavāya* holds between two such entities which though distinct stand in inseparable existence. The real distinction and inseparability of the relata are the two conditions which are same in both the relations. However, in the case of *apṛthaksiddhi* the relata imply the sense of *viśiṣṭaikya* (inclusive unity). This leads to the conclusion that in *apṛthaksiddhi* the sense is that of unison, which means the relation responsible for unison is an internal relation. In other words, the nature of the relata in both the relations is the same while the ultimate purpose is different—the purpose of *apṛthaksiddhi* in Viśiṣṭādvaita is to make the two relata appear as one. *Samavāya* in Nyāya-Vaiśeṣika presents the two relata as two entities occupying the same space.

Taking into consideration these points of similarities Hirianna states *apṛthaksiddhi* as the Viśiṣṭādvaita rendering of *samavāya.* As the conception of *samavāya* gives rise to the sense of duality or plurality the monistic school of Rāmānuja cannot admit the same and hence the school admits *apṛthaksiddhi.* Apart from the name there is also conceptual difference between the two relations.

In Hiriyanna's words the difference and the identical nature of the two are:

> "Tagore, the poet, has somewhere stated that a road between two places may be looked upon either as linking them into one whole or keeping them apart. The situation is the same but explanation is different. Exactly like it seems to be the distinction between *apṛthaksiddhi* and *samavāya.* While the pluralistic Vaiśeṣika looks upon *samavāya* as holding its terms apart, the eventually monistic Viśiṣṭādvaita regards them as unified by *apṛthaksiddhi.*"[17]

However, Rāmānuja opposes the conception of *samavāya* as untenable.[18]

5.5. *Samavāya Differs from Svarūpa (Self-linking) Relation*

It has been stated on many occasions in the foregoing discussions that *samavāya* differs from *svarūpa* (self-linking) relation. The basis of difference between the two lies in the fact that *svarūpa* relation being in the form of its relata varies according to the variation of the objects i.e. the relata, hence it is many. Whereas *samavāya* is one.[19] Moreover, *samavāya* is perpetual relation *(nitya sambandhaḥ),* but *svarūpa* is a transitory one, the relata are produced and destroyed.

Another difference has been pointed out by many scholars that *svarūpa* relation is also in the form of absence *(abhāva),* but *samavāya* does not occur where the absence becomes the adjunct of the relation. This aspect is further elaborated in the course of discussion that *samavāya* is not proved through the absential relation.

5.6. *Svarūpa Is Not a Relation*

Some scholars do not admit *svarūpa* as a relation at all on the ground that it lacks the characteristic of a relation. Gaṅgeśa Upādhyāya, for instance, says that *svarūpa* is not a relation. He says that the self-linking relation by being the nature of the relata and each of the relata being unique having nothing common on the earth, cannot serve as a relation.[20] Relation pertains to the two and it involves in the act of joining.

A character which is unique to 'A' by virtue of which 'A' is differentiated from 'B', cannot unite 'A' and 'B', rather it differentiates 'A' from 'B'. Hence, self-linking relation serving as a relation is contradiction in terms. Moreover, if the qualified cognition has as its cause the relation of the qualifier that relation can be no other than the one and the unitary. The character of the effect is determined by that of the cause. The similar type of effect is determined by the similar type of cause *(anugata-kāryasya anugata-kāraṇa-niyamatvāt).* The qualified cognition, such as 'X' is qualified by quality, activity, etc. is of similar nature. And the similarity in their nature can only be explained, if we assume that all these cognitions have similar generating condition, what the Naiyāyika terms to be inherence of the qualifier in the qualified *(viśeṣaṇa-sambandhaḥ)*. The self-linking relation cannot serve this purpose, because it is discrete in different individuals and lack the capacity of assimilating under one group.

5.7. *Samavāya Differs from Paryāpti*

Though *paryāpti* or the relation of completion is not traditionally accepted one the latter school of Navya-Nyāya has admitted it as a primary relation of *vṛttiniyāmaka* (occurrence exacting) class. Raghunātha Śiromaṇi is credited with conceiving *paryāpti* as a distinct relation.[21] Some scholars consider it as a variation of *samavāya*[22] while others refuse to admit it as a relation at all.[23] However, post Raghunātha scholars of Navya-Nyāya school have conceded the necessity of assuming *paryāpti* as a separate relation.[24] In view of this, the scope of *paryāpti* is to be discussed briefly to establish its distinct identity from *samavāya.*

The ground for admitting *paryāpti* as a separate relation, which, in fact, is only a particular form a *svarūpa* (self-linking) relation is like this:

When we say "this is one pot" there are two pots—the number "oneness" and "twoness" being quality[25] must reside in a substance, and they rest in the pot through the relation of *samavāya.*[26]

The question is—where lies the "twoness"—in the individual pot or the two pots ? The answer is–through *samavāya* "twoness" can reside in each of the two pots. Hence, we can say "the pot is twoness–possessing" *(ghaṭo dvitvavān)*, but surely we cannot say "the pot is two" *(ghaṭo dvau)*. If *paryāpti* is not admitted and only *samavāya* is accepted as the relation operating there, then both the expressions could have been used indiscriminately i.e. "the pot is twoness–possessing" and "the pot is two".[27] It is only the relation of *paryāpti* or the relation of completion makes distinction and restrict the use.

In other words, through *samavāya* "twoness" resides in each of the two pots, but *paryāpti* makes the number "twoness" not to reside in each of the two pot, even when they are together. Therefore, one of the two pots cannot be called "the pot is two" *(ghaṭo dvau)*, only the two pots together can be called "these are two pots" *(ghaṭau dvau)*.

Gadādhara Bhaṭṭācārya has advanced another argument in support of *paryāpti*. His argument is like this: The ether is one and undivided, hence the cognition of 'two ethers' *(ākāśau)* is invalid. But how logically this cognition is proved invalid?

The cognition of 'two ethers' (*ākāśau*) has the relation of *samavāya* as its object, because "twoness" (*saṁkhyā* i.e. quality) is related to ether (substance) through *samavāya*. Thus there is nothing which renders the said cognition invalid and the statement of "two ethers" would have passed as correct and the cognition as valid. It is only *prayāpti* relation which renders the cognition invalid. The number "twoness" cannot exist in the ether, which is one, because the ether by being one does not fulfil the condition of completeness for the occurrence of the relation of completion. The absence of *paryāpti* relation makes the statement of "two ethers" incorrect and the subsequent cognition also invalid. Since "twoness" of the substance is the state of completion for holding the relation of completions *(paryāpti)*[28] and in one ether it cannot hold. But there is no such precondition for holding the relation of inherence.

The necessity of admitting *paryāpti* as a separate relation is warranted by the fact that "one is not two"—says Śivadatta Miśra. He has built up the argument as follows: The cognition of "one is associated with twoness" *(eko dvitvavān)* through *samavāya* relation is valid, however, the cognition of "one is two" *(eko dvau)* is not valid, though *samavāya* is there. Thus the acceptance of the former cognition as a valid one and the non-acceptance of the latter clearly suggest the necessity of admitting *paryāpti* as a separate relation.[29] In fact, why one cognition is accepted as valid and not the other lies in the fact that there is difference between that two and this difference can be understood only by assumption of the two relations, namely, *samavāya* and *paryāpti*.[30]

After taking into consideration all the arguments and the logic behind them for the admittance of *paryāpti* as a separate relation distinct from *samavāya* one is likely to conclude that *paryāpti* is rather a condition precedent for holding *samavāya* leading to a valid cognition. However, *paryāpti* like *saṁyoga* is a quality *(guṇa)* hence it differs from *samavāya* and that is the only relevant point in the above discussion.

5.7. *Vṛtti of Samavāya*

In this context a relevant point, which deserves consideration is, through which relation inherence subsists in a substance ? The substance is a category and inherence is also a category. There must be some *vṛtti* (occurrent) between the two through which inherence subsists in a substance. It cannot be said that between substance and inherence contact *(saṁyoga)* occurs and contact is *vṛtti* for the substance of inherence, because contact is a quality and hence it resides in a subsistence only. The underlying meaning of this statement is that inherence subsists in the substance etc. and as such contact is to reside in inherence, which itself has the substance as its locus, and contact being a quality cannot reside in other than substance.

Nor it can be said that there is another inherence through which inherence resides in a substance, because inherence is one, which cannot be divided.

The existence of a third relation apart from the contact and inherence cannot be conceived. Such a relation will be an internal relation, and, therefore cannot be the instrumental for the subsistence of inherence.

On the question of a separate *vṛtti* for the subsistence of inherence the problem of regressus ad-infinitum has been raised. If the inherence needs the assistance of another inherence and for that matter any other relation, that will also need another relation, and the process will continue which means regressus ad infinitum (*anavasthā*). The inherence does not require the assistance of any other relation for its subsistence in the substance etc. It subsists there by its own right i.e. through its own self.

Śrīdhara postulates two alternatives on the question of subsistence of inherence. Whether inherence without being related to its relata (by some other relation) relates them ? Or, in the alternative, it does so being related to the relata ?

The first alternative cannot be accepted because it will lead to the fallacy of over-pervasion. For instance, inherence relates the yarns and the cloth. Now, if it be held that inherence related the cloth with the yarns without itself being related to either or both of them, the position will be that inherence relates a piece of cotton with a piece of cloth, because the status of inherence as being non-related to the relata will be the same in all cases.

Therefore, the second alternative is to be accepted, i.e. *samavāya* relates the relata being related to them. And the state of *samavāya's* being related to the relata is its own function or *vṛtti.* This cannot be a contact. Even contact is accepted as *vṛtti* for the subsistence of inherence, one shall have to admit another relation for *vṛtti* of contact and thus it leads to the state of regressus ad infinitum.

Jayanta Bhaṭṭa observes that *vṛtti* of inherence is inherence itself. He says that "the relata of a inherence, i.e. the whole and the part etc. are cognised separately and on account of separate cognition they are taken as two different entities. In fact, they do not occupy separate space i.e. the two exist in the same space. For the appearance of the two as one and their being related through a *vṛtti* is conceived, which is called *samavāya.*"[31]

Pārthasārathi has raised the question[32] of occurrence *(vṛtti)* of contact *(saṁyoga)* in the objects of contact *(saṁyogin).* How it occurs ? Is it like the occurrence of universal in the individual or like that of the whole in the part ? According to the Bhāṭṭa school of Pūrva-Mīmāṁsā the universal occurs in the individual without the involvement of the other relation, while the whole occurs in the parts by adhering to other *(vyāsajya-vṛtti).*

Pārthasārathi says that the occurrence of contact differs from the both. It is neither like the occurrence of universal in the individual nor exactly like that of whole in parts. Contact occurs in one object, hence differs from the occurrence of universal. Again contact generates its cognition in one relata of the contact without adhering to the other. Therefore, it is not exactly like the occurrence of the whole.

According to the Mīmāṁsā school, he says, the contact is like that of similarity *(sādṛśya)* and differs in respect of every object of the contact. When we say, "this is like this and this is like this" *(idam anena sadṛśam idam anena)* we cognise similarity of one object in the other with reference to its counter positive *(pratiyogin)*, and as such, it varies according to the object. The contact has given rise to such cognition, therefore, the difference of one contact from the other is to be accepted.

The Mīmāṁsā school does not admit any *vṛtti* for existence of contact.

5.8. *Samavāya is an Eternal (Nitya) Relation*

Samavāya has been defined and admitted as a perpetual or eternal *(nitya)* relation. As a matter of fact its eternal character differentiates it from *saṁyoga,* which is a temporal relation.

Samavāya is cognised as the eternal relation because it has no cause for its coming into existence and it can neither be caused nor destroyed. All positive entities, except the eternal ones, are born in the their positive antecedents, the inherent cause. Śaṁkara asks, if inherence be an effect i.e. caused by some other cause, what is the inherent cause of inherence for its production ? Another inherent cause, or the same inherence? The first alternative cannot be admitted, because it will involve another inherent cause and this way it will lead to regressus ad-infinitum. The second one is also unacceptable, because the same inherence cannot inhere in self. This will expose it to the criticism of self-dependence. *Saṁyoga* and *samavāya* both being relation relates entities and with the destruction of either of the relata or both *saṁyoga* ceases to exist. Thus it stands that when the relata of *saṁyoga* are non-eternal the relation caused by them is also non-eternal. Contact does not hold between two eternal entities *(aja saṁyogābhāva),* hence *saṁyoga* is a temporary relation. But the character of *samavāya* is different—like *sattā samavāya* has no cause. Nobody can adduce cause for *sattā* coming into existence, *samavāya* is also without a cause, hence eternal.

Śrīdhara while explaining this point says that it is quite logical that with the destruction of the relata *saṁyoga* itself is destroyed, because the relata are the inherent cause *(samavāyikāraṇa)* for the production of *saṁyoga,* but in case of *samavāya* the relata are not the inherent cause of the said relation, they are simply adjunct *(pratiyogin)* and subjunct *(anuyogin)* of the relation *(samavāyasya sambandhinau tau na kāranaṁ)*. From the above discussion it becomes quite clear that *samavāya* does not cease to exist even if either of the relata or both are destroyed, because *samavāya* is not caused by them. With the destruction of the relata where does *samavāya* go and how it exist ? It is a matter of cognition and *samavāya* can be cognised to exist in some other loci. The example of universal may be cited to drive home the position. The universal resides in the individual, say, cowness in the cow individual. Where does the 'cowness' go when that individual dies ? The cowness is perceived in some other locus i.e. another individual cow.

Udayana while defining *samavāya* as the eternal relation has laid stress on the eternal character of *samavāya*. The relation of constant absence *(atyantābhāva)* with its locus will also be regarded as an eternal relation, and thus, the said relation will also be inherence. This apprehension has no basis. In the definition of *samavāya* the problem has been discussed to some extent.

5.9. *Is Samavāya an Internal Relation*

Whether or not *samavāya* is an internal relation the position may be examined from the basic point of view of the Nyāya-Vaiśeṣika. The Nyāya-Vaiśeṣika school of philosophy is not only realist but pluralist also. The school postulates the atoms of four kinds of elements, other eternal substances such as ether, soul, etc. and also universal etc. as eternal and real entities. Therefore, neither the relata nor the relation is an abstraction.[33] They are real and disparate. This means the relation is as real as the relata are. From this it is clear that *samavāya* is neither a mode nor state of the relata as stated by the Bhāṭṭas.[34] *Samavāya* is independent of the two relata it relates. How an independent entity can be intimated with others?

One may argue—it is true that *samavāya* being an independent entity has hardly any scope for falling inside the relata, but it can modify them and thus it may be an internal relation,[35] as such there will be no inconsistency. This contention is also inadmissible to the Nyāya-Vaiśeṣika, because he holds that the eternal entities are partless and incapable of being modified, hence *samavāya* cannot effect any modification in the relata.

Another argument, which may be advanced in support of *samavāya* as an internal relation, is like this. Let the ultimate reals, which do not admit modification, remain immune from the modification, but the objects such as the cloth or the pot, which are effects, can be modified by *samavāya*. The modification of the effect has not been experienced. Moreover this hypothesis will go against the causation theory of the Nyāya-Vaiśeṣika, i.e. the theory that the effect is caused anew (*ārambha*), which is conceived against the theory of *pariṇāma* (the cause changes into effect) of Sāṁkhya. In other words, if any modification by *samavāya* in the effect is admitted, it will mean that the cause undergoes changes and the effect is nothing but the changed cause. This the Nyāya-Vaiśeṣika cannot admit.

Samavāya holds between eternal and non-eternal entities as well. It relates eternal substance with quality, for instance, the particles of earth (*pṛthvī*) with the odour; but there is no modification or change, they are incapable of being modified. When it relates an effect, a product to the quality, the effect is not modified by *samavāya*, it remains as before. If any modification is admitted, then there will be two effects, one is pure and the other modified. In any way, the qualified pot i.e. the pot which stands related to its colour does not differ from the pure one.[36] Therefore the question of the effect being modified by the relation of *samavāya* does not arise.

The position may be illustrated by an example. The cloth is related to the yarns through *samavāya*. Both the cloth and the yarns have colour. The colour of the yarns resides in the yarns through *samavāya*. The colour of the yarns is the cause of the colour of the cloth; both cloth and its colour stand related through *samavāya*. Thus *samavāya* holds, through the intermediaries, between the colour of the yarns and that of the cloth. But by no stretch of imagination the colour of the cloth can be said to be modified by *samavāya*. The colour of the cloth is a completely new product which subsists in the cloth through *samavāya*.

Thus it is seen that *samavāya* cannot modify its relata and as such it is not intimate with them. To some extent, like *saṁyoga*, *samavāya* is also an external, which subsists between two entities. However, *samavāya* is not an extraneous one to the relata as *saṁyoga* is and, therefore, cannot be put on equal footing with *saṁyoga*.

Samavāya is both external and internal relation, or it can be termed as a quasi-internal, because one of its relata is always intimate to it, while in *saṁyoga* both the relata are extraneous to that relation and, therefore, *saṁyoga* is entirely an external relation.

The traditional view holds *samavāya* as internal relation. This is one of the grounds on which *samavāya* has been distinguished from *saṁyoga*. There is no harm if *samavāya* is termed an internal relation, but it has some characteristics of an external relation also.

5.10. *The Existence of Absence is not through Samavāya*

"There is no pot on the ground" *(bhūtale ghaṭābhāvaḥ)*—here the ground is qualified by the non-existence of the pot. The qualification is a relation and that exists there through the self-linking relation. If this be considered a different relation i.e. other than the self-linking *(svarūpa)* relation then it will create complicacy.

If the said qualification is eternal, then when a pot is brought there, even then the ground will be regarded as without the pot, because the non-existence is transitory, when a pot is brought to that ground the non-existence of the pot being eternal is deemed to be there. On the other hand, if the non-existence of the pot *(ghaṭābhāva)* will not be perceived in other places also, because as soon as the pot is brought the absolute non-existence of the pot, which is one as a class will vanish in all other places. The result will be that the non-existence of the pot will not be perceived in a place where there is no pot.

Therefore, it is safe to hold that the relation of non-existence, as in the aforesaid instance, is the particular ground associated with particular time. Thus it is a relation of self-linking and not of inherence.

While excluding the absolute absence from the operational range of *samavāya* Vardhamana[37] in his commentary on the *Kiraṇā-*

valī wanted to prove *samavāya* on the ground of cognition of container-containedhood of the two relata, and makes the said cognition dependent on the relation between the two. Thus the dependence on relation being the *hetu* (reason) for the cognition of *samavāya*, the relation of absolute absence with the locus does not stand as the reason *(hetu)* for the cognition of absence, its locus, and the relation between the two. In other words, the relation of absolute absence with its locus[38] is not eternal, if it is presumed to be eternal then we shall perceive, as has been stated above, the absence of the pot on the ground even when the pot is brought there. But nobody cognises the absence of the pot on the ground when the pot is present. Thus, it becomes clear that though the absolute absence is eternal the relation of the said absence with its locus is non-eternal, hence, after the pot is brought to the ground the pot by its presence destroys the relation, which is transitory.

In this context Śaṁkara refers to the views of the Bhāṭṭa who holds that the relation that exists between absence and its locus is *vaiśiṣṭya.* If such a relation be admitted in respect of all varieties of absence, then one would cognise the absence of pot on a ground where the pot exists. The *vaiśiṣṭya* being one, the absence of the pot will be cognised by the cognition of absence of cloth, though in fact pot is there. Neither it can be said that the pot itself as the counter positive of the cognition of the absence of the pot, because *vaiśiṣṭya* being a relation by itself asserts that there is absence of counter cognition. One may say that the relation of *vaiśiṣṭya* resides in an object and it is the locus of absence. This locus has the characteristic of causing such cognition that the pot will not be manifested. This argument is not valid, because after the removal of the pot, the absence of the pot is cognised there.

The opponent further argues: According to you inherence is one and eternal, therefore, why after the destruction of colour there shall not be cognition of colour ? The reply is: The destruction of colour itself causes the cognition of absence of colour. Śaṁkara further points out incongruity if the inherence is admitted as the relation between the absence and its locus.

"There is no pot on the ground"—in such usage there is no necessity of assuming inherence or any other relation, because the self-linking relation is quite adequate to cause the cognition of absence. If the existence of absence be not admitted as in the nature of self-linking relation, this will lead to further complications.

The absolute absence of the pot in "there is no pot" and the mutual absence, such as, "the pot is not the table" (there is absence of pot in the table and also absence of the table in the pot) both are eternal and reside in many objects. The result will be that it will assume the character of the universal. (An eternal object, if resides in many, is to be regarded as universal).

Moreover, if the posterior absence (*dhvaṁsābhāva*) be assumed to be related to an object through inherence, it is to be regarded as caused by the inherent cause, and thus is liable to be destroyed. Whereas posterior absence cannot be destroyed.

Again, the prior absence *(prāgabhāva)* in the same way, not being caused by the inherent cause shall have to be assumed as eternal, which it is not. The reasons for the objection to the admittance of inherence between absence and its locus are like this:

The positiveness cannot be stated as a factor here.

5.11. *Samavāya is One*

It has been said that when *samavāya* is proved, it is proved as an unitary and one. It is the law of logical parsimony or simplicity which establishes *samavāya* as one, in the same way, as the Naiyāyika has proved God as one. The inference which proves the existence of God, namely, "the earth, sprout etc. have intelligent cause, because they are effect" also proves such intelligent cause as one, eternal and all powerful, through the assistance of the inductive reasoning, called logical parsimony *(lāghava-tarkasanāthena).*

The opponents have raised the objection to the effect that if *samavāya* be taken as one there will be confusion in the cognition of categories. If it is one, inherence of action *(karmatva samavāya)* will be present in the inherence of substance, because inherence being one, both inherence of action and inherence of substance, as a rule, should be present (where one is present).

This probability cannot materialise, says Śaṁkara, for the simple reason that the relation of inherence is governed by the substratum-superstratum principle *(ādhāra-ādheya-niyamāt).* Of course, it is true, the inherence that exists between substance and substancehood is the same inherence that obtains between quality and qualityhood, but the substratum differs. What the substratum of substancehood is not the substratum of qualityhood. Substance is the substratum of substancehood while quality is that of qualityhood. Therefore, substancehood is cognised in substance only, qualityhood in quality only and nowhere else.

Presence-absence *(anvaya-vyatireka)* is observed in all cases, i.e. presence of substancehood is cognised only in substance, not in any other locus; again, absence of substancehood is observed in a locus which is not a substance. This principle governs the existence of a particular entity in a particular locus, hence no cause of confusion of categories arises.

In this regard the example of contact may be cited. For instance, in the usages, such as, "the curd is in the can" the contact is the same in respect of both can and the curd i.e the contact operates between the two and so far the relation is concerned both are on equal footing. In spite of their equality it is the cognition that the can is the substratum of the curd, not the reverse. Had the relation alone been the deciding factor, it could have been by both ways i.e. the can as the superstratum *(ādheya)* and the curd as the substratum *(ādhāra)* of the can. But the cognition governs it that the can is the substratum of the curd and not otherwise, because it is the governing principle *(niyama)*,[39] which regulates one.

In the same way the two powers, namely, the manifesting power and the power of being manifested *(vyaṇgya-vyañjaka-śakti)* also are at work. In other words, the manifesting power lies in the substance, quality etc. and the power of being manifested resides in the substancehood, qualityhood etc. and this difference in power makes the two entities different. Thus the manifesting power of substance causes manifestation of the substancehood, not of qualityhood. Similarly the same power residing in quality manifested qualityhood only and nothing else. Because of such restricted nature of the power there is not the least probability of the categories being confused. The basis for assuming such power of the entities is our cognition *(saṁvid),* which alone is our sole guide in cognising a thing.[40]

However, if a qualified cognition does not refer to the relation between the qualifier and qualified as its objective content, or, if such a qualified cognition is not held to have been generated by that relation, or, in other words, if a qualified entity has no reference to the qualifier-qualified relation either as its referent or as its cause, the cognition of a cow and a horse, which are discrete, would have been cognised as a qualified cognition. But neither the cow nor the horse is qualified by either and hence, the cognition of a cow and a horse is not a qualified cognition for the simple reason that one is never related to the other. It is clear, therefore, that a qualified cognition pre-supposes a qualifier-qualified relation. And in such example as "I see red flowers" or "I see a running horse" leads us to the assumption of *samavāya* relation.

We have no contrary cognition in respect of substratum in the above mentioned examples. Because we do not have the cognition, such as substance resides in action, nor, the yarns are in the cloth.[41]

A question arises: since inherence is one, inherence of colour in a pot and inherence of touch in the air will be the same. On account of this, one may say that there is inherence of colour in the air and as such the air would be perceptible by the visual organ.

Such a hypothesis is not correct. Though there is inherence of colour in the air, the air is not the substratum of colour, nobody cognises that the colour is in the air. From the above discussions it becomes clear that the natural power of an object does always serve as the governing principle in all such cases, and hence, there is no apprehension for confusion of the categories, though inherence is one. On the ground that *samavāya* is one nobody should have the cognition of colour in the air, because though the air possesses inherence of colour it lacks colour.[42]

In order to establish the unitariness of *samavāya* Vāgīśvara argues that individual sound inheres in the ether, although the sounds are many, the relation between the ether and the sounds is one. Because it is the relation of ether which determines the relation between sound individuals and the other. Ether is one, hence, the relation, of which ether is a determinant *(ākāśapratiyogika)* is one, and that by that relation all sounds are related to ether.

It can be gainsaid that if the relation of inherence is accepted as one then there will be complete chaos in the objects *(vastuśaṁk ara-prasaṅga)*, because the inherence of sound and the inherence of colour *(rūpa)* will be the one and same, and the result would be, inherence of colour would exist in ether and one would be compelled to admit that ether also has the colour; which is on the face of it, absurd.

To this Vāgīśvara's reply would be that the relation is not an absolute concept, it always takes into account the two relata, one that which is related *(pratiyogin)* and other to which or with which it is related *(anuyogin)* and without prior cognition of these two, no relation is possible, and the cognition is also impossible. When the two determinant factors always differ one would easily be able to avoid the charge of chaos levelled against Vaiśeṣika view *(tasya samasta-viṣaya-śaṁkaratvenaiva parikalpitatvāt)*.

Let us for argument sake admit *samavāya* is one but its nature varies. The nature of inherence of sound differs from that of the inherence of colour. And this will entail plurality of *samavāya*, one differing from the other. Vāgīśvara does not find any logic in this argument and replies that unity will not be violated in *samavāya* as in variegated colour *(citrarūpa)*, a distinct type of unitary colour, in spite of the fact that it involves a number of colours. Once the unitary character of *samavāya* is proved its eternality also stands established. The apprehension that if *samavāya* be taken as one there is likely to be confusion in the cognition of categories *(padārtha-śaṁkara-prasaṅga)* is sought to be removed by the different writers of the Nyāya-Vaiśeṣika system by invoking the rule of container-containedhood *(ādhāra-ādheya niyama)* and the manifesting power of the categories.

Śrīdhara taking recourse to the manifesting power of an object aptly describes that the substance alone has got the manifesting power for manifestation of the substance and so other entity possesses this *(dravyatva-vyañjikā śaktir dravyāṇām eva)*. In spite of different categories being related by *samavāya*, which is one and the same in all cases, this power having been residing at the root of the cognition of entities makes distinct cognition and there cannot arise the question of confusion of categories.

Śivāditya asserts that inherence is one because it has no *jāti.*[43] Elucidating the idea of Śivāditya, the author of the *Mitabhāṣiṇī* says that the uncontradicted cognition of "whiteness is here" like the cognition of "the apples are in the basket"—this along with the parasimony of logic leads to the conclusion that *samavāya* is one.[44] In the *Padārthacandrikā* of Ananta and the *Sandarbha* of Balabhadra the unitariness of *samavāya* has been established on the ground that it is an eternal relation.[45]

Raghunātha Śiromaṇi and some of his juniors hold the view that *samavāya* is not one; it is in the nature of *viṣayatā* (subject-object) relation and, hence, like *svarūpa* (self-linking) relation is many. He asserts that if *samavāya* be taken as one, water will also have to be cognised as a smell-possessing substance. Because what is the inherence of smell in earth is the inherence of moisture in water, and having no distinction in the nature of the said inherences the inherence of the moisture in water will qualify water as the smell-possessing.[46]

The question may arise if *samavāya* is admitted as many how can it be cognised in different entities which *samavāya* relates? Raghunātha replies that the inherencehood *(samavāyatva)* is cognised as the indivisible imposed property, thus there is no impediment in the cognition of *samavāya.*[47]

The upholder of oneness of *samavāya* may further argue that since water does not possess the qualified inherence conditioned by the smell *(gandha-nirūpitatva-viśiṣṭa)* the apprehension that water will also have to be cognised as the smell-possessing one, is unfounded. Raghunātha says that the argument has no force in view of the fact that the so called qualified inherence *(gandha-nirūpitatva-viśiṣṭa)* does not possess any additional quality for such distinct cognition.[48] Moreover, the admission of the qualified cognition in the inherence makes it distinct from the other, that being so, what is the crime committed by *samavāya* for not being admitted as many.[49]

This view of Raghunātha and his followers is mentioned in most of the works of Navya-Nyāya as that of 'the moderns' *(navyāh)* and is refuted by traditional arguments.

In fact, *samavāya* as a category falls in the second group of the categories and is *svātma-sat;* like universal and particular, and is one. Manifoldness of *samavāya* will involve the occurrence of universal *(jāti)* in *samavāya* and for the existence of the said universal *(samavāyatva)* in *samavāya* one more relation has got to be admitted between the two, and that relation will be not other than *samavāya,* because the relation that exists between the individual and the universal is *samavāya* .

5.11. *Oneness of Samavāya according to Gaṅgeśa*

In order to establish oneness of *samavāya* Gaṅgeśa first reports the objection of the opponents as follows:

That there are things which have colour and there are other things which have no colour. We can say that the pot is blue, but we cannot say that the air is blue, because air has no colour. Now if *samavāya* is said to be one then this determination that " 'A' has colour" but " 'B' has no colour" will not be possible, because on the Nyāya supposition of the unitariness of inherence, inherence of any quality, and that of the *rūpa* (colour) will be the same.

Air being a substance must have some quality although it is devoid of colour. And if inherence is held to be one, the inherence of colour should exist in the air. Consequently, the visual perception of the air would have been possible. It can be said *samavāya* associates colour only with the pot and not with the air, because air is colourless. The question will necessarily arise:

Is it the nature of associating colour with something 'X' ? Or, is it the very nature of inherence ?

If it is so, then the character of associating taste *(rasa)* with "Y" cannot be its (inherence) nature, because these two characteristics sharply differ.

In reply to all these charges of opponents Gaṅgeśa asserts that although the air has an inherence of colour, the constant absence of colour *(rūpātyantābhāva)* exists in it (air), which, i.e. constant absence of colour does not exist in the pot. You cannot ask why it is so? Because it is the very nature of the loci (*adhikaraṇasvabhāvāt*), the air and the pot that one possesses colour, the other does not. And such cognition cannot be ruled out since there are uncontradicted perceptual experiences.

5.12. *Is Samavāya Perceptible?*

The opponents have attacked *samavāya* on the ground that it is neither perceptible nor inferable. Vyomaśiva, Śaṁkara, Vāgīśvara, Śrīdhara and more particularly Vallabha have dealt with these aspects of *samavāya*.

It is noted that there is difference between the Nyāya and the Vaiśeṣika schools on the question of perceptibility of *samavāya*, while the Naiyāyika says *samavāya* is perceptible the Vaiśeṣika asserts that it is not, *samavāya* can be cognised by inference only.

The question of perceptibility of *samavāya* is intimate with its cognition. The question is: The cognition of *samavāya* is a qualificand cognition and it is dependent on the cognition of the qualifier *(liṅgi-jñānotpattau)*.[50] What is the qualifier in the qualificand cognition of *samavāya* ? It is clear that there is no qualifier and qualificand in the case of *samavāya*, hence it cannot be cognised by perception.

Vyomaśiva asserts that *samavāya* is not perceptible, but it can be inferred. The reason why *samavāya* is not perceptible is like this. When we cognise "the cloth is in the yarns" we have the cognition of only the superstratum *(ādheya)* and the relation that relates the superstratum with the substratum. The relation with the relata may be perceptible in an indeterminate *(nirvikalpa)* state of knowledge, not otherwise.

Samavāya can be inferred. From the cognition of "this is here" one can infer existence of *samavāya*. For instance, "the cloth is in the yarns", the cloth stands related to yarns, hence there is a relation between the two. The cognition of "this is here" leads to the above inference, it does not lead to the perception of *samavāya*.[51]

Following the *Vaiśeṣika* views Vāgīśvara states that *samavāya* is not amenable to perception. It is neither amenable to our sense perception since it is a relation which unites not only the perceptible entities, like the pot and the blueness, but it also holds between two entities of which one is perceptible and the other non-perceptible entity, such as, sound and the ether. Cognition without an object is an impossibility and the ordinary cognition in the form of "blueness exists in the pot" or "the activity of running in the horse", or "humanity in the human being" etc. points to some determinant relation which Vāgīśvara calls *samavāya.* Vallabha following the Nyāya system says that it is perceptible. Whenever, universal or its individual is perceived simultaneously the relation of inherence which unites them is also perceived. And to perceive *samavāya* we need not require to perceive it either as qualifier or as substantive, but it is perceived per se.

Had it not been a case of perception, such usages as "I see a cow in my front", or "this is a cow" would have remained inexplicable. In the cognition "this is a cow", "this is co-existent *(samānādhikaraṇa)* with "cow"; rather in that case the perception would have taken the form of "this" "this" and "cowhood" "cowhood". You cannot say in such cases "cowhood is a relatum of inherence". We have the cognition of the two sharing the same locus *(samānādhikaraṇya)* and indeed the Vaiśeṣika would not try to explain this situation through some other relation. Likewise, such cognition as "this is cow", which can be formulated "this is the relata of cowhood" would not require any other relation.

To this the Naiyāyika replies that in such cognition as the "cowhood is the relata of inherence", we have indeed the cognition of a relation, and this will not lead us to regressus ad infinitum, because here the cognition of the relation is super-imposed and not real. One may ask: Why not then in the case of "cowhood" and individual cow, the relation be considered as a case of superimposition ?

The reply would be—that here a relation postulated because there is no impediment to its postulation, whereas, where *samavāya* itself is a *samavāyin* (the relatum of *samavāya*) we cannot logically postulate another relation, for the simple reason that it is barred by the possibility of the regressus ad infinitum.

To this the reply would be as follows:

It will not be a case of regressus ad infinitum, because the cognition of the relation in the present instance is a case of super-imposition. A question may arise: In such cognition—"this is a cow" the notion of the relation may also be said to be a case of super-imposition. To this the Vaiśeṣika argues that such notions of relation can be considered as super-imposition which are contradicted by a succeeding notion. Uncontradicted experience cannot be considered as a case of super-imposition. The contradiction in the present case is regressus ad infinitum. If, however, the opponent does not see any fault where regressus ad infinitum is involved, the Vaiśeṣika is ready to leave it unquestioned.

The Vaiśeṣika holds that while *samavāya* is not perceptible the cognition of container-containedhood of the part and the whole, the substance and the quality etc. is based on perception. In fact, on the ground of perceptual cognition of the container-containedhood of the yarns and the cloth *samavāya* is established by the Vaiśeṣika.

In the instances, such as, "the cloth is in the yarns" the relation of *samavāya* that exists between the two is not perceived, but what is perceived is the containedhood of the cloth limited by the yarnhood, and conditioned by the locushood of the yarns, which is limited by the relation of *samavāya (tantutvāvacchinnā-dhikaraṇatā-nirūpita-samavāya-sambandhā-vacchinnaḥ paṭaḥ).* In other words, the containedhood (*ādheyatā*) of the cloth appears as the qualifier of the cloth in the process of perception.

Let us take another example, say, "the white pot" in this perceptual cognition the inherence of the while colour in the pot is not perceived. But the qualifierness *(prakāratā)* of the white colour is limited by the relation of inherence, hence the inherence is not perceived because of qualifierness, qualificandness etc. the property of the knowledge are not perceptible.

The Naiyāyika holds the view that *samavāya* is perceptible and says that when the two relata of the relation which relates them is perceived, the relation also got to be perceived. Thus the cognition of "the cloth is in the yarns" is a perceptual one.

Gaurinatha Shastri explains the perceptibility of *samavāya* in a different way. The Naiyāyika's view of the perceptibility of *samavāya* is to be understood as the perception of the inseparably connectedhood of the relation and not the relation as an eternal one, says Shastri. However, he has neither explained the reasons nor quoted any authority.

The Vaiśeṣika says that the logic of assertion is that nothing can be cognised by perceptual cognition what is not the counter-positive of the prior and posterior absence, and *samavāya* being an eternal entity cannot be the counter-positive of the said absence, hence *samavāya* as an eternal relation is not perceptible.

The intention of the Vaiśeṣika can be understood from the very nature of *samavāya* . *Samavāya* subsists in its relata without the mediation of another relation, hence it is a self-occurrent *(svātma-vṛttika)* one, which condition implies that it is not related to the sense organ either by contact or any other way. In absence of such a relation between *samavāya* and the sense organ it cannot be an object of visual perception.

The inference advanced by the Naiyāyika for establishing perceptibility of *samavāya* being contradicted by the perceptual cognition stands vitiated.

5.13. *Samavāya by Inference*

(A) Mānamanohara

Vādi-Vāgīśvara, Vallabha and Gaṅgeśa have established *samavāya* by the argument based on inference. Since their arguments are class by themselves they deserve special treatment. Their arguments have been summarised and produced separately.

Vāgīśvara takes up the question of whole and part and puts it into the terms of inference.

(i) Controversial entity is related to the whole, that is, the pot, because it is a substance like the soul.

(ii) Controversial entity i.e. the parts are related to whole through an eternal relation, because they are substances like ether.

The first inference seeks to prove a relation between the parts and the whole while the second one proves the eternality of the relation.

What Vāgīśvara wants to make out is this; the soul is a substance and all-existent, and, hence it is related to anything which is a whole like a pot. The soul is also a substance and the parts are being of the nature of substance are related to the whole.

In the second inference he seeks to prove that the hypothecated relation is eternal and that is why the illustration of ether has been given, and, in fact in the Vaiśeṣika position the relation between ether and the sound is eternal; the Bhāṭṭas also admit the same although in their opinion sound *(śabda)* is a substance which is in eternal contact with the ether. Therefore, the Bhāṭṭas cannot disown the *sādhya,* (probendum, the thing to be proved), and there is no deficiency in it.

Vāgīśvara then refers to the views of some other scholars whose argument is like this:

Contact is different from that relation (*samavāya*) from which it is different, because it is a knowable.

This proposition Vāgīśvara does not find reasonable and hence presents a number of probable alternatives but none of them appeals to him. Vāgīśvara asks, is it a fact that one shall have to admit, *samavāya* as independent relation because the cognition of sharing the same locus would not be possible ? But sometimes it happens even though two entities are related they cannot be said to have shared the same locus; for example, the rope and the pot. They might be related but such position as *"rajjuḥ ghaṭaḥ"* is neither plausible nor admitted. Also in the case in which two entities are not related, for example, the mountain Vindhya and the Himālayas *(Himvad-Vindhyayośca)* the cognition of sharing the common locus *(sāmānādhikaraṇya)* does not occur. The underlying meaning is that the absence of cognition of sharing the common locus is equal in both the cases i.e when two entities are related or not. Therefore, the cognition that two entities share the common locus does not, in any way, presupposes a relation between the two.

Now, the other alternatives are as follows: There must be a relation different from *saṁyoga,* because *saṁyoga* presupposes mutual difference between the two relata while *samavāya* suggests difference-cum-identity. Vāgīśvara holds that this position is untenable; the difference between the pot and its colour is obvious, but how can their identity be determined?

What is after all identity? It cannot be the negation of difference, because in that case identity and difference cannot co-exist, for the simple reason they are mutually contradictory. Or, shall we presume that identity is opposite to difference? For, accepting this position, the meaning of opposition is to be defined.

(a) Is this opposition in the nature of identity and difference? or,

(b) Is it due to their individual locus? or,

(c) Is it due to their opposite functioning?

Whatever may be the case, identity is always opposite to difference. When identity contradicts difference they cannot co-exist.

In the case of the pot and its colour, the pot is not other than the colour and hence there is no mutual absence between the two. This statement does not sound logical; when we say one is different from the other you admit that there is mutual absence. It is wholly impossible to assume that "there is difference but no mutual absence" because difference and mutual absence are synonymous *(tayoḥ paryāyatvāt)*.

Vāgīśvara made out the point that identity and difference being mutually contradictory cannot have the same locus and hence *samavāya* cannot be the relation of identity-cum-difference. However, one may argue that the difference is not an independent attribute but, is of the nature of the things which are different. If this be so, identity and difference can be mutually compatible. To this Vāgīśvara replies that the cognition of difference is dependent upon the cognition of the counter-positive, that is, the cognition of things which are different. But to cognise the nature of an entity one does not require to cognise anything else. Hence, difference and the nature of the object, which are different, cannot be identical. Therefore, the mutual incompatibility of identity and difference stands.

He further argues that an object which is denoted by other term, is bound to be different from the object denoted by other term because the terms differ.

Vāgīśvara further states that *samavāya* is one, and once it is proved so, it will also be proved as an eternal one.

In this context he raises the question, if *samavāya* is perceptible or it can be known by inference only, and replies that *samavāya* is not perceptible.

Vallabha in his *Nyāya-Līlāvatī* brings out a detail analysis of the concept of *samavāya* . At the outset he puts the argument of the opponent that *samavāya* can neither be proved through perception nor by inference.

In fact, the Vaiśeṣika does not consider *samavāya* to be perceptible and hence the opponent's main point of attack is to show that there is no valid reason through which *samavāya* can be proved. Hence Vallabha shows the probability of logical reasoning as follows:

Such qualified cognition that "this cow has cowness", or, "the cloth is in the yarns" entails the postulation of some relation between the two. Such usages result from the uncontradicted experience and points to some positive entity, which unites the two, and thereby resulting in a qualified cognition. This can be illustrated from our ordinary experience.

We have such experiences as "the pot is on the floor" and all of us have uncontradicted experience that the two are mutually related. Here a question may be asked—if a relation is not perceptible how can the two relata be perceived as related? To this Vallabha replies: That the qualified cognition is due to the cognition of the qualifier and the qualified, and in fact, nothing more is needed over and above the two. For example, when we say "there is no book on the table", for such usuages what we require is the experience of the book and the table, and we do not seek any further assistance of a relation between the two. Although some relation has to be postulated, even if that is not perceptible. The relation as a cause for such a qualified cognition as above has to be inferred even if it is not perceived. A question may be asked—how is it that in our cognition one thing appears as qualified by the other though their mutual relation does not appear to our senses?

The reply of Vallabha to this question is that the qualified usages refer to the qualifier and qualified, as such their mutual relation is super-imposed. The relation of *samavāya* is a case of super imposition *(āropita-sambandha-gocaraḥ);* the relation of *samavāy* cannot be the case other than a super-imposition, because it is super-sensible *(atīndriya)* and also because of the fact that the possibility of other relation is ruled out *(taditarasyābhāvāt).*

Vallabha next introduces a discussion on qualifier and substantive *(viśeṣaṇa viśeṣya).* One must have a definite idea of these two concepts before one analyses a qualified cognition which is the sine qua non for postulating *samavāya* as a relation. The qualifier is that which is secondary in comparison to the substantive.

There is the relation of two things container and the thing contained, as in the case of a man holding the staff *(daṇḍī puruṣaḥ)*; the man is the substantive, the locus of the staff and he creates the resistance so that the staff is not fall en down, and herein lies the relative importance of the man, the container, then the thing contained. The staff loses its importance in the hands of the man holding because in spite of having the quality of heaviness *(gurutva)* its falling down is checked by the man. Naturally, the man enjoys the supremacy over the staff, which is in his hands.

In the same way, when we say "the yarns are possessed of the cloth" *(paṭavantas-tantavaḥ)* the yarns, which are the inherent cause of the cloth, stand as substantive, whereas the cloth, the effect, is the qualifier. But if I say, "the cloth is in the yarns"—the qualifier and the substantive would be just otherwise. So in the case of relation of universal and the individual *(jātivyakti),* the individual would be substantive *(viśeṣya)* because it is the manifester, while universal would be the qualifier *(viśeṣaṇa)* and is manifested.[52]

In the case of absence, for example, when we say "there is no book on the table" or "the table is possessed of the absence of the book" the table is the substantive and the "absence" is the qualifier. On the other hand, if we say, "the absence of the book occurs in the table" then the absence of the book becomes substantive and the table becomes qualifier.[53]

A question may be raised here: Can we in all cases of qualifier-qualifiedness *(viśeṣaṇa-viśeṣya-bhāva)* postulate a relation? Suppose, when *samavāya* itself is a qualifier or substantive, leading to a qualified cognition, we do not have to postulate another relation beyond *samavāya*. In order to solve this incongruity Vallabha says that such usages as "the cloth is possessed of inherence of yarns" *(tantusamavāyavān paṭaḥ)* or, "these two have inherence-relata" have no doubt the nature of the qualifier and the substantive, but it is super-imposed and not in the real sense of the term. In fact, the term qualifier and qualificand have different connotation in different context.

5.14. *Gaṅgeśa proves Samavāya through Inference*

Gaṇgeśa in his *Tattvacintāmṇi* dealt a crushing blow to the critique of *samavāya*. According to him the existence of inherence can be proved through three inference.

Inference—I

"Such qualified cognition as something is possessed of quality or activity or universal refers to the relation of qualifier, because it is a qualified cognition, as for example "here is a staff-holder *(daṇḍin)*."

To be more explicit, when I cognise a man as a "staff-holder", I must have cognised the relation between the man (staff-holder) and the staff. Similarly, when I cognise a flower as red, or, a running horse or the man having manhood I must assume the relation between the flower and redness, or between the horse and its activity of running, or between the man and manhood.

A qualified cognition, after all, the product of the cognition of the qualifier and its relation with the qualified. Here a question may be raised: The inference proposed by the Naiyāyikas is based on defective reason. For example, in the case of cognition of absence we have also a qualified cognition. Absence always refers to its counter-positive and locus. For example, when I say "there is no book on the table" the absence of the book, the counter-positive, exists on the table. Such statement should also refer to a relation between the absence of the book and the table, because the cognition referred to is a qualified cognition.

The opponent wants to make out that no such relation between the absence of the book and the table can be cognised. Gaṅgeśa remarks that in such cases of absence existing in its locus, the Naiyāyika admits a relation, called adjectivity *(viśeṣaṇatā)* which is a type of self-linking relation *(svarūpasambandha).*

Now the question may arise that if in the case of *abhāva* (absence) the self-linking relation serves the purpose of linking the locus and the absence of container and contained (*ādhāra-ādheya*) and, thereby results the emergence of a qualified cognition then such instances for which *samavāya* relation is assumed, can also be explained by the already accepted self-linking relation.

To this Gaṅgeśa replies that such cognitions as qualified by quality, activity or universal, which are the subject of inference and in which the reason of the inference i.e. the character of the qualified cognition exists, proves the existence of *samavāya* relation. To be clear, the very character of the qualified cognition proves the existence of *samavāya* relation. In other words, the very character of the subject proves the character of the thing to be proved *(pakṣa-dharmatā-balena)* and such relation which is proved through the very character of the subject, is to be one and unitary. That is to say, if *samavāya* is proved, it is to be proved as an one and unitary relation, where as the self-linking relation is innumerable, because this relation is of the nature of its relata (not being separate from them) which are also innumerable.

Gaṅgeśa further records the viewpoints of one of his predecessors, whom he calls '*navya*' (modern) who modified the inference of *samavāya* as follows[53]: The inference may be put as, A(X,Y).

Inference—2.

> "guṇakriyā-jātiviśiṣṭabuddhiḥ sambandha-viśeṣaṇa-sambandhaviṣaya-nirviṣayakabhāva-viśeṣaṇaka-viśiṣṭabuddhitvāt, itara-nirūpaṇa-nirūpya-viśeṣaṇaka-viśiṣṭa-buddhitvād vā; ato abhāvādi-viśiṣṭabuddhau na vybhicāraḥ."[55]

"The qualified cognition, such as the flower being qualified by redness etc. has its objective content or referent relation(with the qualifier) which is different from the relata, because it is a qualified cognition, of which the qualifier is a positive entity having no further reference."

Inference—3

"Because it is qualified cognition of which the qualifier, the cognition of which, is dependent on something extraneous to it."

The motive behind the modification of inferences, as above, is to exclude the possibility of reason *(hetu)* being fallacious, and in the case of a qualified cognition of absence *(abhāva)* to exclude *abhāva* as also to differentiate self-linking relation *(svarūpa sambandha)* from *samavāya* . The nature of *sādhya* (the probandum) has been modified in this inference to exclude the self-linking relation, since the self-linking relation is the nature of relata and, therefore, in the case of a qualified cognition of a positive entity *(bhāvapadārtha)* the mutual relation between qualifier and qualified is something distinct from both the two i.e qualifier and qualified.

Hetu (reason) as modified in the above inference also excludes the possibility of the discrepancy in the *hetu*. That is to say, in case of a qualified cognition of absence the absemce is qualified because an absence always refers to an object which is negated, so as absence has always a counter-positive *(pratiyogin)* by which the absence is determined. The cognition of absence pre-supposes the cognition of its counter-positive *(pratiyogin)*, so as absence is always determinable by something else other than it *(itaranirūpya)*. As in the case, "the ground is without the pot" that is, there is absence of the pot on the ground, the "absence" is determined by the pot. And if in the inference *hetu* is modified as that it should not have a qualifier, the cognition of which is dependent on the cognition something other than the self, or, if I attribute the qualities with the adjunct, that it should be a positive entity, or it should not refer to a counter-positive, then automatically the opponent's charge of discrepancy in *hetu* with reference to cognition of absence is replied.

So the inference is based on universal concomitance between *hetu* and *sādhya* and such concomitance is unconditional *(anaupādhika)* and hence such a reasoning is *(prayojaka)* capable of proving *sādhya*.

Gaṅgeśa then presents the logical arguments of the Vaiśeṣikas as follows:

The perceptual cognition of quality, action and universal is a product of sense-object relation, because it is perceptual cognition which is a product, as far example, the perceptual cognition of a staff-holder. Now this inference establishes that there must be some sort of relation with the sense-organ, so that the respective perceptual cognition occurs. But quality, action and universal are not directly perceived. They are perceived only through the mediacy of their respective locus i.e. the substance which is qualified by quality, action or the individual (substance, quality and action) qualified by corresponding class character. Thus when the direct relation is excluded and a relation being a necessary condition of perceptual cognition, we must infer the existence of some indirect relation which involves *samavāya*. Thus in the perception of the above attributes the Vaiśeṣika admits the relation contact-cum-inherence (*saṁyukta samavāya*). In the same way when I perceive a locus, I also perceive the class character, for example blueness inherent in the blue colour. Thus the relation in this perceptual cognition will be contact-cum-inherence-cum-inherence (*saṁyukta-samaveta-samavāya*).

Here also the self-linking relation cannot serve any purpose, because that being discrete and individualistic in character cannot be a unifying factor.

Now the Bhāṭṭa may ask—in the case of qualified cognition of absence if the possibility of contact and inherence is excluded, why not accept a separate relation called *vaiśiṣṭya* (qualifiedness) which unites the absence with its locus. But that is not possible in view of the fact that if the relation called *Vaiśiṣṭya* is held to be one like *samavāya* then where there is the absence of pot but the presence of a piece of cloth then there would be the objection of the perception of the absence of the piece of cloth, because on the Bhāṭṭa supposition of unitariness or oneness of *vaiśiṣṭya*, the *vaiśiṣṭya* of the absence of the pot and that of the absence of a piece of a cloth would be one and the same.

The Bhāṭṭa cannot say that the *vaiśiṣṭya* of absence of a piece of cloth and the absence of a pot is different, and hence even though there is the *vaiśiṣṭya* of absence of cloth, the absence of cloth is not there. Consequents the absence of cloth would not be perceived and the alleged objection would not arise.

To this the Naiyāyika replies that although the Bhāṭṭa avoids this difficulty by postulating the difference in *paṭābhāva-vaiśiṣṭya* (characteristic of the absence of a piece of cloth) and *paṭābhāva* (absence of a piece of cloth) but difficulty will arise in the following case.

The *paṭābhāvābhāva* (the absence of the absence of cloth) is also an absence, and that being an absence should also exist through *vaiśiṣṭya* relation where the cloth exists, because *vaiśiṣṭya* is one and unitary. So the objection, namely, where cloth exists there should also have been the cognition of absence of the cloth, holds good, because the *vaiśiṣṭya* of *paṭābhāvābhāva* (characteristic of the absence of cloth) and that of *paṭābhāva* (absence of cloth) is one and the same.

Moreover, the *vaiśiṣṭya* relation is unique in each individual instance of absence, hence, it lacks the capacity to unite *abhāva* and its locus under one relation. And if the Mīmāṁsaka presses for acceptance of *vaiśiṣṭya* relation why not accept the *vaśeṣaṇatā* relation which is already accepted, although the defect of lacking in capacity to unite will be the same in both the cases. The Bhāṭṭa admits *viśeṣaṇatā* relation in the case of perception of *vaiśiṣṭya*, and the Naiyāyika thinks where is the necessity of postulating another relation in addition to *viśeṣaṇatā.*

It may further be argued that in fact the relation between the colour and the pot is not *samavāya,* but the relation of identity *(tādātmya).* Our perceptual experience says that in the cognition of 'the man is a staff-holder' *(daṇḍīpuruṣaḥ)* or "this is a blue pot" *(nīlo ghataḥ),* the staff-holder is identical with the man and the blue is identical with the pot.

It is not a fact the term 'blue' means the blue but it means blue-possessor *(nīlamat)* and by that, we have the identity of the blue and the pot *(nīla* and *ghaṭa)* because the blue-possessor, the pot. In case of *daṇḍipuruṣa* (staff-holder) however, by the suffix 'in' added to the *daṇḍa* we understand the relation of qualified and, hence, there is no necessity of assuming a separate relation called *samavāya.*

And if the relation of identity is assumed between the two, co-existence between the two meanings is also possible.

Now there are two types of co-existence. One relates to the meanings and the other to the words. In the case of verbal co-existence the two words must have the same-ending as in the case of *(nīla* and *ghaṭa*) and this co-existence is possible because the limitor *(avacchedaka)* of the qualifierness *(viśeṣaṇatāvacchedaka)* and the limitor of the qualificandness *(viśeṣyatāvacchedaka)* are related to the same. That is to say, in the present case the staff holderness and manhood have the same locus i.e. the man. This existence in the same locus is the root cause of the verbal occurrence *(sāmānadhikaraṇya)* and any sort of relation of concurrence is on the basis of the relation of identity.

But the Naiyāyika may ask: The blueness and the potness have different *pravṛttinimitta* (cause of application), that is, the condition of denotation, so how can there be identity of the two? The opponent replies that in spite of the difference in the *pravṛttinimitta* they have the same identical reference. Gaṅgeśa in his criticism concentrates on the opposition's theory of identity based on the unity of the reference. Mīmāṁsaka asserts that the word white and the cloth have the same locus and hence there is identity between the two. To this Gaṅgeśa retorts that in case their identity of reference is admitted, the two term "white" and the "cloth" could not be used simultaneously. For example, we do not use such expressions as–*ghaṭah kumbhaḥ* (pot-jar), where the two terms refer to the self-same object. Moreover, in case of sameness of the reference a blindman, when he touches a piece of cloth could have cognised colour of the cloth also, or, when he does not cognise the colour he should not have also cognised the piece of cloth.[56] In the same way in a saffron coloured piece of cloth white colour would not be cognised, or, if he does not cognise white colour in that piece of cloth, he should not have also cognised the piece of cloth itself.[57]

Moreover when 'A' asks 'B' to bring a piece of white cloth, he would have brought anything white, no necessarily a piece of white cloth. Moreover, as such expression, namely, "not cloth is the cloth" *(apaṭaḥ paṭaḥ)* is itself contradictory. Similarly the expression, namely, "this piece of cloth is not white" would have also been self-contradictory, because in the opponent's theory the word white and the cloth have the same locus. Furthermore, in the Vaiśeṣika theory of baking a pot in heat produces the colour in the pot. Before the pot is baked it had dark colour, while it is red afterwards. Now in the same pot, when it comes into contact with the fire, the dark colour is destroyed and the red colour is produced. Now if we follow the opponent's theory, the conclusion would be that with the destruction and emergence of the two colours, namely, destruction of the dark colour and the emergence of the red colour, the first pot would have been destroyed and the second pot would have emerged. Or, on the other hand, if the opponent says that the same pot is there, then he should not have admitted that one colour (dark) ceases to exist and other colour (red) emerges.

The opponent says that with the destruction of the colour the pot is also destroyed and with the emergence of a new colour a new pot is produced, and we identify it to be the same pot from our experience *(pratyabhijñānāt).*

The opponent may assert in reply that the two words 'white' *(Śukla)* and 'pot' *(ghaṭa)* can be simultaneously used because the words have different ground of application *(pravṛttinimitta).* The word 'white' has the white-universal or the generic property of white *(Śuklatva)* as the ground for its application and this ground is different from the substance *(dravya)* which is the ground for application of the word 'pot'. When the grounds of application of words differ, their conjoined use is justified. Although when a blind man perceives a piece of white cloth by tactual sense organ, he does not perceive the white colour in it.[58]

The opponent further asserts that this whiteness is identical with the corresponding substance in which there the colour exists and in which there is a self-linking relation between whiteness and clothness.

To this Gaṇgeśa retorts if whiteness, sweetness, perfumeness, hotness etc. *(Śuklatva-madhuratva-surabhitva-uṣṇatva* etc.) exist in their respective substances and consequently they are said to be identical with their respective substance, the sense organ by which a substance, say, a piece of cloth is known through the tactual sense organ, such property as *śuklatva* (whiteness) should have also been known by the same sense organ.[59]

But we know that each sense organ has its own field of knowing. A piece of cloth can be cognised by the tactual sense organ, on the other hand whiteness can be known by another sense organ (eye) by which the white colour is cognised. A generic property is known by the same sense organ, which is competent to know the corresponding individual. So the fact is that one sense organ is competent to apprehend whiteness while the other sense organ is competent to apprehend clothness goes to prove that the quality and substance are not identical.[60]

Moreover, in case of their identity, such cognition as "the piece of cloth has white colour" *(paṭasya śuklaṁ rūpam)* would not have been possible, rather we would have cognised as "the cloth is blue colour (*paṭo nīlamiti*)".[61]

The opponent however shifts his position and says that it is not the relation of identity, but "identity-cum-difference" *(bhedābheda)* which holds between quality and substance.[62] It is not absolute identity *(atyantam abheda)* but identity-in-difference. This concept of difference has made it possible to use the two words 'white' and 'cloth' to be used jointly, while the sameness in their reference *(eka-pravṛtteḥ)* proves their identity. This identity-in-difference is established through our perceptual cognition and cannot, therefore, easily be done away with. The difference is admitted by both the Mīmāṁsaka and Naiyāyika, while identity is the exclusive concern of the Mīmāṁsaka, which he proves on the basis of co-occurence *(sāmānādhikaraṇya)*.

Had it been a case of absolute identity or absolute difference, in either case co-occurence would have been uncalled for. Hence, the best way to get out of this dilemma is to admit identity-cum-difference.

Of course, the Naiyāyika may ask that the identity and difference are two contradictory qualities and contradictory qualities are mutually co-existent with the absence of the other. How can they have the same reference or locus? To this the opponent replies–that in case of conjunction the Naiyāyika also admits that a property can have concurrence with its absence, for example, "the pot is on the ground"—the pot occurs only in a part of the ground and in other parts its absence occurs. These are called properties of non-pervasive occurence. We have also uncontradicted experience that at one time the pot is dark and at another time, when heat is applied to it, the same pot becomes red. So the red pot has mutual absence *(anyonyābhāva)* in the dark pot. At the same time we use such expression that the same pot is now red and not dark. Hence difference and non-difference can exist in the same entity and, therefore, there is no incongruity if we say that the difference and the non-difference can have the same reference or locus.

5.15. *Anyonyābhava cumbheda*

The mutual absence is of non-pervasive occurence; difference *(bheda)* is mutual absence *(anyonyābhāva)* and can exist with its absence. In the same way constant absence *(atyantābhāva)* can equilocate with its absence. Thus the relation between the quality and substance can be of identity and difference.

Gaṅgeśa considers the position of opponents untenable. The Naiyāyika thinks that property like, conjunction is of non-pervasive occurence, and, are known as such. But here the Naiyāyika introduces the concept of limitor *(avacchedaka)* and explains that in case of conjunction the counter positive and its absence may co-exist, but in relation to different limitors. For example, there is a monkey on the tree but so far as its branches are concerned, it is absent in the same tree, when the roots are concerned. The dark pot, that is the pot delimited by darkness, has mutual absence in the red pot i.e. the pot limited by redness. In the same way there is mutual absence of *nīla* in the *ghaṭa,* as such, the pot determined by the potness has mutual difference. As one has the mutal absence of the other, the two, *nīla* and the *ghaṭa* must have different references. It may be that some pots are blue, but not all.

In Nyāya terminology, we may say, the mutual absence of blue *(nīla)* does not exist in the pot as limited by potness *(ghaṭatva).* Because when the mutual absence of blue exists in the pot, absence of that mutual absence *(anyonyābhāvābhāva)* cannot exist in it, of course, with regard to the same limitor i.e. the potness. The counter positive and its absence can never have equilocator nor do we cognise it as such. The Naiyāyika thinks that mutual absence or difference is of pervasive occurence i.e when 'X' is different from the pot, it is different from all individual pots. Hence the question of existence of absence of difference of blue in the pot as limited by potness does not arise. Even if we do not cognise the mutual difference between blue and the pot we have such cognition as *nīlo ghaṭaḥ,* (the blue pot). This shows that there is difference between the two.

The opponent may however argue: Let there be difference between blue and the pot, because one has the mutual absence of the other, but there can be identity between the two, because identity *(abheda)* is not the absence of the difference *(bheda),* but something positive. There is no contradiction between the two, since *abheda* is not the negation of *bheda.* Hence they can co-exist without any reference to the difference limitor *(avacchedakabheda).*

To this Gaṅgeśa replies: For the cognition of identity the cognition of absence of difference is not the cause. Therefore, in the expression *nīlo ghaṭaḥ* (blue pot) we refer to the relation between blue and the pot and that relation is inherence.

Of course, the opponent may contend that in that case as we have the cognition *daṇḍī puruṣaḥ* (the staff-holder) we should have also cognition such as *nīlo ghaṭaḥ* (the pot having the blue colour). Gaṅgeśa does not find any difficulty in accepting *nīlo ghaṭaḥ* as usual expression, but he says that we can easily delete the suffix *'matup'* and extend the meaning of *nīla* to the *nīlavat* (colour-possessing) and by such extension of meaning it is possible to super-impose the identity between the two in spite of their established differences.

The opponent further tries to do away with inherence as a distinct relation by taking refuge to the relation of qualifierness *(viśeṣaṇatā),* a relation which has been accepted by the Naiyāyika also in the perception of inherence and absence. So let there be the relation of *viśeṣaṇatā* in the perception of sound and in the perception of colour (that is, the locus of colour is related to the sense organ, namely, eye, and through that the colour is perceived).

The Naiyāyika can say that even in the case of *viśeṣaṇatā* and in the case of qualifierness the sense organ contact *(indriyasambaddha-viśeṣaṇatā)* the inherence should also be taken into consideration.

To this the opponent replies: let there be inherence, but the relation of qualifierness to function as a relation does not inherence. The relation of qualifierness itself can serve as an independent relation. If you want to accept inherence, that is also another form of qualifier relation and neither a separate nor an independent relation.

Gaṅgeśa states that the case of perception of sound etc. it is the basis of that inherence relation we may think of qualifierness, but it has no independent contribution of its own. In the perception of sound the fact is that we perceive sound through inherence relation and the sound is looked upon as qualifier of the ear organ, because the ear organ is nothing but *ākāśa* (ether) and the sound is held to be quality of ether.

The opponent says: The Naiyāyika should not accept qualifierness as a relation in the perception of absence, inherence may serve the purpose. Because the Naiyāyika's ground for postulating inherence is also applicable in the case of perception of absence, namely, the qualified cognition pre-supposes cognition of the relation between qualifier and qualified. The Naiyāyika cannot say that this will involve difficulty, because, inherence relates positive entities and consequently absence will turn out to be a positive entity, because the same argument may hold good in case of perception of absence. As the absence of the pot is the qualifier (the absence of the pot qualifies the ground) so also the colour qualifies the substance, its contents. So, if you (the Naiyāyika) admit *samavāya* in one case and *viśeṣaṇatā* in the other case, why not admit the same (*samavāya*) in the other case (relation between absence of the pot and the ground) also ? That is to admit either of the two relations, i.e. inherence or qualifierness in both the cases.

Moreover, the prior-absence *(prāgabhāva)* and the posterior-absence *(dhvaṁsābhāva)* should also inhere in the locus of this respective counter-positive. For example, if I say "a pot will be produced" on the ground, the ground is the locus and the prior-absence of the pot should inhere in that ground. In the same way, the positive absence of a pot should (e.g. a pot is destroyed on the ground) also inhere in the ground or in that stage of time, because in a particular point of place or time we cognise the posterior absence of the same after it is destroyed. But a posterior absence is never destroyed although it is produced, so in the case of posterior absence we cannot say it is destroyed due to the destruction of its inherent cause. Only a positive entity is destroyed when its inherent cause ceases to exist.

The Naiyāyika may retort that if we accept the position that absence also exists through the relation of inherence, the difficulty will arise in the cases of mutual absence and eternal absence which are held to be eternal. These absences being eternal, if held to inhere in the locus of their respective counter-positive, which obviously will be more than one, they would hardly differ from universal which are eternal inherent in many.[63] The opponent cannot say that the universal are positive entities and these will differentiate them from the constant absence and mutual absence, because that will involve logical complexity, in view of the fact that an additional qualifier, namely *bhāvatva* (positiveness) would have to be added in addition to already accepted two qualification, namely, *nityatva* (obligatory-hood) and *aneka samavetatva* (being in many). Nor that the Naiyāyika says in case of qualified cognition of absence there are some special characteristics, which we do not find in the case of a qualified cognition of a positive entity and this is the ground for which absence does not exist through inherence relation, while a positive entity can exist.

The opponent here points out that although absence exists through inherence relation still the objection of its being identical with the universal should not arise, because if absence is a *jāti* (class) it should fit in the hierarchy of universal into *parā* (superior) and *aparā* (inferior). For example, we have *sattā* (existence), *dravyatva*(substancehood) and *pṛthivītva* (earthness) in the gradation of universal. One is higher than the other. Existence is more extensive than the substancehood while substancehood is more extensive than the earthness. Now, if absence is a *jāti* it should be either more extensive or less extensive than any one of the three. If they are less extensive, than in a particular pot we would have the cognition of absence of existence, substancehood and earthness. If on the other hand they are more extensive, than one would not have cognised absence of potness in universal.

In reply to these arguments and counter-arguments Gaṅgeśa rejects the possibility of absence being inherent anywhere. He says that when something, say, a pot inheres in some locus, for example in the parts of the pot, we say that is locus i.e. parts are inherent cause of that whole product and it is an admitted fact borne out by our perception that anything which is a product is destroyed due to the destruction of its inherent cause. Adhering to this principle if we say that absence also exists through inherence relation then that locus would be its inherent cause, and in case of a posterior absence, at least one will be compelled to admit that posterior absence will also be destroyed, a position which any sane man would hardly accept, because it is a well-known fact that there is no destruction of posterior absence. Destruction has no end.

It will be of no use saying that the question of destruction does not arise because destruction is not a positive entity, and positive entity is only destroyed, because it will lead to further logical complexity and this principle does not apply in the case of prior absence, which is destroyed with the emergence of a product. Hence, the plea of the opponent will not hold good and the opponent will have no other alternative but to accept the Nyāya position that absence does not inhere. On the other hand, if posterior absence does not exist through inherence relation it would be logical to admit that although posterior absence is a product, is not destroyed, because the reason of its destruction, namely, the destruction of its locus i.e. in which it inheres, is absent.

The opponent cannot say that the reason why that the destruction of something is not destroyed, lies elsewhere. It is not the fact that the destruction of the posterior absence is barred for the reason that if the destruction of a pot is destroyed, the same pot will be produced.

To this Gaṅgeśa replies—the equilocation of the condition that produces the effect irrespective of the fact that the production of something would be unwholesome. Hence, the reason why destruction does not inhere lies in the fact that in that case it would have been destroyed due to the destruction of its inherent cause, because it is the inherent cause in which something inheres. Had it inhered then due to series of destruction of those inherent causes we would be involved in a cumbrous situation. If it is ruled that the destruction of a pot inheres, it should inhere in its own locus i.e. the parts of the pot *(kapālas)*. Now continuing this series of destructions, the destruction of the parts of the pot would likewise have inhered in parts of those parts and the ultimate parts, which are called atoms, and the atoms being imperceptible the ultimate destruction of the pot would have also been imperceptible. A situation which any sane man would not accept.

Moreover, if the destruction of a pot is held to inhere in the parts of the pot which the opponent would be compelled to admit, we would have not cognised the destruction of the pot on the ground and such expression as "the pot is destroyed on the ground" would have been meaningless.

The opponent cannot say that the destruction of the pot exists simultaneously in the parts of the pot as well as on the ground. Because in that case one would have not cognised that the pot is destroyed without perceiving the parts of the pot. Because as per opponent's supposition the destruction occurs in the both by *vyāsajya vṛtti* (adhering to each other in occurrence) and unless both are cognised the destruction would not have been cognised.

Thus Gaṅgeśa argues against the possibility of absence existing through inherence relation. He takes into account the posterior absence only to contradict the opponent's objection that inherence unites absences *(abhāva)* also and not simply a limited numbers of positive entities as instantiated by the Vaiśeṣika, namely, generic attribute and individuals, material bodies and the constituent parts, qualities and motions with their substrata, particularity and the eternal substance.

Notes and References

1. saṁyoga-nāśako guṇo vibhāgaḥ —TS. p.19.

2. saṁyogasya vibhāgāntatvaṁ vibhāgavinaśyatvaṁ dṛśyate na samavāyasya. —*Kiraṇāvali*, p. 776.
3. Ibid., p. 777.
4. yaḥ sambandha iha pratyayahetuḥ sa samavāyaḥ. —PPBh, p. 35.
   iha dravye dravyatvam ityākāraka-pratyaye hetuḥ sambandha-maryādayā bhāsamāna ityarthaḥ. —JS. on PPBh, p. 35.
5. pratītibhedād bhedo' sti deśabhedastu neṣyate /
   tenātra kalpyate vṛttiḥ samavāyaḥ sa ucyate // —NM, p. 63
6. yayor dvayor madhye ekamavinaśyad aparāśritamevāvatiṣṭhate tāvayutasiddhau. yathā avayavāvayavinau guṇa-guṇinau kriyākriyāvantau jāti-vyakti-viśeṣa-nityadravye ceti. —TS, p. 61.
7. This point has been discussed in some detail in the section *sāmānya.*
8. The Nyāya-Vaiśeṣika considers the material cause as *samavāyi-kāraṇa,* which is rendered as 'inherent cause' according to the theory of *ārambhavāda.* The material cause is called *upādāna-kāraṇa* is Sāṁkhya to fit in the theory of *pariṇāmavāda.*
9. NM., p. 693.
10. na punaḥ samavāyasya samavāyo' sti. iha samavāya iti na syāt. —NV. 2.1.33, p. 484.
11. arthāntaraṁ paṭāt tantraḥ tadhetutvāt tūryādivat iti —NVT. p. 513.
12. "abhinna eva candramasi dvaitāropavat" —NL. p. 720.
13. "adhigatānyatvānām aviṣvag bhāvenāvasthitānām ihedamiti buddhiryataḥ sambandhād bhavati sa samvāyākhyaḥ sambandhaḥ." —VV.
14. "iheti cānayā buddhyā samavāyo na gṛhyate"
    ādhāra-grāhiṇī caiṣā samavāyā-pratiṣṭhitā //
15. SV., Śūnyavāda, p. 156.
16. "tantuṣu paṭasamavāyaḥ paṭe rūpasamavāya iti pratītiḥ katham iti cet, svarūpa-sambandhena." —Upaskāra, p. 127.
17. Indian Philosophical Studies, 1.
18. Śrībhāṣya II.ii. 12-16.
19. "anatasvarūpāṇāṁ sambandhatva-kalpane gauravāt lāghavād eka samavāya-siddhiḥ." —SM., p. 88.
20. "na ca svarūpa-sambandhaḥ, teṣām ananugatatvād-anantatvācca." —TC., p. 680.
21. Ingalls, *Materials for the study of Navya* —*Nyāya*, p. 77.
22. "nanu paryāptiḥ samavāyaḥ." —Jāgadīśī, p. 262.
    "nanu paryāptiḥ samavāya eva." —AVNDP, p. 272.
23. "atha paryāptyākhya-vilakṣaṇa-sambandha eva aprāmāṇikaḥ, tat kathaṁ sambandhatā?" —Vyva., p. 162.
24. "paryāptiścāyam eko ghaṭaḥ imau dvau ghaṭau iti pratīti sākṣikaḥ svarūpa-sambandha-viśeṣaḥ." —AVNDP, p. 262.
25. "sparśaḥ saṁkhyā parimiti ..." —*Bh.P.* -*kārikā* 4.
    "rūparasagandhasparśāḥ samkhyā ... guṇāḥ." —KS., 1.1.6.

26. *Bh.P., kārikā,* 10.
27. "anyathā dvau dvitvavān-iti pratītiraviśeṣa-prasaṅgād iti bhāvaḥ." —AVNJ., p. 262.
28. "dvitvādi-svarūpasyaiva dvitvādi-paryāptitayā abhimata-siddheḥ." —Vyva p. 263.
29. "eko na dvau it pratiteḥ prāmāṇya-nirvāhāya paryāpti-sambandha āvaśyakaḥ. —Śivadatta Miśra's commentary on Vy. va. PM., p. 81.
30. "samavāyena eko dvitvavān iti pratīterabhyupagamena eko dvau–iti pratīteranabhyupagamena paryāpterapi pratīyamānatvāt." —Ibid, p. 81.
31. NM., p. 677.
32. SD., under i.1.5.5 *sūtra* of Jaimini.
33. Bradley, *Truth and Reality,* pp. 150-51, 289.
34. "nacāpyayuta-siddhānāṁ sambandhitvena kalpanā." —SV, 4.146.
35. For this type of internal relation, see Joachim, *Nature of Truth,* pp. 11-12, 46 and also *Appearance and Reality,* p. 617.
36. "viśiṣṭaḥ suddhānnātiricyate." —SM.
37. Kiraṇāvalī-prakāśa, ph. 145-46.
38. Accordng to the Prābhākara school the absence is nothing but the form of its counter-positive.
39. "vidhiratyantam aprāpte niyamaḥ pākṣike sati." —Ny.
40. pp.
41. The Buddhist criticises the Nyāya-Vaiśeṣika on this point by saying that the notion like "the cloth is in the yarns" has been invented by you and nobody except you has such cognition. Rather the common usage is quite contrary to this, i.e. "the yarns are in the cloth". Everybody says, "the horn is in the cow" nobody says "the cow is in the horn".
"paṭas-tantuṣvihetyādi śabdāśceme svayaṁ kṛtāḥ.
śṛṅgaṁ gavīti loke syāt śṛṅge gaur-ityalaukikam." —PV.
42. SM. p. 88.
43. Sap. p. 51.
44. "iha kuṇḍe badarāṇīti pratyayavat ityanumānena lāghava-tarka-sanāthena eka eva sidhyati." —Mitabhāṣiṇī, p. 18
45. "(ekatvaṁ) svānyonyābhāva-samānādhikaraṇa-padārtha-vibhājakopādhimatvam." —Balabhadra-sandarbha, p. 148
46. "samavāyo' pi ca naiko jalādergandhādimatva-prasaṅgāt, parantu nānā iva." —PTN, p. 71.
47. "samavāyatvaṁ tu punaranugatam akhaṇḍopādhiriti." —Ibid.
48. "viśiṣṭaḥ śuddhān nātiricyate."
49. "tathā-vidha-viśiṣṭa-nirūpitādhikaraṇatayā atiriktatve kimaparāddham vibhinna-samavāyaiḥ." —PTN, p. 71
50. "atha vā gṛhītaṁ viśeṣaṇaṁ viśeṣyasya jñānotpattau liṅgañca liṅgijñānotpattau vyāpriyate samavāye tu tadrūpatā nāsti iti tadgrahaṇe pramāṇābhāvaḥ. —VV, p. 121.

51. "tasmād ihabuddhyanumeyaḥ samavāyaḥ, natu iha-buddhau pratyakṣaḥ."
—Ibid.
52. "samavāyi-kāraṇatvañca tantāder viśeṣyatvaṁ samavāyi-kāryatvañca paṭāder viśeṣaṇatvam. samavāyitve sati vyañjakatvañca vyaktināṁ viśeṣyatvaṁ, vyaṅgyatvañca viśeṣaṇatvam." —NL, pp. 713-14.
53. "abhave'pi tat pratiyogyadhikaraṇatvaṁ viśeṣyatvam, abhāvatvañca viśeṣanatvam." —Nyāya-Līlāvatī, p. 714.
"etacca ghaṭābhāvavad bhūtalam ityatra draṣṭavyam.
bhūtale ghaṭābhāva ityatra tu vaiparityena yojanīyam." —NLP, p. 714.
54. In the present state of our knowledge we fail to trace this syllogism to any one of the pre-Gaṅgeśa works. It is likely that this inference might have been put forward by some one who might have flourished in between Udayana and Gaṅgeśa. Most of the literature of this period, particularly the Nyāya system of philosophy have been lost to us.
55. *Tattvacintāmaṇi*, p. 660 (Tirupati ed.)
... sambandhi-bhinna-viśeṣaṇa ... (Delhi ed.)
56. "andhasya paṭagrahavat rūpagrahaḥ, rūpāgrahavat paṭāgraho' pi vā syāt."
—.T.C., p. 676.
57. "mahārājatake paṭāgrahavat (śuklāgraha) śubhrāgrahavat paṭāgraho' pi bhavet." —Ibid., p. 676.
58. "andhādinā śuklādigrahe śuklatvādīnām agraha upapadyate suklatvādi-jāteśca dravyeṇābhedo na samavāyaḥ kintu svarūpa-sambandha eva."
—T.C., p. 676.
59. "dravya-vṛttitve dravya-grāhakatvādibhiḥ grahaṇa-prasaṅgāt."
—T.C., p. 677.
60. "rūpatvādīnāṁ dravya-vṛttitve pratiniyatendriya-grāhyatā eva na syāt, yogye vṛttitvena jāter grahaṇa-yogyatvābhāvāt." —T.C. p. 677.
61. "abhede ca kathaṁ paṭasya śuklam rūpamiti bhedabuddhiḥ, paṭo nīlamiti buddhi-prasaṅgaśca." —Ibid.
62. "vayaṁ to bhedābhedavādinaḥ." —T.C., p. 677.
63. "evam anyonyātyantābhāvayor nityatve aneka samavetatve ca jātitva-prasaṅgāt."

Chapter 6

The Critique of Samavāya

6.1. It has been mentioned in the foregoing chapters that the Nyāya-Vaiśeṣika concept of *samavāya* has been criticised and rejected by the Sāṁkhya, the Mīmāṁsaka, the Vedāntin, the Buddhist and the Jaina. The arguments against *samavāya* are varied and from different standpoints; they veer round two basic objections:

First, there is no necessity of assuming a separate relation called *samavāya*, the purpose for which it is admitted can be well served by the self-linking relation, the qualifier-qualified relation, etc. Secondly, assumption of *samavāya* for relating two relata and its subsistence in them leads to *regressus ad infinitum*.

The Sāṁkhya holds that the effect is not different from the cause, therefore, the question of relating the cause with the effect does not arise and *samavāya* is not required. He further says that if *samavāya* is to be regarded as identical with the effect and the cause, then would it not be more logical to regard the effect itself as identical with the cause for the sake of brevity?

The Mīmāṁsaka considers that the relation which exists between them is the self-linking (*tādātmya*). The Bhāṭṭa Mīmāṁsaka takes great pain in repudiating *samavāya* by establishing the state of identity-cum-difference between *jāti* and *vyakti*.

The Vedāntins, both Advaita and Viśiṣṭādvaita do not admit *samavāya*. Śaṅkarācārya lays his finger accurately on the weakest point in the *samavāya* theory, namely, the inconsistency of calling *samavāya* a connection between two distinct things, and, at the same time regarding it totally different from *saṁyoga*. The Rāmānuja Vedāntin by admitting *apṛthaksiddhi*, similar to *samavāya*, rejects it. Vallabhācārya in the *Aṇubhāṣya* criticises *samavāya* and replaces it by the relation of *tādātmya*.

6.2. *The Sāṁkhya Critique of Samavāya*

The Sāṁkhya does not subscribe to the causation theory of the Nyāya-Vaiśeṣika nor does he admit universal as distinct from the individual and whole from the parts and thus he refuses to admit *samavāya*, which exists between cause and effect etc. He rejects *samavāya* on two major grounds:

(i) *Samavāya* cannot be cognised, and

(ii) It is not an eternal one, because the relata of this relation may be non-eternal, cognition of the relation between *sañjā* (name) and *sañjin* (the object denoted by it) does not lead to the cognition of similarity (*sādṛśya*), the basis for the admittance of universal. Since universal is not cognised the relation, which relates it also cannot be cognised.

The word and the meaning both are non-eternal, and hence how the relation that holds between two non-eternals can be regarded as eternal? On the other hand, the relation being non-eternal how it can bring the recollection of an object of the past and link it with an object that is in the present? The simple meaning of this question is this: Only an eternal thing can be the instrumental in cognising a quality of an object of the past with which it had an association, and, which has also an association with an object of the present. Without this the cognition of similarity is not possible.

Further, in order to constitute a relation the two relata of the relation must be cognised as separate entities. If it is cognised as identical it leaves no scope for the operation of a relation.

On the other hand, if it is held that the relation is eternal, then it presupposes that the relata must always remain related. There cannot be any point of time when the two relata remain separated, because the relation is eternal, which exists while relating the two.

In the absence of any conclusive proof leading to the cognition of an eternal relation between *sañjnā* and *sañjin* the relation between them cannot be accepted as an eternal one.

6.3. *The Mīmāṁsā Critique of Samavāya*

Kumārila takes exception to the concept of *samavāya* as accepted by the Nyāya-Vaiśeṣika. He asks, what is after all this *samavāya* relation? The Naiyāyika says that when two inseparable entities are so related that one is in the other, or, in other words, one is the container and the other is the thing contained, then they are related through *samavāya*. So *samavāya* is a determinant relation of two things to be looked upon as the container and the thing contained.

Here Kumārila points out that no such relation between the container and the thing contained is apprehended in entities, which according to the Nyāya-Vaiśeṣika is related through inherence. We never apprehend in the form that 'cowness' exists in the cow. On the other hand, our cognition takes the form "this is a cow". This shows that *jāti* (universal) and *'vyakti'* (individual) are identical. The relation of the two things, container and contained is possible only when two are exclusively different, as in the case, when we say "here is a book on the table".

Kumārila further continues that the Nyāya-Vaiśeṣika while defending *samavāya*, has used the term *'ayutasiddha'*, or, in other words, the primary characteristic of the two relata of inherence should be such that they cannot exist separately. Here Kumārila asks: "What is after all this *ayutasiddhi*?" Does it mean that the two relata have no activities independent of the other (*pṛthag gati-matva*), or, the two relata have no two separate loci? In the case of the parts and the whole both these two characteristics do not apply. For example, I can move my hand without moving my body. So the activity of one does not entail the activities of the other. Hence, they become *yutasiddha* and not *ayutasiddha*.

If I adhere to the second interpretation, namely, that the relata would be *yuṭasiddha*, if, and only if they have two separate loci, but this would apply to the case of the part and the whole, because the whole exists in its parts and parts exist in their parts. Hence, it is evident that the whole and the part (*avayavin* and *avayava*) have two separate loci and consequently they are *yutasiddha*. In the same way, potness (*ghaṭatva*) exists in the pot (*ghaṭa*), and the pot, in its turn exists in its parts, hence the respective loci of potness and the pot is different.

It thus becomes evident that the Nyāya-Vaiśeṣika's attempt to prove the relation that supposed to exist between parts and whole, universal and individual etc. as *samavāya* falls through.

Main purpose behind such argument is to show that neither in the whole and the part nor in the universal and the individual, the relata of *samavāya* can be said to be absolutely different, which would have provided ground for the said relation.

6.4. The Nyāya-Vaiśeṣika, however, meets this objection and replies that the relata of *samavāya*, namely, universal and the individual (*jāti-vyakti*), the part and the whole (*avayava-avayavin*) cannot be identical, for the universal (*sāmānya*) generates similar notion, while individual (*vyakti*) generates discriminating notion. *Sāmānya* is unitary so also inherent in all individuals, while individuals are mutually exclusive. For example, the purpose that is served by a whole cannot be served by its parts. Had they been identical, they would have served the same purpose.

To this the Bhāṭṭa Mīmāṁsaka replies that our cognition should be the main proof of whether two things are identical or exclusively different. Had they been totally different we would have cognised them as 'this' and 'cowness' the way as we cognise two things as "this is a chair" and "this is a table". Hence, one must admit that they cannot be absolutely different.[1] On the other hand, our experience tells us that it is in the 'cow individual' (*go-vyakti*) and not in the 'horse individual' (*aśva-vyakti*) the 'cowness' (*gotva*) is perceived. Or, in other words, 'cowness' generates a notion similar to its ownself in the cow individual and not in the horse individual. This becomes possible if we assume that the two are identical. Otherwise 'cowness' would have generated the notion of the cow in the horse individual (*aśva-vyakti*) also.

Of course, the Bhāṭṭa does not deny that in spite of identity the two relata of inherence are mutually different; when we say "this is a cow", 'this' relates to an individual cow present before me and the 'cow' refers to the universal cowness. Otherwise, 'this' and the 'cow' would have been synonymous, hence, reference of 'this' and 'cow' must be different. Thus to the Mīmāṁsaka the relation of *sāmānya* or *jāti* to the individual is of "identity-cum-difference".

A question may pertinently arise: Identity and difference are two mutually exclusive attributes. How is it that they would co-exist or function as one? To this the reply of the Bhāṭṭa would be that although the two are mutually exclusive properties still their co-existence can be admitted, since it is a fact of our experience.

When I say it is a piece of silver, I cannot say at the same moment it is not a piece of silver, both are contradictory attributes, hence both are mutually exclusive. But in the case under reference "this is a cow" we have two different types of cognition one assimilating, the other discriminating. 'This' refers to an individual and the 'cow' refers to a cow universal, it is proved by our experience. That the two different attributes may co-exist, if there is no contradiction between the two—unlike silver and non-silver.

6.5. Kumārila further cirticises *samavāya* by saying that the basis of *ayutasiddha* cannot prove *samavāya*. If *ayutasiddha* means that before the occurrence of the relation the relata do not come into existence, no relation can hold non-existent relata, hence the relation itself is negated; on the other hand, if it is conceded that the relata are already there prior to the ocurrence of *samavāya*, then they must have existed separately, and any relation that holds between two such entities is the relation of *yutasiddha*, i.e. those which are capable of existence independently.[2]

Thus on the basis of *ayutasiddha samavāya* is not proved. Kumārila poses the oft-repeated question—if *samavāya* is identical with or different from its relata, and he finds fault with all the alternatives that may be advanced in reply to the above question.

As Kumārila is primarily concerned with proving the notion that it is *dharmin* (the quality possessor) which is cognised by the people by a particular term, he refutes the Buddhist contention that the cognition of 'cow' by the term 'cow' in the cow individual, is like the cognition of forest by the tree. He says that there is a permanent entity which is associated with when a particular quality disappears and other quality emerges, that is the quality possessor (*āvirbhāva-tirobhāva-dharmakeṣu anuyāyi yat, taddharmī*). He states that one can cognise the quality possessor even before one cognises the quality. Umbeka in his commentary explains that the quality possessor (*dharmin*) can be cognised even when the quality is not cognizable. For instance, in the twilight though one does not cognise the whiteness of the row of cranes, one cognises the row of the birds.[4]

At the same time Kumārila refuses to accept absolute separate status of *jāti* from *vyakti* and refutes *samavāya*. He concludes that though *jāti* has no separate existential character except substance etc. still it is to be accepted.[5] Umbeka says that the individual is cognised as qualified by *jāti*. Thus the Bhāṭṭa kills two birds by one stone—the refutation of the Buddhist doctrine against *jāti* and the Nyāya-Vaiśeṣika concept of *samavāya* by postulating some sort of identity between universal and the individual. Pārthasārathi Miśra sums up the position like this: In fact there is no separate entity of *jāti* except *vyakti* and one entity with two characters is cognised.[6] Thus the position does not warrant admittance of *samavāya*, hence, it stands refuted.

6.6. Pārthasārathi explains this position of *samavāya* that it is a relation of which the superstratum causes the same cognition in the substratum and that is *samavāya*.[7]

Pārthasārathi in his *Śāstradīpikā* while discussing the ineffective reason of inference says that the reason (*hetu*) becomes contradictory when it contradicts the property-possessor (*dharmin*) but it does not become so when it contradicts a particular property *(viśeṣadharma)* of the property possessor. In this context the question of inherence is discussed—whether it is a *viśeṣadharma* or otherwise.

Inherence is a separate entity other than the substance, quality, action, universal, and particular because it gives rise to the cognition of "this is here", like the contact. In this instance the probandum (*sādhya*) is "other than the five categories" but the reason proves something which is just opposite the probandum.

The contact exists in every object and is many, hence the reason proves something other than inherence and that it is many. Thus the reason contradicts the very being of the quality in the quality-possessor and its particularity, that is one.

This is not justified, because the cognition of "this is here" is not seen in 'inherence' i.e. the property-possessor. Hence the question of supporting or contradicting does not arise. Had it resided in inherence it could not contradict the same. When it is in opposition it can contradict the same, but on account of being resident there, it cannot reside in the opposition.

If it is said that inherencehood is contradicted, it should be decided if inherence-hood is different from the inherence-possessor. In case of difference, even if inherencehood is contradicted, by this, the property-possessor is not contradicted. That the property-possessor cannot be contradicted otherwise, as has been stated above. Thus on the ground of contradiction of the property-possessor (*dharmiviśeṣa*), i.e. the oneness of inherence is contradicted, which does not constitute a defect of the reason. The intention of the statement is this:

That the cognition of "this is here" is the reason for the inference of subsistence of inherence, and at the same time, the said reason contradicts the particular qualification of inherence i.e. inherence is one. Even if it is admitted that the reason contradicts the oneness of inherence that does not stand in the way of the Vaiśeṣika, who wants to prove that inherence is a category, which is different from the other five categories.

When inherence is proved as a separate category, that does not mean that inherence is one. Therefore, the reason, which does not prove the oneness of inherence is not vitiated.

6.7. Nārāyaṇa, a follower of the Kumārila school of Pūrva Mīmāṁsā, calls in question the cognition of *samavāya*. He asks, whether it can be perceived through the sense organ, or inferred?

It may be argued that it is perceptible, because the quality and its locus, for instance, the white colour and its substratum, the cloth, have the co-presence and co-absence with the visual organ. This means *samavāya* is the content of the above qualified cognition and thus it is proved that *samavāya* can be cognised through perception.

This argument is not valid, says Nārāyaṇa, because *samavāya* itself is disputed and hence it cannot be said that *samavāya* is the content of the above cognition. Had it been a pre-established fact then only one could have advanced the above argument.

For perception of an object there must be contact of the object with the visual organ. Now, may we ask, what is that contact of inherence with the visual organ? It cannot be qualifier-qualificandness (*viśeṣaṇa-viśeṣyabhāva*) and existence of other types of contact is barred. Nārāyaṇa then criticises the inference advanced by Prabhākara, which is:

The cognition of "cowness in the cow" is conditioned by the substratum-superstratum relation, because of the cognition 'this is here" like the cognition of "there is rice in the pot".[8]

This inference is not proved, says Nārāyaṇa, because the reason of the above inference i.e. "this is here" is a deviating one; we have similar cognition in the instances, such as "there is no pot on the ground". The relation of absence to the ground is not *samavāya* though we have the cognition of "this is here":[9]

Another inference may be like this: what is under dispute is conditioned by qualifier-qualificandness, because it is a qualified cognition like the cognition of the staff-holder.[10]

No doubt this is a qualified cognition, but the above inference is vitiated on account of the deviation of the reason, because we have qualified cognition in the instances, such a "the pot is destroyed".[11] The assertion is that the qualified cognition does not lead to the inference of *samavāya*.

Bhavanātha's statement that the appearance of a thing, though it did not come and though it was not there, as dependent on an object, which is produced, leads to the cognition of *samavāya*.[12]

Now may we ask what is the factor that leads to the cognition of *samavāya*? Is it pervasion of appearance by inherence or, is it unintelligible without the cognition of *samavāya*?

There is no such pervasion, because two are not seen together elsewhere and hence pervasion of appearance by inherence cannot be cognised. For the cognition of the pervasion of an entity by another, both are to be seen together elsewhere.

The appearance cannot be said to be unintelligible because it can be cognised through non-difference which admits difference (*bheda-sahiṣṇuṇā abheden-opapatteḥ*).

Nārayāṇa further questions the very nature and occurrence of *samavāya* i.e. what relates *samavāya* to its relata, which are stock in trade of all the opponents of the Nyāya-Vaiśeṣika school.

His other objection is to the concept of *samavāya*: if there is no relation for relating *samavāya* with its relata then with reference to a cow one would use "mass, cowness and inherence" discarding the ephemerical usage such as "this is a cow".[13]

His solution is that what holds between quality and the quality-possessor, the whole and the part, is the relation of identity (*tādātmya*).

6.8. *The Vedānta Critic of Samavāya*

Bādarāyaṇa in his *Brahama-sūtra* while refuting the *paramāṇu-kāraṇavāda* (atom as the cause of the universe) says that even acceptance of *samavāya*, the theory that the universe is created from the atoms, does not stand scrutiny.[1]

Śaṁkara following the *Brahama-sūtra* has taken up the question of *samavāya* as an independent relation in the context of rejection of *asatkāryavāda* (non-existence of the effect in the cause) and also *paramāṇukāraṇavāda* (the atom is the cause of the universe) and establishes that *samavāya* is not a logical proposition.

Śaṁkara says that the cause and the effect, the substance (*dravya*) and its attribute (*guṇa*) which are held by the Naiyāyika to be related through *samavāya* are actually cause of self-linking relation (*tādātmya sambandha*). Because in these instances neither we can comprehend that an effect is different from its cause nor we can assert that the substance differs from attributes, or, in other words, they can never be cognised as separate entities like the horse and the buffalo whose initial difference is evident. So when the two entities are cognised as identical and inseparable it would be logical to assume the relation, that exists between the two, as the self-linking relation (*tādātmya sambandha*), which is an accredited type of relation.

Moreover, if the Nyāya-Vaiśeṣika concept of *samavāya* is accepted it will involve a number of difficulties.

Suppose 'X' and 'Y' are related through *samavāya*, let us call it 'R'. Now, if 'R' relates 'X' and 'Y', then as a rule 'R' must be related to both 'X' and 'Y', which will lead to the assumption of another relation, let us call it 'R^1' through which 'R' would be related to 'X' and 'Y'. Again that 'R^1' is to be related to its relata through another relation, let us call it 'R^2'. In this way 'R^2' would also require another relation for being related to its relata. The result would be the *regressus ad infinitum*.

If, however, the Naiyāyika seeks to get rid of this difficulty by saying that there is no necessity of assuming 'R[1]', (another *samavāya*) for the relation of *samavāya* to its relata, that is to say, that *samavāya* does not require the services of another *samavāya* in order to be related with its relata. This will be tantamount to saying that *samavāya* is not related with its relata while mutually relating the two, or, in other words, 'R' (*samavāya*) no doubt relates 'X' and 'Y' mutually, but 'R' itself is not related either to 'X' or 'Y'. Such a position cannot be accepted, because in that case the two relata will never be related. From this it will follow that the part and the whole, the substance and the quality etc. could remain unrelated, because the relation which would relate them (part with the whole etc.) is not related to its relata, and that which is not related to its relata, cannot, in any way help the two relata to be related.[2]

6.9. The Naiyāyika may however argue that *samavāya* is itself a relation (*svayaṁ sambandha-rūpatvāt*), therefore, it does not require the agency of any other relation to be related to its relata. *Samavāya* by virtue of its own nature as a relation is related to its own relata the way the universal existence (*sattā*) occurs in three categories *dravya* (substance), *guṇa* (quality) and *karma* (action) for which they are cognised as existent (*sat*). *Sattā* itself also exists and for that the Naiyāyika does not say that it requires the help of another *sattā* (beingness), but it is known as *sat* (existent) by dint of its own nature. The same way, *samavāya* is related to its relata, but not through another relation. By virtue of its nature i.e. the very nature of the relation that *samavāya* stands related to its relata without seeking assistance of another relation.

To this Śaṁkara queeps why not apply the same logic to *saṁyoga* also? Because *saṁyoga*, after all, is a relation and as such it would have been related with its relata without the assistance of *samavāya*. In fact, the Naiyāyika holds that when two entities 'X' and 'Y' are related through *saṁyoga*, the relation *saṁyoga* exists in its relata through the assistance of *samavāya* because *saṁyoga* is held to be a *guṇa* and its relata, the *saṁyogin*, are *dravya* and the *guṇa* must reside in a *dravya* through a relation.

Vācaspati, however, offers an apparent solution on behalf of the Naiyāyika and subsequently refutes it. He says that the opposition may argue that *saṁyoga* is a product (*kārya*) and a product is always dependent for its emergence on its inherent cause. Naturally *saṁyoga* must be related with its inherent cause on which it is dependent through an inherent cause. (There being only three causes, the other two, viz. *asamavāyi kāraṇa* and *nimitta kārana* are precluded).

To this postulation Vācaspati replies that in case of eternal conjunct (*aja-saṁyoga*) this argument of dependence does not hold good. Contact (*saṁyoga*) is not always a product, because there are *saṁyoga* which are eternal (*aja*) and in such cases of eternal *saṁyoga* they will not require the assistance of a *samavāya* to be related with their relata. [In the case of contact between Time and Space (*dik-kāla-saṁyoga*) both Time and Space being eternal the contact which relates them is also eternal].

Moreover, why do not you take contact as one and eternal like inherence? The cognition of inherence depends on that of the relata. Even when the relata differ or cease to exist, inherence, according to Naiyāyika, neither differs nor ceases to exist. But on the other hand, it is held to be eternal and unitary. In the same way, contact also can easily be held undifferentiated, one and eternal, although its cognition depends on those relata, which differ. In that case, however, the argument of the Naiyāyika that contact being a product must be related to its relata through inherence does not hold good. If, however, to avoid this difficulty *samavāya* is held to be different when its relata differ, or, if it is said that it is non-eternal, then the Naiyāyika would be compelled to admit that *samavāya*, which is a product, is emerged from the accessory causes only; because postulation of inherence cause would be an impossibility for the simple reason that it would involve *regressus ad infinitum*. Then why not admit the same in the case of *saṁyoga*, a product, which is generated from the accessory causes only and does stand in the need of an inherent cause. Thus the postulation of *samavāya* as a relation stands vitiated.

Moreover, the cognition of the relata is the basis for the cognition of a relation, when the two relata are cognised as essentially identical (*tādātmya*), no one can assume a relation between two identical entities.

6.10. Citsukhācārya in his *Tattvapradīpikā* has attacked *samavāya* mainly on two points, namely, the *lakṣaṇa* (definition) and *pramāṇa* (proof) of *samavāya* and he concludes, since neither the definition of *samavāya* is possible nor the proof of its existence is available, *samavāya* cannot be accepted as a separate entity distinct from substance etc. (*lakṣaṇāsamabhavāt pramāṇābhavācca na samavāyasya dravyebhyo bheda-siddhiḥ*).[3]

In order to reject the concept of *samavāya* Citsukha first puts the argument of Śrīdhara from his *Nyāyakandali*, following Śrīdhara Citsukha quotes the *Bhāṣya* of Praśastapāda and explains the term *ayutasiddha* (inseparably connected).

When the two relata of the relation do not exist without the other, i.e. separate container and containerhood is not cognised that is inseparably connected (*ayutasiddha*) and this leads to the cognition of *samavāya*, such as, in the case of yarns and the cloth. Though the yarns do exist in their parts, the cloth does not exist anywhere except the yarns, and hence, the condition of *ayutasiddha* is fulfilled. In this way the relation that exists between two non-eternal, and eternal entities, can be explained.

The phrase *iha pratyahetuḥ* has been included in the definition of *samavāya* in the *Praśastapāda-bhāṣya* to exclude certain relations from the scope of *samavāya*. This provision excludes the *vācya-vācaka-bhāva* relation that exists between the ether and the word which denotes the ether. Again, the expression *ayutasiddha* in the definition of *samavāya* excludes the relation that obtains between the can and the curd; because they also convey the sense of container-contained (*ādhāra-ādheya*). And this is all what the author of the *Nyāya-Kandalī* (Kandalīkāra) has said in support of definition of *samavāya* and for its acceptance as a category.

6.11. All these arguments are fallacious, says Citsukha. *Samavāya* cannot be established by describing it as *ayutasiddha* for the simple reason that the relation of qualifier-qualifiedness will crop up in the scope of the definition of *samavāya*. It has been stated that the relation that holds in quality and substance, activity and activator, the parts and whole, the universal and the individual, the particular (*viśeṣa*) and the thing that possesses the particular, is *samavāya*. But this also will not hold good, because the same objection is inevitable.

If, however, the argument is like this that the concept of "this is here"occurs in *samavāya* only and nowhere else, even then the over-pervasion of the definition in such cases as "the sound is in this ether" (*iha ākāśe śabdaḥ*) remains as before, for the simple reason that the words *'iha'* and *'ākāśa'* stand as quality and substance, contained and container and they also convey the sense "this is here" (*iha idam*), and hence, there is over-pervasion.

Moreover, the phrase *ādhārādheya-bhāva* (container-containedhood) in the definition of *samavāya* is redundant and it does not serve any purpose, because, the other part *ayutasiddha* etc. serve the desired end.

Pointing out the fault in the definition of *samavāya* as defined by Praśastapāda and as explained by Śrīdhara Citsukha calls in question the definition given by Udayana.[4] It will be like this:

(a) When we say "there is no pot on the ground", this is an instance of qualifier-qualifiedness relation (*viśeṣaṇa-viśeṣya-bhāva-sambandha*) and the above definition of *samavāya* will over-pervade this. Because, though the ground exists in its own locus, there is no other locus (except the ground) of *abhāva* (absence) and hence, the concept of *ayutasiddha* is here. Moreover, the cognition of "this is here" (*ihedam pratyayaḥ*) and the container-contained relation are also cognised. This over-pervasion cannot be excluded by a qualifying clause as the relation of a positive entity (*bhāva padārtha*). Because, in the instance "the cloth has its colour" or in other words, "the cloth is qualified by the colour", which is a relation of qualifier-qualified and of positive entity, will be covered by *samavāya*.

The definition that the eternal relation is *samavāya* (*nitya-sambandhaḥ samavāyaḥ*) is also equally faulty, because on that premise the qualifier-qualified relation will also come under *samavāya* relation.

If it is further argued that the pot and its colour both are ephemeral (colour is the qualifier and the pot is the qualificand) and as such the relation that exists between the two non-eternal entities is also non-eternal, and therefore, the definition of *samavāya* will not over-pervade the qualifier-qualified relation. Of course, such argument has some force, but the relation that obtains between two eternal relata, such as, between the soul and soulness is also a qualifier-qualified relation and the counter-positives of the relation being eternal the relation that exists between them is bound to be eternal. Thus, the over-pervasion of the definition of *samavāya* (i.e. *nitya-sambandhaḥ*) remains as before.

Moreover, if it is said that when the two relata of the relation are non-eternal the relation is also non-eternal, acceptance of such a position will make *samavāya* also non-eternal; *samavāya* exists between the pot and its colour (both are non-eternal), and, hence, *samavāya* is also bound to be non-eternal.

6.12. Citsukha then proceeds to point out the imperfection of the definition of *samavāya* given by Śivāditya in his *Saptapadārthī*. That even though in such cases the qualifier is modified to be a positive entity (*bhāva padārtha*) as postulated by Śivāditya[5] the position remains unchanged. Because, such contact, which is eternal (*aja-saṁyoga*), i.e. not born either from one of the two relata, from the both, or from the contact itself, will be covered by the definition of *samavāya* as given by Śivāditya.

However, Vātsyāyana does not admit eternal contact (*ajaā saṁyoga*).[6] But such a contact cannot be denied, because it is established by proof (*pramāṇa-siddhatvāt*). The contact of self with the ether is an instance of eternal contact (*aja-saṁyoga*). The inference to prove such a contact will be:

> "The self is in contact with the ether, because it is capable of having contact, like the pot."[7]

The author of the *Mānamanohara* anticipating such an inference raises the question of *upādhi* (imposed property) and states that the above inference stands vitiated due to *upādhi*.[8]

To this proposition the reply is that activity and manifestedness cannot be construed as *upādhi*; the absence of *upādhi* and the absence of *sādhya* (probandum) should have the same concomitance (*vyāpti—upādhyabhāva-sādhyābhāvayorapi vyaptireṣṭavyā*), otherwise there will be no concomitance of *upādhi* and *sādhya*. Here pervasion in absence *(vyatirekavyāpati)* is cognised, and hence the imposed property has no locus.

Citsukha further asks what are the means of knowledge (*pramāṇa*) for admitting *samavāya*? Is it perception or inference? It cannot be perception for the simple reason that *samavāya* cannot be perceived. How *samavāya* can be perceived? If it is said that "the cloth is here in these yarns" (*iha tantuṣu paṭaḥ*) and it is perceived it does not stand scrutiny.

In order to be perceived *samavāya* must either generate the concept of container or contained or that of both. In the first alternative, it will create the notion of container in both cloth and the yarns *(iha tantuṣu paṭeṣu),* and in acceptance of the second alternative both cloth and the yarns will be cognised as the things contained (*paṭaḥ tantuḥ*) and in the third alternative both yarns and the cloth should have been cognised both as container and contained and, that is too, without any discrimination. It thus stands that *samavāya* is not perceptible.

It also cannot be argued that the concept of universal and the individual being qualified by the universal (*jāti-jātimantau*) will be the means of knowledge for perception of *samavāya*. Because it also cannot stand the scrutiny for its validity. In this concept one may ask whether *samavāya* exists between universal and the individual through both, or, through other agency, or, by itself i.e. independently? The admission of the first alternative will lead to the defect of *ad-infinitum* and so also is the case with the second alternative, and acceptance of the third alternative will make the position more complex, since in that case *samavāya* is supposed to exist without any relation to its relata.

6.13. *Asatkhyāti*

Now an argument has been advanced to the effect that without being related by any other relation, the relationship between the universal and the individual will be cognised through *samavāya* and, as such, the defect of *ad infinitum* does not arise.

To this reply is this: Acceptance of such a proposition exposes the very concept of relationship, that is, the universal and the individual will appear related without being related by a relation. Moreover, it will lead to the *asatkhyātivāda*, that is to say that notion of relationship of *samavāya* will be there without its presence. This means, substituting the concept of *anyathākhyāti* by *asatkhyāti*.

The underlying meaning of the above argument is this, that there is a relation between the universal and the individual and that relation relates the two. We call it *tādātmya* (self-linking) and you may call it *samavāya*. Now, if it is said that the relata are related without the agency of the relation (as *samavāya* in your case) then the individual would also appear to be qualified by the universal without having the function of relation.

If without the existence of *samavāya* the action of *samavāya* be accepted in the relata, then it amounts to the cognition of a thing in its absence, which means cognition of a thing which is not real. This is *asatkhyāti*. This cannot be said as *anyathākhyāti* i.e. the cognition of a thing in a different way from its own nature, but here both are real i.e. the mother of pearl and a piece of silver, but *samavāya* is not perceptible in other places also. Hence without taking the risk of accepting the theory of *asatkhyāti samavāya* cannot be accepted as perceptible.

Samavāya cannot be proved by inference also, because there is no exclusive mark (*liṅga*) for it. The inference will be:

> "Controversial cognition of 'this is here' presupposes a relation, since nothing prevents that cognition, like the cognition of "these fruits are in this basket".

The meaning of this statement is this that the existence of potness in the pot presupposes a relation and that relation makes the cognition of potness in the pot. This is like the cognition of "the fruits are in the basket". But such an inference does not prove any new relation. The relation of qualifier-qualified and container-contained are already there and these are cognised.

It may be argued that the qualifier-qualified relation which is said to be the basis of *samavāya* can be inferred, and thus *samavāya* is cognised. It is true, such an inference may hold good, but in the instance "there is no pot on this ground" (*iha bhutale ghaṭābhāvaḥ*) there is no second relation other than the qualifier-qualified one.

Citsukha then refutes the inference forwarded by Vallabha in the *Nyāyalīlāvatī*: "When we see a cow we have the qualified knowledge that "the cowness is in this cow." Such a qualified knowledge is positive in character and the knowledge is not hindered by any other outside element. Therefore, the inference:

The qualified knowledge "the cowness is in the cow" is subject to a relation, like "the pot is on the ground".

Again, when we see a cow, the cowness of the cow and that which is before us have co-locushood and such a knowledge emanates from the knowledge of the relation that exists between the cow and cowness, like the stick and the earring are connected with Devadatta. Here again the same defect of *siddha-sādhana* (proving things already proved) will crop up i.e. it proves only qualifier-qualifiedness.

The objection to *siddha-sādhana* may be avoided by postulating a proposition that the qualifier-qualifiedness is not a relation at all, because that does not exist on two, and unless an attribute exists on two, it cannot relate two entities and, as such it is not a relation at all. On the other hand, if it be argued that it resides in both, then there will be no distinction between qualifier and qualificand, both will appear either as qualifier or qualificand. The same will be the position so far container-containedhood is also concerned. This being so when a new relation is proved by inference there cannot be the defect of *siddha-sādhana*, because that is not already cognised as a relation.

Let it be so; in spite of the fact that the qualifier-qualifiedness resides in both the relata the distinct knowledge of container and contained is always there. For instance, when we say "the fruits are in the basket" or "the cloth is in the yarns" we have the distinct knowledge that one is container and the other is the thing contained. The term of inherence equally rests on the yarns and the cloth, even then by dint of their own virtue the yarns create the notion of container and the cloth that of the contained. Hence, in respect of qualifier-qualifiedness also the distinct notion will be there, and as such acceptance of *samavāya* by inference will expose it to the defect of *siddha-sādhana*.

6.14. *Is Samavāya Independent or Dependent?*

Existence of *samavāya* is again tested by posing the question, whether it is independent or dependent. The first alternative cannot be accepted, because acceptance of it will lead to the condition that an entity remaining elsewhere relates two entities, which is not possible. Acceptance of the second alternative will lead to the *ad infinitum* i.e. that *samavāya* in order to be dependent on its relata will need the assistance of another *samavāya* and so on.

If, however, it is said that in order to relate the two relata *samavāya* subsists in its relata without having assistance of another relation and, due to the presence of *samavāya* the relata unite, and thus the question of *ad infinitum* does not arise, then the same condition shall have to be conceded in respect of *saṁyoga* also. It means that *saṁyoga* would not require the assistance of any other relation for its subsistence, which the Naiyāyika cannot accept.

Citsukha further discusses an inference and points out the over-pervasion of the reason (*hetu*) in the inference by various ways. He also says that there is no incongruity in accepting an eternal relation between two non-eternal entities.

The non-eternal substrata of *samavāya*, which you accept as eternal, do not affect the eternal character of *samavāya*, similarly the relation of qualifier-qualified which is eternal may exist between two non-eternal entities. He solves the problem of the relation that may be conceived between qualifier and qualified, as follows:

Those who accept *samavāya* as a relation say that *samavāya* by virtue of its nature is related to its relata, and is not in the need of assistance of another relation. The same logic may be applied to in respect of qualifier-qualified-relationship. The qualifier and the qualified (*guṇa-guṇyādi*) by their nature are related and they themselves form the ground for taking them so. If this position is conceded to the qualifier-qualified relation there will be no more necessity for admitting *samavāya*, which suffers from the defects of assuming more *(kalpana-gaurava)* and ad-infinitum *(anavasthā)*.[9] Thus for want of proper definition and exclusive means for the cognition of *samavāya* as a category separate from substance etc. is not proved, and hence, cannot be accepted.

6.15. Rāmānuja while explaining the *Vedānta-sūtra*[10] which refutes the atoms as the cause of the universe says that acceptance of *samavāya* as a relation in the process of the emergence of the universe will lead to the *regressus ad infinitum*, i.e. acceptance of one *samavāya* makes it obligatory that there should be successive *samavāyas*. He then cites the example of cause and effect, the parts and the whole, such as the yarns and the cloth and states that they are identical. The yarns by combining together takes a different shape and assume different functions.[11]

Sudarśana Sūri raises the question of existence of identity-cum-difference *(yugapad-bahutvaiktva)* because the yarns are many in number and the cloth is one which means they are mutually different and identical. It also cannot be said that difference and identity are mutually contradictory, because there is no contradiction everywhere between the two. They become contradictory when the question of existence and non-existence is involved.[12]

The yarns are cognised as identical with the cloth and not as a different entity. However, in fact, one thread is different from the other thread, the two threads cannot be identical. What is meant by the identity of threads with the cloth is that the cloth is not a different entity from the combined threads.

The purport of the above statement is to show that since the parts (the yarns) and the whole (cloth) are identical-cum-different the necessity of admitting the relation of *samavāya* does not arise.

He further questions the Vaiśeṣika definition of *ayutasiddha*, the ground for admitting *samavāya*. He asks if the universal and the individual are cognised as the entities inseparably related and *samavāya* is admitted to hold between the two, another *samavāya* will be needed for relating the first *samavāya* with its relata. Though *samavāya* is supposed to be intimate, it stands in the need of another relation.

If, however, it is presumed that *samavāya* by its own right, without the assistance of anything else, inseparably related to its relata, is it not better to admit that the universal, quality etc. possess that quality? Because in the former case one has got to admit *samavāya* first, which is unknown, then its unique feature. In the latter case, it is more a simple process to admit those entities endowed with the said unique quality.

6.16. Vallabhācārya in his *Aṇubhāsya*, while explaining the two *Vedānta-sūtras* relating to pre-existence of the effect in the cause[13] and refutation of the theory of atomism,[14] criticises the Nyāya-Vaiśeṣika concept of *samavāya.*

He argues that if inherence is admitted for relating the effect with its cause in that case existence of the effect in the cause must be conceded, because the relation requires two for its existence. Moreover, for the subsistence of inherence in its relata the question of another relation arises and acceptance of another relation leads to *ad infinitum.*[15] On the other hand, if the effect is presumed to be created without being related to the cause, then the effect will be illusory like the cognition of silver in the conch shell (*śuktikā-rajatavat*).

Vallabhācārya further attacks the concept of *samavāya* by refuting the thesis of emergence of *dvyaṇuka* (dyad) from the combination of atoms. He bases his arguments on the traditional concept of relation that it requires two for its existence. While the atom is in existence *dvyaṇuka* is yet to emerge and hence the condition for holding *samavāya* is not satisfied. *Samavāya* is eternal and as such it must have the two relata for its existence (*sa ca nityaḥ sadā sambandhi-sattāmapekṣate*).

According to Nyāya-Vaiśeṣika theory of *asatkāryavāda* (pre-non-existence of effect in the cause) *dvyaṇuka* being an effect cannot exist prior to its production, and as such there is only one relatum, i.e. the atom for existence of *samavāya.* If, however, it is said that *dyaṇuka* exists prior to its production, the very notion will negate the theory of *asatkaryavāda*; on the other hand, if it is not there *samavāya* cannot stand only on one leg, i.e. on atom (*samavāya-hāniḥ ityubhayataḥ pāśā-rajjuḥ*).

Puruṣottama further explains the position by saying that inherence cannot be said to exist first in the atom and then after the production of *dvyaṇuka* it resides there also i.e. the other relatum of inherence, because to warrant such presumption the existence of inherence in the atom is not proved by any of the four *pramāṇas,* viz. perception, inference, word and similarity. He elaborates his objection to *samavāya* in a more vigorous way in his work the *Prasthāna-ratnākara,* where he criticises the term *ayutasiddha* and says that inherence cannot be cognised on that basis.[15]

Śrīharṣamiśra, who is quoted by Puruṣottama, questions the connotation of *ayutasiddha*, if it means "dependence on others"? And does it imply the relation? What is that relation? It can neither be contact nor inherence, because the term 'dependence on others' involves inherences and taking recourse to it for the cognition of inherence leads to the defect of self-dependence (*ātmāśraya*).[16]

Vallabhācārya and his followers admit *tādātmya* (self same) relation between such entities which are passed as inseparably related. The relation of *tādātmya* is cognised by perception. The relata of the said relation are perceived and that perception has concomitance (*vyāpti*) with the perception of the relation.

5. *The Buddhist Critique of Samavāya*

6.5.1. Śāntarakṣita in his *Tattvasaṁgraha* rejects the concept of *samavāya* and refutes the argument of the Nyāya-Vaiśeṣika. With a view to countering the arguments he puts the Nyāya-Vaiśeṣika viewpoints first.

(a) A relation is to be accepted between two entities such as parts and whole, quality and substance, etc. because our cognition is "the cloth is in the yarns", "colour is in the pot", which presupposes a relation between the two. This relation is inherence.

(b) The inherence is one and eternal, because it is causeless. Even though the entities which are related by the inherence are destroyed, the inherence is not destroyed. Only the effect is destroyed. Hence, inherence is eternal. Since it is one and eternal it differs from contact (*saṁyoga*) which is non-eternal and many.

(c) Śāntarakṣita quotes Praśastamati in order to say that though inherence is one, there is no apprehension of the five categories being confused in their cognition. Inherence of substance would not be felt in quality, because the substance only has the manifesting power of substance, so also the quality does manifest quality and nothing else.

Śāntarakṣita then proceeds to refute the above contention one by one.

The so-called notion—"the cloth is in the yarns" (*ina tantuṣu paṭah*) is the invention of the Nyāya-Vaiśeṣika to fit in his doctrine (*svasiddhāntānurāgeṇa*), nobody other than him accepts it. The notion implies container-containhood i.e. one is the substratum and the other is the superstratum. Such notion is only possible, if the two entities regarded as container and contained, are cognised as separate entities. For instance, in the cognition "the apples are in the basket", the basket and the apples are two different entities and also cognised as such and, therefore, the basket is the container and the apples are the things contained. But the yanrs and the cloth are neither really different entities nor cognised as different. It means there is no locus for the inherence i.e. the proposed *sādhya* (the things to be proved) is not established (*sādhyadharmī na siddhaḥ*).

The Nyāya-Vaiśeṣika says that inherence is causeless. There is no cause of inherence. One who does not recognise a cause, how can he conceive an *effect* which presuppos a cause? Kamalaśīla in his commentary on the *Tattvasaṁgraha*, shows that the entity does not come into existence, simply because such a thing is conceived. The cognition is not after the entity, it is independent of it (*naiva icchānāṁ vastu-svabhāvānurodhaḥ svātantrya-vṛttitvād āsām*). Such a proposition will lead to *ad-infinitum.* Moreover, what is conceived as something by you, may be conceived otherwise by the others.

None but the Nyāya-Vaiśeṣika cognises that the cloth is in the yarns. Every one cognises that the contrary is the case, for example, in the tree there are branches, in the mountain there are bolders (*vṛkṣe śākhāḥ śilāścāge ityeṣā laukikī matiḥ*). Moreover, the cognition of the branches in the tree is not due to inherence, but due to the cognition of all parts of the tree without break (*agākhya pariśiṣṭāṅgo nairantaryopalambhanāt*). In view of this the cognition that "the cloth is in the yarns" is contradictory and how such contradictory cognition be considered as the ground for accepting inherence as a separate category? Further, it has been established that the whole is nothing but the assemblage of parts. There is no separate whole except the aggregation of parts.

One may ask how could we have the knowledge of colour in the pot? How the residence of colour in the pot can be explained without accepting the relation between the colour and the pot? In other words, the colour, the smell, the touch, the activity—all these are attributes of substance. They are to reside in the substance through a relation i.e. inherence. If inherence is not admitted subsistence of attributes in the substance cannot be explained.

The reply is: for the knowledge of colour in a pot, one does not require the assistance of inherence. It is the nature of the pot to have colour. So, the so called inherence is nothing but the nature of the thing itself. In other words, the colour is identical with the pot (*ghaṭa-svabhāvaṁ rūpam, na ghaṭādyātmakam*). The fact is that the pot and the colour do not share the same locus, hence both colour and the pot are cognised in different loci. For instance, the word colour represents all colours residing in the pot, cloth etc. Similarly, the pot represents all pots of blue colour, pots of white colour, pots with activity etc. When we say "a white pot", whiteness rejects the other colours as well as white colour residing in other locus, and thus it becomes a particular. Thus, the cognition, such as whiteness in the pot, is caused by the words, not by inherence.

6.5. *Oneness and Eternality Refuted*

If inherence is one and eternal in all entities (*yadyekastrailokye samavāyaḥ syāt*) connected by it in this way, such as parts and whole, quality and substance, universals and the individuals etc., then cloth will also be cognised in the halves of the pot, cowness in the elephant because they are also inherent of something and inherence is one. It may be argued that there is a special power which distinguishes one from the other. The special power which is supposed to be imparted to the substance etc. will also be created in the particular substance according to inherence. The inherence being one would be the same in everything, then how can it be said that its power is fixed only with reference to a certain thing and not to everything. The underlying meaning of the argument is this: Let there be one inherence in everything, but there is difference of locus which will create different cognition. The cloth does not reside in the halves of the pot, hence the cloth will not be cognised in the halves of the pot (*kapāla*). But this logic has no force. What the Naiyāyika calls inherence, on the strength of which he has stated that the cloth resides in the yarns, is that inherence not present in the halves of the pot (*kapāla*) so that the cognition of cloth will not be there. What is the inherence of cloth in the yarns, the same inherence of cloth is present in *kapāla*. Hence, why there will not be confusion of the five categories, because the substance and quality etc. reside through the same inherence.

The Nyāya-Vaiśeṣika here argues that even though the inherence is one there will not be confusion of the categories, because the cognition of substratum and superstratum rules it. Although the substratum is the differentiating factor, you cannot say that inherence will vary from locus to locus, because in all categories the cognition of inherence is one. It is known by the process of presence and absence *(anvaya-vyatireka)*. For instance, though *saṁyoga* (contact) is one between the can and the curd, the substratum-superstratum rule operates and makes the cognition of locus in the can only, and, not in reverse. In the same way, there lies the manifesting-manifested power in the entities connected by inherence. Therefore, the oneness of inherence will not stand in the way of the categories functioning separately.

To this Śāntarakṣita and Kamalaśīla reply:

After assuming the inherence to be one there is no scope to invoke the substratum-superstratum rule. The principle that substancehood resides in the substance, qualityhood in quality etc. is entirely yours, we do not subscribe to this. You have restricted substancehood to substance alone by the device of inherence. But in fact inherence of substancehood is bound to be present in inherence of qualityhood *(guṇatvādi jātyā teṣām sambandhāt)*.

In this way the confusion of categories is unavoidable. On the other hand, if inherence of substancehood is assumed to be different from that of qualityhood then the manifoldness of inherence, like that of contact, is to be accepted.

The presence of the same inherence implies cognition of the same notion i.e. the cognition of substancehood in quality, because when the cause exists intact there cannot be the absence of effect. Therefore, here the substratum-superstratum relation becomes inoperative.

The different powers such as the power of manifesting and power of being manifested are also conceived on the strength of inherence and the conception is not based on the Buddhist doctrine of knowledge. Moreover, inherence connects two eternal entities also. How the manifesting-manifested power could be caused in the eternal entities?[1]

The example of can and curd i.e. contact between these two, cited to indicate the substratum-superstratum relation is not acceptable to us. In other words, what you have stated that though contact is the same between the can and the curd, only the can is container, not the curd. But we do not accept it. Let there be one kind of contact between the two, still the probability of confusion is there.

6.6. *Samavāya Cannot be Eternal*

The inherence cannot be eternal, because if the connection of a pot with its parts is eternal then the pot should also be eternal. The pot and its parts being in *samavāya* they would reside eternally in the eternal inherence. But neither the pot nor its parts are eternal.

The Naiyāyika may however argue that *kapāla* (halves of the pot) are the materials of the pot, when these materials are being separated or destroyed – the pot is also destroyed. Hence, though there is the eternal presence of inherence due to the absence of accessory and other causes the pot etc. cannot be considered to be eternal.

The Buddhist replies that the above argument is not valid. Because *kapāla* (the halves of the pot) has its constituents with whom it stands related through inherence, those materials also have their constituent materials, with whom the former stand related and the process goes on. These materials being the *samavāyin* (inherent) are related through inherence relation, and, hence the constituent materials are not destroyed. If you say, they are destroyed, the inherence will also meet the same fate. This will make inherence non-eternal.

Moreover, when the part and the whole are destroyed, how can inherence connecting the part with the whole remain? After the destruction of the relata the relation cannot exist. Thus like contact *(saṁyoga)* which is destroyed at the next moment after the destruction of the relata, inherence would also be destroyed and hence would be non-eternal.

On the other hand, so long contact exists, the relata also exist. In the same way, if inherence exists, the relata of inherence must exist.

Moreover, the Nyaiyāyika says that when colour is destroyed, the inherent smell remains in the pot. This means if one relatum is destroyed, the other relatum exists and the relation resides there. But then this logic should apply to contact also.

No, it is not applicable, says the Nyāya-Vaiśeṣika. The relation of contact differs from relatum to relatum and, hence it is non-eternal, but inherence being one remains even if one relatum is destroyed. Thus it is eternal.

The Buddhist says—now this must be answered first whether this inherence of smell is the same as that of colour. If the answer is in the affirmative, the question would arise, how colour disappears, if not, inherence cannot be one, which is sought to be established. The Nyāya-Vaiśeṣika's attempt, therefore, to prove *samavāya* on the ground that it is one and permanent does not succeed.

The Jaina Critique Of Samavāya

The Nyāya-Vaiśeṣika concept and definition of *samavāya* has been severely criticised and refuted by the Jaina school of philosophy. Akalaṅka and Māṇikyanandin, the two pioneers of the school, have touched the subject in their work. It is Prabhācandra, who, in his work *Prameyakamala-mārtaṇḍa*, the commentary on the *Nyāyamukha-parīkṣā* has dealt with the subject at great length. Prabhācandra makes an all out effort to refute the concept of *samavāya* and he finds fault with the definition of *samavāya*. He concentrates on the nature of relation, its function etc. and states that *samavāya* does not satisfy the norms. He has not paid attention, it seems, to the epistemological aspect of Nyāya-Vaiśeṣika philosophy. Prabhācandra not only finds fault in the definition but in oneness of it. He also states that *samavāya* can neither be perceived nor inferred; and finally he resorts to the of repeated argument that *samavāya* cannot subsist in its relata without the mediacity of another relation of *samavāya* , which leads to *ad infinitum*.

He has taken the trouble of reproducing all the arguments put forward by the scholars of the Nyāya-Vaiśeṣika school who flourished before him, and shatters all of them into pieces. Though not quite convincing his laborious and lengthy argument shows that he believes more in logical jargon than its real import.

The reference he makes to different works and authors whom he quotes, and refutes is helpful for the study of *samavāya* and other concept of the Nyāya-Vaiśeṣika school and hence reproduced and given in the appendix. Here a few basic points are mentioned.

He says there is no perfect definition of *samavāya* and there is no valid proof, perception or inference for cognition of *samavāya*. The concept of *ayutasiddha* is erroneous and the cognition of "this is here" *(ihedaṁ pratyayaḥ)* is a fallacious reason and hence it does not prove *samavāya*. The inference cited for proving *samavāya* is only the inference in absence *(vyatirekānumāna)*, and in absence of positive inference *(anvayānumāna) samavāya* cannot be proved.

He also states that *samavāya* is many and for subsistence of one *samavāya* in its relata it needs another, which in its turn still another, and thus it will lead to *ad-infinitum*. He calls it a self-linking relation which relates quality with substance etc.

He descends into polemic and says that *samavāya* is one of the six categories of the Vaiśeṣika while the Naiyāyika admits sixteen categories. Besides there are two more, *pramāṇa* and *prameya*–therefore, the assertion by Vaiśeṣika that categories are six only including *samavāya*, *(ṣaḍeva padārthāḥ)* is not correct. He after stating views of the Nyāya-Vaiśeiṣika takes up them one by one posing a of number alternatives to them, and refutes all.

The nature of his criticism can be seen when he puts the question:

(I) Has *samavāya* been defined in scriptures ? or,

(II) Is it a matter of practical experience?

He rejects the first alternative and takes up the second one. He in a lengthy argument demolishes the concept of *ayutasiddha* and says there cannot exist a relation between two inseparably related things. His argument in this respect similar to that of Kumārila. He also questions if the state of inseparably related one is the basis of *samavāya* why the cognition of "this is here" *(ihedaṁ pratyayaḥ)* is added?

He establishes that *samavāya* is not perceptible. For instance, an object in order to become perceptible must possess unique character *(asādhāraṇa-rūpatva)* and magnitude, just as the pot, which has a distinct character of its own and also magnitude *(pṛthu-buddhno-darādyākāravat)*. But inherence is not such. He examines if *samavāya* possesses uniqueness and says it does not. He puts the question as to what relates *samavāya* to its relata, posed by many opponents, and he adds one more thing *adṛṣṭa* (unseen) as a factor which might be stated as an agency which might operate between *samavāya* and its relata, and he rejects it.

Similarly, the point that qualifier and qualificand must be related through some relation is also discussed.

What is significant that he after reproducing views of the Nyāya-Vaiśeṣika school he himself meets the probable initial objection to the statement, and then makes vigorous effort to demolish them.

Thus he rejects the concept of *samavāya* by refuting all arguments of the Nyāya-Vaiśeṣika school.

Notes and References

1. *yadyekāntato bhinnaṁ viśeṣyād syād viśeṣaṇaṁ svānurūpāṁ sadā buddhiṁ viśeṣye janayet katham ?"* —SV.v. 142.
2. *nāniṣpanasya sambandho niṣpattau yutasiddhatā.* —SV.v. 146.
3. *nanu dharmātirekena dharmiṇo' nupalambhanāt tat-saṅghāta-mātraevāyam gavādiḥ syād vanādivat.* —Ibid, v., 151.
4. *yathā pradoṣasamaye śuklagrahaṇe' pi balākāpaṅktir-avadhāryate.* —SVTT. p. 158.
5. *pārarū yam na tasyāstītyaprāmāṇyam na yujyate.* —Ibid v. 158.
   jātiviśiṣṭatayaiva nityamavagamāt na mithyātvam —Ibid., TT. 152.
6. *nahi jātirnāma vyakterarthāntara-bhūtam kimapi tattvam, api tu vastveva hyekam ubhayātmakaṁ vyāvṛttyanuvṛtti-rūpatayā buddhyate.* –SD. p. 75.
7. *"yena sambandhena ādheyam ādhāre svānurūpām buddhim janayati, svākāreṇa bodhayatītyarthaḥ saḥ sambandhaḥ samavāyaḥ"*.—Ibid p. 100.
8. *iha gavi gotvam iti pratyayaḥ adhikaraṇa-adhikartavyatā-sambandha nibandhana, iha pratyayatvāt, iha ghaṭe taṇḍuḷa iti pratyayavat.* —MM, pp. 289-90.
9. *iha bhūtale ghaṭo nāstīti pratyayena vyabhicārāt anupapannam.* —Ibid.
10. *vivāda-padam viśeṣaṇa-viśeṣya bhāva-sambandha-nibandhanaṁ, viśiṣṭa-jñānatvāt daṇḍīti jñānavat.* —Ibid.

11. *vinaṣṭo ghaṭa it pratyayena vyabhicārād upekṣaṇīyam.* —Ibid.
12. *āgama-sannidhi-vihīnasyāpi utpanna-vastu-para-tantratayā bhānam samavāya-janakam.*
—Bhavanātha quoted by Nārāyaṇa.
13. *paraspara-sambandhābhāve sati yaṁ gauriti vyavāharaṁ apahāya piṇḍa-gotva-samavāya iti vyavahāra-svīkāra-prasaṅgāt.* —MM, p. 290.
14. *samavāyābhyupagamācca sāmyādanavasthiteḥ.* —VS. 2.2.13.
api ca kāryakāraṇayor dravyaguṇādīnāñca aśva-mahiṣavadbheda-buddhyabhāvāt tādātmyam abhyupagantavyam. —SBh. 2.1.18.
15. *nahi asambaddaḥ samavāyibhyām samavāyaḥ samavāyinau sambandhayet* —Bh.M. 18.4.2.
16. TD., p. 341.
17. *na syādayuta-siddhyādi samavāyasya lakṣaṇam viśeṣaṇa-viśeṣyatva-sambandhe vybhicārataḥ.* —TT, p. 332.
18. *nitya-sambandhah samavayah.* —SP. p. 51.
19. *nājaḥ saṁyogo'sti nityapārimāṇḍalyavat pṛthag-anabhidhānāt".*
—VBh., p.212.
20. *ākāśam ātmanā saṁyujyate, samyogitvāt, ghaṭavat.* —TD., p. 340.
21. *tatra kriyāvattvasya mūrtatvasya paratva-apartvayor vā upādheḥ ātmākāśena na saṁyujyate, amūrtatvād, rūpādivat.* —MMH., p. 54.
22. *ato yathā samavāyasya svabhāva-sāmarthyād eva ātmani paratra ca sambandha-vyavahāra-hetutvam, evam guṇa-guṇyāderapi svabhāva-sāmarthyād eva sambandha-vyavahāra-hetutva-upapatteḥ na kalpanā-gauravānavasthā-duṣṭa-samavāya-svīkārāvakāsaḥ.*
—*TP*, pp. 340-41.
23. VS. 2.2.13
24. *yathā tantava eva vyatiṣaṅgaviśeṣabhājaḥ paṭa iti nāmarūpa-kāryāntarādikaṁ bhajante ...* —Srbh. 2.1.19,p. 260.
25. *nahi bhinnābhinna-śabdavācyaṁ sarvaṁ dūṣyam api tu yatra bhāvābhāva-virodhaḥ.* —Commentary on Śrībhāṣya 23.19, p. 260.
Pārthasārathi, however, observes that contact of yarns *(tantu-saṁyoga)* means occurrence of contact in a pair of yarns, whereas the cloth exists in inumerable yarns. —SD., p. 197
26. *yukteḥ śabdāntarācca* —VS., 2.1.18
yuktistāvat samavetameva kāryam sat utpadyata iti sambandhasya dviṣṭhatvāt nityatvācca kāraṇāntareāpi paramparayā sambandhā sambandhotpattau mithyātvam eva. —ABh, 2.1.18, p.81.
27. VS., 2.2.13.
28. Puruṣottama commenting on the *Aṇubhāṣya* says that if the inherence subsists in the relata, say, the cause, the way *sattā* exists in the first three categories of the Vaiśeṣika, the inherence being eternal will remain always associated with the cause and everything will be produced from everything.
29. He says that according to the Kaṇāda theory of creation and destruction of the World every effect, which is produced, is destroyed in *pralaya* (delu-

sion) and the subjunct of *samavāya* being effect (all relata are not effect) are destroyed, but *samavāya* being eternal is supposed to exist. Thus human being is not able to cognise *samavāya* in absence of its relata, and, on the other hand, it cannot be cognised as a temporal relation also.

30. *yad yad dravyaṁ yad-yad-dravya-samavetaṁ*
tat tadātmakam iti vyāpteḥ.

31. *vyaṅgya-vyañjaka-sāmarthya-bhedo'pi samavāyataḥ*
nānyatastu sa nityānām utpādānupapattitah. —TS., p. 271; v. 851

Chapter 7

Reply by the Nyāya-Vaiśeṣika to the critique of Samavāya : Samavāya Established

All the followers of the Nyāya-Vāiśeṣika school beginning with Praśastapāda down to the modern writers marshalled all kinds of arguments to refute the objections raised to the concept of *samavāya* by the opponents and up strong defence for protecting it.

The objections and the replies to the objections are produced to some extent in the course of discussion in the previous chapters. What is intended here is to pick up core of the contention of the opponents and put the replies of the Nyāya-Vaiśeṣika precisely to those points.

The basic objection to the concept of *samavāya* by the Sāṁkhya lies in the fact that according to him the effect is not really different from its material cause *(upādāna-kāraṇa)* out of which the effect is produced, hence *samavāya* , which is conceived as an intimate internal relation for relating the effect with the cause stands unwanted.

Samavāya is originally conceived as the relation between cause and effect *(ihedamiti yataḥ kāryakāraṇayoḥ)* and, therefore, the Nyāya-Vaiśeṣika has got to prove that the effect is an entirely new and different entity from its inherent cause *(samavāyi-kāraṇa)* in which it originates. The difference in the approach to the cause-effect relation of the Sāṁkhya and the Nyāya-Vaiśeṣika schools can be appreciated from the terminology itself, while the Sāṁkhya prefers to call the material cause *(upadāna-kāraṇa)* , the Nyāya-Vaiśeṣika terms it *samavāyi-kāraṇa.* The Nyāya-Vaiśeṣika establishes that the effect is a different entity from its cause, so also the whole from its parts and the universal from the individual, where it resides.

The Nyāya-Vaiśeṣika holds that the cloth (effect), which is produced in the yarns (cause), is not the transformation of the yarns into a separate form, named cloth. The cloth as a new entity originates in the yarns.

He says that the cloth and the yarns cannot be taken as one. First of all, there is mutual contradiction between the two. The cloth differs from the yarns by its nomenclature, in form and the purpose served by it. The yarns which are not cloth cannot be cognised as cloth. The application of the term cloth, in its primary sense, to the yarns is barred and there is no reason for taking it in the secondary sense or as the suggestive one.

Moreover, in order to cognise two things as identical there should exist something which is common to both the entities. It is seen that this is the requirement for the false cognition *(mithyā pratyaya)* also. Thus the common property is the basis for the cognition leading to the identity of the two and there is nothing common in the cloth and the yarns,[1] which are effect and cause respectively.

Other objections to the causation theory of the Nyāya-Vaiśeṣika by the Sāṁkhya and other opponents are the problem of the same weight and the occupation of the same space by the cause and the effect. According to the Nyāya-Vaiśeṣika theory of causation the effect emerged in its *samavāyi-kāraṇa* is a new entity possessing all the qualities of a substance, hence, the effect is supposed to have its own weight, colour, etc. Consequently, the effect after being produced, resides side by side with its cause, therefore, the two (cause and effect) together should have much more weight than that of the cause alone. Similarly, the cause and the effect should have occupied two different spaces.

For instance, the cloth is an effect and the yarns are its cause, which have their own weight. After the cloth is produced, which is a new entity, it resides in the yarns. Now the weight of the yarns along with the cloth should have been more, if not double, of that of the yarns.[2]

The same way, the cloth should have occupied a space, different from the space occupied by the yarns.

The Buddhist points out that two substances having separate essence and separate quality of their own and residing simultaneously as the cause and the effect cannot occupy the same space. That the notion of two material substances occupying the same space nullifies the basic character of material substance, because it is the very character of the matter to resist the penetration of another matter to the same space. The resisting character of matter to another matter *(rūpa)*, according to the Buddhist terminology, is *sapratighatva,* and this stand in the way of assuming the effect, and for that matter the whole, as a separate entity. The effect and the whole not being different from the cause and the parts, respectively need not be related by any relation.

These objections have been met by Uddyotakara, Jayanta, Śrīdhara, Vācaspatimiśra and others logically effectively. The totality of the argument is like this: What is considered as the cause is not always cause, it is an effect in respect of other causes i.e. its parts. For instance, the yarns are the cause of the cloth, but yarns themselves are the effect so far their fibres *(aṃśu)* are concerned and the process goes on this way till it rests on atoms. The weight of the effect is inclusive[3] of the weight of its cause in every stage. For instance, the weight of the yarns, which are the effect in respect of their parts, fibre *(aṁśu)* includes the weight of the fibres. Thus the weight of the cloth includes the weight of the yarns and hence the question of additional weight does not arise and the objection has no force.

The objection as to occupying the same space by two entities, i.e the cause and the effect is unfounded, says the Nyāya-Vaiśeṣika. The cause and effect are admitted to be two different entities only because the cognition of the effect differs from that of the cause. In this sense they are two, but they do not occupy two different space. Hence, the question of occupying different space does not arise as they stand related by *samavāya,* says Jayanta.[4] This implies that the difference of the two is more of ontological nature than physical.

All the arguments of the Nyāya-Vaiśeṣika lead to the point that the effect is different from its cause, the whole from its parts and for relating the two *samavāya* is a must.

The Vedantins of all shades of views do not subscribe to the Nyāya-Vaiśeṣika theory of causation and do not admit *samavāya* for relating the effect with the cause or whole with parts.

The example of cloth and the yarns is cited by the Vedantin to explain the relation that exists between Supreme Being and the world. The position is like the existence of the yarns in the cloth as its material cause. If the cloth is to be taken as different from the yarns, the yarns from their fibres, thus where the process will rest? The cloth is the body of the yarns, since they exist as the cloth.[5]

Vallabhācārya objects to the admission of *samavāya* as the relation holding between cause and effect from another point of view. His contention is that if *samavāya* is admitted as the relation holding between cause and effect it pre-supposes pre-existence of the effect in the cause, the acceptance of which negates the doctrine of *asatkāryavāda* (theory of non-existence of effect) of the Nyāya-Vaiśeṣika. The Nyāya-Vaiśeṣika cannot have both cake and loaves, he is either to stick to *asatkāryavāda* and give up *samavāya* or accept *samavāya* at the cost of *asatkāryavāda.*[6]

The Nyāya-Vaiśeṣika asserts that acceptance of *samavāya* does not effect the least the doctrine of *asatkāryavāda. Samavāya* does not pre-suppose the existence of the effect in the cause, because both emergence and occurence of *samavāya* takes place at a time[7] and there is no sequence of time between the two actions. Thus, for the occurence of *samavāya* the effect need not be present in the cause to suggest negation of *asatkāryavāda.* Hence, the above charge is due to the misunderstanding of the functioning of *samavāya.*

The nihilist Buddhist not only refutes *samavāya* but refuses to admit the concept of relation also. He refuses the occurence of any relation and for that matter occurence of *samavāya* between quality and quality, possessor, in the instances, such as 'blue pot'. When we say "blue pot" we mean the blue colour as residing in the pot, it means that the colour is in the nature of the pot and the two terms mean identity. Inherence is not required for the cognition of the blue colour in the pot.

The Nyāya-Vaiśeṣika refutes this criticism by saying that one is qualifier and the other is qualificand and there must always be a relation between the two. To the Nyāya-Vaiśeṣika they are not grammatical subject and predicate, but they are logical and epistemological entities. When we say *"nīlo ghaṭaḥ"* it means *"nīlatva-viśiṣṭa-nīlarūpavān ghaṭatva-viśiṣṭghaṭaḥ"*, i.e. "the pot possessing blueness and potness". This implies a relation between blueness and potness and that is *samavāya.*

The Buddhist does not admit universal as an entity and as such he refutes the existence of *samavāya* for relating universal with individual.

The Buddhist argues—does universal 'cowness' reside in the cow or non-cow? If it resides in the cow (which is already known as a cow) what is the use of postulating universal (cowness), because cow is already there. On the other hand, if it is conceded that 'cowness' resides in the 'non-cow' the horse, elephant etc. that are non-cow, would also be known as cow, which is quite absurd.

The Nyāya-Vaiśeṣika asserts that it is due to the misunderstanding of facts. Uddyotakāra replies to the above objection as follows:

That an entity is neither a cow nor a non-cow before the universal 'cowness' subsists in it. It becomes cow when stands qualified by 'cowness'. Both the notions, cow and non-cow refer to a qualified entity and in order to be a qualified entity the qualifier must be present. Without the qualifier nothing can be cognised as a qualified entity. In the above instance prior to the subsistence of the universal 'cowness' the animal does not exist at all. Nobody can term an entity, which is not in existence, either as cow or non-cow, and whenever it exists, it stands connected with universal 'cowness'.

He draws a similarity to the subsistence of *sattā* (the character of being) i.e. what exists and what does not exist. That the character of being is neither with an already existing thing nor with a non-existing thing, whenever a thing comes into existence it stands connected with the character of the thing. Hence, no one can ask whether it subsists in an already existing thing or non-existing thing.[8]

The Buddhist further raises the objection to the doctrine of universal and says that universal cannot be cognised as a distinct entity and different from particular i.e individual. Universal is supposed to subsist in a number of individuals in the same fashion and same form. The question is, if universal resides in an individual in its entirety, universal being exhausted there, cannot be cognised in other individuals of that class, if it (universal) resides in parts, on where it could exist completely. Thus how one would have the cognition of cow universal in every animal, called cow?[9]

Moreover, existence means maintaining its own nature. An independent entity is not required to depend on other entity for its manifestation. But according to the Nyāya-Vaiśeṣika universal is manifested through the medium of individual. The position is, if universal has its own independent character it needs no medium for its manifestation, on the other hand, if it lacks that character, no medium whatsoever will be of any help for its manifestation.

Universal is not an entity possessing gravitation that it needs a medium for resisting its fall.

If, however, universal is stated to subsist in the individual through the relation of *samavāya* it makes the matter still worse. The assumption of universal is yet to stand the test of logic, and for this bold assumption taking recourse to another assumption is quite absurd. It lands the Nyāya-Vaiśeṣika in an unenviable position similar to that of speaking a chain lies to justify one lie already uttered.

The same way, there is no whole as distinct from the parts, and it is all the more absurd to assume a relation for relating that unproved whole with the parts. That the cloth is in the yarns etc. is due to your own infatuation while the cognition of the people is quite contrary to it.

The Nyāya-Vaiśeṣika replies to the Buddhist objections by saying that the question whether whole resides in the individual partly or wholly is quite unfair. Uddyotakāra points out the unfairness of the question by postulating the followings:

Should we ask: "Does the tree reside in the perceived parts partly or wholly?" And the answer is that the tree is an integrated whole and not a cluster or conglomeration of parts, and resides on its own right. Hence, the answer to the above question will be like this:

(a) some of the parts forming the whole occurs in some parts of the whole, or

(b) some of the whole occurs in some parts. Hence the question is absurd.

(This aspcct has been discussed in some detail under 'Whole and Part').

That universal resides in the individual and manifested on account of being resident there does not lead to the conclusion that universal is non-existent. Our cognition of a thing, say, a cow, as a cow it presupposes the existence of an universal which is common to one and all individuals of the species, and that cognition is at the root for the acceptance of universal. Universal and individual are in an inseparable relational tie, hence the question of manifestation separately does not arise. (That on the question of separate existence of universal from individual the Bhāṭṭa Mīmāṁsaka has followed a middle path i.e. the state of identity-cum-difference between universal and individual, and that the Prābhākara Mīmāṁsaka differs from the Bhāṭṭa and more or less toes the line of the Nyāya-Vaiśeṣika by asserting universal to be different from its locus and perceptible, has been stated in the foregoing chapters).

The Buddhist further attacks the concept of *samavāya* on the ground that it cannot be perceived. The existence of a relation holding between two relata may be admitted if it is perceived. It is not perceived and hence, nobody is obliged to admit it.[10]

The Rāmānuja Vedāntin also joins the issue, of course, from a different angle. Veṅkaṭanātha argues: We do not perceive inherence, the relation that holds between two inseparable correlates, in addition to the nature of the two relata. So it is wrong to hold that inherence is proved by perception.[11]

The Jaina also asserts inherence cannot be perceived. Prabhācandra argues that it is established that when an entity possesses a unique character of its own the entity becomes perceptible on account of that character, such as grossness and magnitude of the pot. Nothing of the sort is associated with inherence. Hence, inherence is not perceptible.

The reply given to this objection by the Naiyāyika differs from that of the Vaiśeṣika. While the Naiyāyika holds that *samavāya* is perceptible the Vaiśeṣika maintains that it can be cognised only by inference (*iha buddhyānumeya*). The onus of refuting the charges levelled against the perceptibility of *samavāya*, therefore, lies with the Naiyāyika who takes up cudgel to demolish the arguments of the oppositions.

He asserts that the qualified cognition of an entity presupposes a relation between two entities and that the said relation is perceived by the perception of the relata of the relation. Thus *samavāya* is perceived like any other relation. The process of perception of *samavāya* is like this: Universal 'cowness' resides in the individual cow by the relation of inherence; the particular cow which is before us is cognised by our sensory organ because there is a sense-object contact. Now by the perception of the cow individual and the cow universal[12] inherence which holds between the two is also perceived. Thus the arguments of the Buddhist and that of the Jaina that inherence is not perceptible as a relation *(sambandha-buddhyā na pratyakṣa)* stand refuted.

According to the Vaiśeṣika *samavāya* is not perceptible because it is beyond the contact of the sense organ, and knowable by inference only.[13] It is beyond the reach of the senses, because the sense-object relation is only of six kinds.[14] That *samavāya* is not perceptible is sought to be established by the following arguments:

That an entity in order to be perceptible must be different from others. Now the question is, where lies this difference? In the property or in the object? If it is said, that it is in the object, then inherence cannot occur with reference to an object which is not present. On the other hand, if it is stated to be in the properties, what are those properties? They are, those, which are affirmed, which are denied, and which are independent of the two. For instance, smell is affirmed of earth and denied to the others. Smell inheres in the earth. There cannot be inherence between the two which are independent of each other. If inherence is assumed to be independent there must be some relation for relating it, which means *ad-infinitum*. Hence it is better to stop at the first inherence.

Praśastapāda points out that though *sattā* (beingness) is also self occurent in the substance, quality and action the position differs from that of *samavāya* so far perceptibility is concerned. While the former is perceptible the latter is known through inference (*iha buddhyānumeya*) only.[15] The reason for this lies in the fact that beingness by its subsistence in substance too occurs in the object of perception, but this cannot be said in respect of *samavāya.*

Śrīdhara further points out the difference between contact and inherence. Though both are relations contact is perceptible on account of perception of its relata as two different entities and contact is caused by both or either of them, but in respect of inherence its two relata are perceived as being one. This position leaves no scope for perception of inherence by the senses.[16]

Bhāsaravajña on the question of perceptibility of *samavāya* makes an attempt to strike a compromise. While enumerating the kind of sense-object relation he says that five kinds of sense-object relation includes absence and inherence also, because the above five is of the qualifier-qualificand nature.[17] But it is to be noted that inherence not always becomes perceptible.[18] Here he differs from Vyomaśiva, who being true to the Vaiśeṣika faith says that the relation is beyond the perception by the senses.[19]

One of the main objections raised by all the opponents to the concept of *samavāya* is, how it is related to its relata? What is *vṛtti* (occurent) of *samavāya* for its subsistence in its relata? In other words, how does it subsist in its relata being related or without being related? If it subsists without being related, then everything can subsist on everything. If it subsists by being related, what is that relation? If by some other relation, that will also need some other relation; if it needs another *samavāya*, it will lead to *regressusad-infinitum.* Moreover, according to you (Nyāya-Vaiśeṣika) *samavāya* is one, there cannot be second of it.[20]

Veṅkaṭanātha following Rāmānuja argues that if inherence, in addition to the nature of the relata is assumed to account for the relation of two inseparably related entities another inherence to be assumed. If, however, inherence is assumed to be related to its relata by dint of its own merit, the two relata may also do so, and substance and attribute, whole and part etc. are mutually related to each other by their own merit.

The Nyāya-Vaiśeṣika by refusing to admit this position would be obliged to admit inherence between cognition and its object, which he does not. Moreover, inherence being a common relation for relating the substance to attributes may also relate cowness to horse, there being no law to restrict the operation of inherence. If on the other hand, the unique character of the inseparably related entities are accepted, which relates each other, this characteristic precludes the possibility of such absurdities. Hence, it is neither necessary nor obligatory to admit *samavāya* in addition to the unique character of such entities which are inseparably related.

The reply given by the Nyāya-Vaiśeṣika to the above charge is simple but bold. He replies that *samavāya* is related to its relata of its own (*sva-vṛtti*) and no other *vṛtti* (occurent) is required for this purpose.[21] This *sva-vṛtti* (self-linking character) of *samavāya* is conceived to riggle out of the criticism, which however, later on developed into a full-fledged relation, named *svarūpa*. This relation is not over and above the two relata i.e. identical with them. Praśastapāda establishes the self-linking character of *samavāya* by comparing it with the subsistence of *sattā* (being) in the first three categories i.e. substance, quality and action, which are admitted as *sattāsamavāyin* (possessed of being). For the subsistence of *sattā* in those three categories there is no other *vṛtti*, because it subsists of it own.[22]

Praśastapāda built up his thesis of self-linking character of *samavāya* on the ground of its imperceptibility. Because unlike *sattā* inherence has no occurent to be perceived by senses.[23] Śrīdhara while asserting self-linking character of *samavāya* explains that being in the nature of occurent (*vṛttyātmaka*) *samavāya* is related to its relata on its own and no other *vṛtti* or relation is required for it. He further points out that though *saṁyoga* is also of occurent nature it is produced (*kṛtaka*), hence needs another relation for its subsistence, but *samavāya* is not produced, it is an eternal (*nitya*) relation.[24] The purport of the statement is this that whatever is produced has a cause behind it and the effect is to subsist on the cause by some *vṛtti*, or, in other words, *saṁyoga* being a product is to be related to the relata through a relation, but *samavāya* has no cause, because it is not produced.

The Nyāya-Vaiśesṣika in order to avoid the defect of *ad infinitum* admits *svarūpa* relation. The assumption of *svarūpa* relation though saved the situation it landed the Nyāya-Vaiśeṣika in a position which needed more defence to protect it.

A relation is different from its two relata (*sambandhidvya-bhinnatve sati*) but the solution of the Nyāya-Vaiśeṣika goes against this traditional concept of relation.[25] However the Nyāya-Vaiśeṣika does not consider this heurastic device as going against the basic concept of relation. Following Nyāya-Vaiśeṣika one may ask—why this solution sounds so odd? Is it like one's being one's own father? Does it amount to climbing upon his own shoulders?

This apparent odd associated with the assumption of *svarūpa* relation lies in the fact that the relation is accepted as universal but the Nyāya-Vaiśeṣika does not accept relation as universal, and hence, there is no contradiction in assuming *svarūpa* relation, which without any other relation is capable to generating qualified cognition.[26] The Nyāya-Vaiśeṣika justifies his assumption of *svarūpa* relation by asserting that though the relation is different from the relata there is no *priori* necessity that the relation should be numerically different from the relata and *svarūpa* is such a relation which is not different from its relata. The real intention is that the first relation (*svarūpa*) is not different from the relata, and on the other hand, is not different from the subsequent relation (*samavāya*), hence, there is no necessity of repeating it.

Like all other relations *svarūpa* relation relates the adjunct to the subjunct but unlike others it also relates itself to the subjunct. This character of *svarūpa* relation saves the Nyāya-Vaiśeṣika from the embarrassment of assuming multiplicity of entities.[27] B.K. Katilal terms this characteristic as—"bypostatics abstraction" and he quotes Manley Thomson—"bypostatics directs our attention but does not presupposes a separation in existence." (*Philosophical Review*, p. 288).

He further explains this position as follows:

"When we say consider his relation to his father", we are not presupposing three separate existing entities, the father, son, and the relation without paying attention to the father or the son as he would in response to "consider the father" or "consider the son".

According to the Nyāya-Vaiśeṣika a property of an entity is the qualifier, which is indicated by an adjective. For the sake of convenience we may call it 'intrinsic'. Such a property can be construed not only to physical entity but of any term, and in fact, it is construed as a separate entity. In this way such a property is construed of the term, which itself is an abstract. This is done by adding the suffix of *tva* or *tā*, and it has become possible due to the genius of Sanskrit language. However, the process may go on reducing the rendering an unintelligible jargon.

It implies that the so called property is to be related to its substantive term by a relation. What is that relation? The assumption of a relation implies another relation and a multiplicity of relation becomes unavoidable. To avoid this the Nyāya-Vaiśeṣika adopts *svarūpa* relation, and this unique device of the system makes it logical that such properties unless they are construed as a *jāti* (universal) which is a separate real, are to be related to their locus by dint of their own right. In other words such intrinsic properties, except *jāti* are related through *svarūpa* relation, and no other relation is required for the purpose. This also enables the Nyāya-Vaiśeṣika to do away with the assumption of such abstract as separate real entities.

The said properties, as we have pointed out in the discussion on relation, are divided into two classes. One is *jāti* (universal) and the other is *upādhi* (imposed property). According to the Nyāya-Vaiśeṣika universal is a category and real and as such ontologically different from its locus i.e. *vyakti* where it is manifested. All such other properties which are not construed as *jāti* are termed as *upādhi* and to be identified with its locus. This function of identification is served by *svarūpa* relation and here lies its difference from *samavāya*. The position may be summed up like this: There are three entities where *samavāya* occurs, namely, two relata inseparably related and the relation (*samavāya*), which is real as the relata are. The said relation relates the relata and the relation itself is related to them through *svarūpa* relation, which has no separate reality from the relata and hence no more relation is needed for relating it to the relata. This is the position in respect of *jāti* for its relation to its locus. However, in case of *upādhi* the position differs; *upādhi* has no independent reality apart from its locus, hence, no other relation occurs between them.

The concept of *svarūpa* relation and its occurence for relating certain abstract entities, though served as a good device it involves some other problems. *Svarūpa* relation seems to hold between *upādhi* and its substantive, *upādhi* having no reality apart from its substantive. But it also holds between *samavāya* and *samavāyin,* both reals. In order to maintain a distinction *samavāya* is stated to be related by its own characteristic (*sva-vṛtti*) while *upādhi* is related by *svarūpa* relation.

In historical perspective two different developments can be noticed in this context. First, in order to defend the concept of universal from the attack of the Buddhist the Nyāya-Vaiśeṣika made an attempt to well define *jāti* and also to reduce its extension i.e. limited the instances of *jāti.* Secondly, some of the late mediaevel writers of Navya-Nyāya headed by Raghunātha Śiromaṇi tried to reshuffle the categories of Kaṇāda, who found it difficult to reconcile acceptance of *samavāya* as a separate category. He also assumed that *samavāya* is not one, but many.[29]

The existence of *samavāya* appears similar to that of absence (*abhāva*)[30] and, therefore, the two are to be discussed to point out the exact nature of them. Occurrence of inherence is criticised on this point by many.

In the instance of occurrence of *samavāya* at the first step we get the permanent relation of inherence and then in the second step when the occurrence of inherence is enquired into, we get *svarūpa* relation. But in the case of absence, particularly in the case of constant absence, which is regarded as permanent, we do not go into for such process and no two relations are involved.

For instance, in the case of "there is no pot on the ground" nobody construe a relation that connects absence to its locus as a separate entity as is done in case "the white cloth" (*śuklaḥ paṭaḥ*) where inherence operates and, which is admitted as a separate entity. In case of absence it is *svarūpa* relation and nothing else.

The question is—why this difference? Why do we not do with *svarūpa* relation alone and thereby omit the concept of *samavāya*? The reply given to this is *lāghava,* i.e. the logic of parsimony.

But on an analysis it seems *lāghava* alone is not behind this difference in approach. First of all, *samavāya* is a relation while *abhāva* is not. Secondly, while the former is a positive entity, *bhāva padārtha*, the latter is a negative one, *abhāva padārtha.*

The thesis of *lāghava* is based on assumption of that *samavāya* being one is the same in all instances of its occurrence, while *svarūpa* being in the nature of its relata is many. The intention is that where two relata are construed as two separate entities having relational tie, it is easy to admit the relation as a separate entity, which occurs in every case.

However, the opponent may argue that the law of parsimony can be invoked in his favour, because he assumes one category less, i.e. *samavāya* from the scheme of categories. However, the Nyāya-Vaiśeṣika asserts that *samavāya* is to be admitted for explaining other doctrines and as such it is better to avoid multiplicity of assumption of *svarūpa* relation in all cases.

Absence (*abhāva*) is a category. The positive property can be treated as occurring in some substantive i.e. locus. The absence of that entity is regarded as a single whole property occurring in that locus. As we have pointed out above that there is a difference between occurring of a positive entity to its locus and that of the negative entity. Thus the occurance of positive entity may take the form of contact, inherence etc. depending upon the nature of the two relata, but occurence of absence in the locus is always the same i.e. *svarūpa.* This *svarūpa* relation is in the nature of *viśeṣaṇatā* (qualifierness). An absence of something is often looked upon as the qualifier of the locus. For instance, "there is no pot on the ground" (*bhūtale ghaṭo nāsti*), the ground is qualified by the absence of the pot (*ghaṭābhāvavad bhūtalam).*

It is thus established that *samavāya* cannot relate absence to its locus, nor *svarūpa* can be a substitute for *samavāya* for relating positive entity to its locus, which are in permanent relational tie.[31] *Svarūpa* (self-linking) relation is nothing over and above the relata and as such an absence may also constitute a self-linking relation. For instance, when we say "there is no pot on the ground" the absence of a particular pot (the pot which is at some other place) holds a self-linking relation with the ground, for the reason that the self-linking relation exists in the form of the relata. In the above instance both the ground and the absence of the pot are present.

This assertion is not correct, says the Nyāya-Vaiśeṣika. The concept of a relation is based on a qualificative knowledge, and hence, 'X' can be said as the self-linking relation if it generates a qualificative knowledge and at the same time it does not come under any relation, which is well defined and with distinct character.

Self-linking relation has got the capability of generating qualificative cognition without the assistance of any other relation. This characteristic distinguishes it from other relations. Gaṅgeśa laid emphasis on this characteristic of the self-linking relation.[32] While commenting on the definition of self-linking relation Jayadeva Miśra points out that the relata of the self-linking relation must be endowed with the capability of generating qualified cognition.[33] The existence of absence in its locus does not fulfil the said requirement.

Though absence exists in its locus through the relation of qualifierness (*viśeṣaṇatā*) and the self-linking relation is also referred to as the relation of qualifierness that does not provide the ground for construing existence of absence as the self-linking relation, because qualifierness is not a definition. All qualifiers are related to the qualificand by some way or other. On the other hand, whatever is related to an entity is not always qualifier of that entity.

Jayanta makes the position clear like this: It is wrong to say that everything related to something is qualifier. When we say the man is with the staff (*daṇḍī puruṣaḥ*), the staff is the qualifier and the man is qualificand and both are related by the relation of contact (*saṁyoga*), but this cannot be said in all cases of contact. For instance, when a person touches the staff by his feet or he carries the same on his head he cannot be described as the staff-holder (*daṇḍin*), therefore every related thing is not the qualifier and thus does not constitute the relation of qualifierness. On the other hand, every qualifier is not a relation.[34]

The Bhāṭṭa holds that the relation that exists between absence and its locus is *vaiśiṣṭya*.

This argument is not valid. If such a relation be admitted in respect of all varieties of absence, then one would cognise the absence of the pot on the ground where the pot exists. *Vaiśiṣṭya* being one, the absence of pot will be cognised by the cognition of absence of cloth, though in fact pot is there. Neither it can be said that the pot itself as the counter-positive of the cognition of the absence of the pot, asserts that there is absence of counter-cognition.

One may say that the relation of *Vaiśiṣṭya* resides in an object, and it is the locus of absence. This locus has the characteristic of causing such cognition that the pot will not be manifested.

This argument is not valid, says the Nyāya-Vaiśeṣika, because, after the removal of the pot, the absence of the pot will be cognised there.

The opponent further argues: According to you inherence is one and eternal, therefore, why after the destruction of colour-there shall not be cognition of colour? The reply is: The destruction of the colour itself causes the cognition of absence of colour.

The Buddhist further attacks *samavāya* that it can neither be one nor permanent. If there were only one inherence in all the three words (*yadyekas-trailokye samavāyaḥ*) then the notion of 'cowness' would also be present in the horse, so also the substancehood in quality. If it is said to be otherwise, *samavāya* would be many like *saṁyoga*.

If it is permanent where does it go when one or both of its relata disappear? Where it subsists when one of the relata is yet to come into existence, for example the effect.

A relation can relate two existent entities and *samavāya* being a relation should conform to this norm. But it is stated that *samavāya* subsists between cause and effect, the effect which is yet to be produced.

The Nyāya-Vaiśeṣika replies that *samavāya* differs from *saṁyoga* by its nature and, therefore, it is not correct to say that *samavāya* is also many. For instance, when contact exists between two entities, does that existence mean a property of the contact or of the effect? Obviously it is a property of the effect and not of the contact. Since there are numerous effects to which this contact belongs, the relationship of contact must apply and hence it is many. If, on the other hand, existence is said to be property of contact, it would need another contact and thus involves the defect of *ad infinitum*. No such things can be said against *samavāya*. The character of *samavāya* explains that it subsists of its own (*tattvaṁ bhāvaḥ*) and, hence, it is one.

That inherence relates things which are yet to be produced is not correct. It relates as soon as it is produced or in other words, the thing is produced being related.

The existence of inherence even when one of the relata or both disappear is like this:

When the relata cease to exist, all that ceases to exist is the circumstances that is responsible for the manifestation (*khyātinimitta*) of inherence, and not inherence itself. Because inherence is not an effect, hence is neither produced nor ceases to exist. It is seen that an effect has a substratum, if inherence is an effect, what is its substratum?

The position is—if inherence were an effect it could only be produced along with that effect which is the relatum. This means that the effect i.e. relatum which is produced would be without a substratum at the moment when it is being produced, because an effect (relatum) can exist in a substratum through inherence, which is yet to be born; if it is said, inherence is produced before the effect comes into existence and it relates the effect as soon as it is produced. The question would be—at that moment where inherence would subsist? Thus it is not an effect and as such is permanent.

The intention of the objection that if inherence belongs to entity which is not present, how could we determine which kind of properties are meant.

Uddyotakāra replies that inherence pertains to that kind of properties, which are denied and not to those which are affirmed or independent. The meaning is that only those things which are not present i.e. that those were in the past and those that will be in future can be denied at the time when inherence appears.

If it is an entity of the past or future how the expression *"ghaṭo bhavati"* can be justified. The expression *"ghaṭo bhavati"* (the pot exists) is synonymous of *"ghaṭo jāyate"* (the pot is being produced). It thus proves that the pot which is being produced is not present, it means that we affirm which is actually not present.

Uddyotakāra retorts that it is not correct. What is meant by the expression *"ghaṭo bhavati"* or for that matter *"ghaṭo jāyate"* stands for "*ghaṭo vidyate*" (the pot is known). When we affirm the existence of the pot, it means the pot is in the process of production, because the pot is constructed of several parts and the word pot stands for them. Since some of the parts of the pot are already there, they are things accomplished and they are responsible for the use of the expression—the pot is in existence (*ghaṭo bhavati*), meaning *ghaṭo vidyate*.

Some of the opponents criticises the concept of *samavāya* that it cannot be *nitya* relation, because its relata are always not permanent.

This objection is not valid, says the Nyāya-Vaiśeṣika. It is a permanent relation in the sense that it relates adjunct to the subjunct in such a way that the adjunct cannot exist without occurring in the subjunct. For instance, 'cowness' can never exist without being related to cow.

It may be further pointed out that in the instance of occurence of inherence the subjunct of inherence continue to exist even when the adjunct is not there or ceases to exist.

For instance, when the cloth is destroyed the yarns exist, or, when the motion of the body stops, the subjunct of the motion i.e. the body remains at rest and without the adjunct. Thus it is evident that the adjunct of *samavāya* cannot continue to be an entity of its own without being related to its subjunct. It is to be noted that the Nyāya-Vaiśeṣika points that subjunct of *samavāya* relation, which is a substance, can conceivably exists even without the adjunct, say, a particular. But the opposite state cannot be conceived. The colour cannot be conceived to be existent without occurring in any locus. In this sense the term *ayutasiddha* and the relation that holds between the two i.e. *samavāya* as *nitya* are to be understood.

Prabhācandra's critique of *samavāya* in his *Prameya-kamala-mārttaṇḍa* has been given briefly in the previous chapter and details in the appendix. His hair-splitting and lengthy argument against the concept of *samavāya* may be summed up as follows:

(a) The notion of inseparably related (*ayutasiddha*) is erroneous; applicable to contact (*saṁyoga*). Contact is a relation, which is related by itself, but at the same time it needs another relation.

All the alternatives suggested by Prabhācandra that inherence is related to its relata through some other agency or other relation are to examined for refutation. The four alternatives put forward by Prabhācandra are:

(a) contact, or
(b) another inherence, or
(c) the qualifierhood, or
(d) unseen (*adṛṣṭa*)

(a) It cannot be contacted, because contact resides in the substance and as such it is a quality; inherence is not a substance, therefore, contact cannot reside there.

(b) Another inherence is also ruled out, because inherence has been accepted as one by you. It is explained by the aphorism of Kaṇāda *"tattvaṁ bhāvena"*.[17]

It is also not the qualifier i.e. to say, inherence cannot be proved on the ground that it is the qualifier of the cognition. The substances are relata of inherence. When two entities are related by some other relation (other than inherence, such as contact, self-linking) then only we may have the qualified cognition. For instance, when we say "the man is with the stuff" there is the contact of the man with the stuff and we may have the qualified cognition. Otherwise everything will be qualifier or the qualificand without discrimination. Moreover, if the qualified cognition is accepted without a relation, then this will make inherence and other relation redundant, because the quality and the quality-possessor will be cognised as such without a relation. Inherence will not be cognised as the qualifier of the inherent.

When we say "these two are in contact" we cognise contacthood of the two. Without the property of contact, the contact will not be the qualifier of the entities which are in contact. It is not cognised that inherence is related to the inherent through some other relation. Moreover, if the qualifierhood of inherence is entirely different from inherence and the inherent, then what will be the exacting factor? If it is said that inherence will do this, then it will be a case of mutual dependence. When the exacting nature of inherence is established, then only the exacting nature of the qualifier can be cognised. Again, on the assumption that the qualifier possesses the exacting nature, the exacting nature of inherence is cognised. Thus one depends on the other. Moreover, this is to be first ascertained whether this qualifying nature of inherence is a separate category in addition to the accepted six, or is identical with one of them?

If the answer is, it is an additional one, the question arises, whether it is a positive entity or a negative one? It cannot be a positive entity, because acceptance of this as a positive entity in addition to the six will contradict the established principle of that school, "the categories are only six" (*ṣaḍeva padārthāḥ*).

Neither it can be accepted as a negative entity, because nothing of the sort is admitted. If preferring the second alternative it is presumed as identical with the said six, categories, may we ask, of the six with which one it is identified? It cannot be a substance for the simple reason that quality does not reside in it. For that matter it is not a quality also, because the quality resides on the substance. It can neither be an action it will not reside in action, because the rule is "the action does not reside in action" (*akarma karma*).

It cannot be included in the category of universal, because universals reside only in three categories, namely, substance, quality and action, whereas inherence reside in universal also.

It also cannot be identified with particular (*viśeṣa*). The particular resides in the eternal entities, but this qualifyinghood (*viśeṣaṇabhāva*) is found to be present in the non-eternal entities also. Moreover, if it is taken to be as a particular, then its absence in inherence (*samavāya*) will be obvious. Again, when this becomes a qualifier of many inherents (*samavāyin*) at a time, inherence shall have to be accepted as many.

The qualifying nature of inherence is the qualifier of many objects at one and the same time, hence inherence is bound to be many, like the staff and the earrings in respect of a person, there it is many. ("The man is staff-holder", "the man is with earrings" in such cases the contact of the staff is different from that of the earrings, and hence the contact is manifold).

From the above argument it is proved that inherence cannot be related to its relata through its qualifying nature.

Inherence is not related through the unseen (*adṛṣṭa*), because *adṛṣṭa* cannot be a relation. This has been admitted by you also.

Adṛṣṭa is self-occurrence (*ātmavṛtti*) without residing in inherence and inherent, how it can reside in two entities? Moreover, this will contradict the accepted principle that relation takes place in six different ways (*ṣodhā sambandha-vāditva*). This will be in addition to the six.

If, however, it is said that inherence is related through *adṛṣṭa,* then let the quality with the quality-possessor be related through *adṛṣṭa,* what is the compelling necessity for assuming inherence?

Moreover, there is another objection to this: *Adṛṣṭa* itself without being related to inherence cannot be the reason for the relation of inherence with its relata. If it is assumed that an unrelated thing relates, then everything can relate everything.

On the other hand, if you say that *adṛṣṭa* is related to inherence, may we ask, through which relation and how? If *adṛṣṭa* is related to inherence through inherence, then this will involve mutual dependence. When inherence is proved, then only the relation of *adṛṣṭa* with inherence can be asserted. Again, when this is proved then only the related *adṛṣṭa* may serve as the reason for the relation of inherence with its relata.

If on the other hand, it is said that inherence is related to its relata by some other relation, that will destroy the entire edifice of inherence that it is related to its relata of its own. Thus it is established that inherence is in no way related to its relata. It also cannot be said that inherence exists without being related. Presumption of this will contradict the principle laid down that the six categories possess dependence (*ṣaṇṇāmāśritatvam*).

If inherence is not related how can it possess the character of a relation, which is altogether a different entity.

If may be due to the cognition of the relation. If it is so, Lord Maheśvara may also generate the cognition of the relation.

Inherence without being related how it can be the cause for the cognition of the relation of the two relata? The contact of two fingers, which is different from the cloth and the pot does not serve as the cause for the cognition of a relation between them. The following inference will be contradicted if, the relating faculty of unrelated entities is admitted. The cognition of the relation in the instance such as, "the knowledge is in this self" is not the cognition of such relation which is not related to its relata, because it is a cognition of the relation, like the cognition of the relation of the staff with the person.

Moreover, the question is: Whether the proposed inherence is supposed to exist between two inherents or non-inherents? If you say that inherence exists between two non-inherents then inherence will occur between the cloth and the pot. If on the other hand, inherence exists between two inherents, on what basis they are termed as inherent? For the existence of inherence or on their own. If it is due to inherence, then this will lead to mutual dependence. After inherence is proved, the relata can be termed as inherents, and when they become inherents, the relation that exists between them can be called inherence.

Now the question arises—whether inherencehood of inherence is identical or different with its relata? It cannot be identical, because assumption of that will involve the ether as inherence. For instance, the ether and the sound are related by inherence, thus, if the said inherence is not taken as different from the other and the sound, they too should have been regarded as inherence. On the other hand, if you say that it is different, in that case, the two inherents will not be involved in inherence. Assumption of another relation for the subsistence of inherence will lead to the *regressus ad infinitum*.

If the existence of inherence is due to the inherents that will be the case of mutual dependence. When it is proved that the inherents have the character of inherence, the inherence is proved; and on account of the existence of inherence, the relata are termed as having the character of inherence. If you say the inherents (relata) are on their own have the character of inherence, what is the necessity of assuming inherence?

It cannot be said that all these objections are there in respect of contact *(saṁyoga)* also, because without accepting the entity which emerges as a result of contact, the occurence of contact is not possible. If, however, it is said that contact occurs through the agency of another contact, the aforesaid objections can be levelled against it.

What is stated that the qualityhood etc. are different from the entities, which are being connected *(saṁyogidravya),* and as such is a separate entity, is not correct.

The question may be asked:

Whether the quality to be taken as the superstratum because (i) it is very insignificant, or (ii) due to the action of the quality-possessor, or (iii) simply for the reason that it appears as the superstratum?

The first alternative is not possible, because that will make universal, which is of the great magnitude, is a non-superstratum. For that matter, the second alternative is also not possible. The third alternative is only apparently good, because, it is advanced without analysing its nature. The quality etc. does not appear, as a rule, as the superstratum. For instance, the colour in a pot is cognised as subsisting in and out of the pot. In the instance of can and curd the superstratum i.e. the curd is not cognised as existing outside the can.

You may say that though the colour etc. is superstratum, the relation between the colour and the pot is not a separable one. The absence of separable relation is the cause for the non-appearance of the colour as residing in the pot.

This has no justification, says Prabhācandra. The separable relation is not the cause of the cognition of an entity as subsisting on the top of the other. Otherwise, two standing bamboo poles which are separably related, so also the water and the milk, which though mixed, can be separated, will have to be cognised as superstratum and being on the top of the other.

Thus Prabhācandra has dealt a slashing blow to the Vaiśeṣika concept of *samavāya* as a distinct relation:

(a) The relation that holds between the yarns and the cloth is self-same *(tādātmya);*
(b) That *samavāya* does not conform the norms of relation;
(c) That *samavāya* is not perceptible;
(d) That the inference for the cognition of *samavāya* is defective;
(e) That *samavāya* like *saṃyoga* is many and cannot be one;
(f) That *samavāya* cannot subsist on its own;

(g) That subsistence of *samavāya* cannot be termed as the state of qualifier-qualificandness, because that cannot be a category in addition to accepted six.

All the above mentioned points have been discussed and the replies of the Nyāya-Vaiśeṣika are put, which seem hardly necessary to repeat here. The objections as to the various defects of the inference, such as the deviation of the reason *(anaikāntika hetu)* ineffectiveness of the probandum *(sādhya-vikalatā)* need not be refuted one by one, because all these have been dealt with in the *Tattvacintāmaṇi* by Gaṅgeśa, which are reproduced in the the chapter "Concept and Definition". It will be seen that Gaṅgeśa refuted all the criticism relating to the inference of *samavāya* and provided the correct inference.

Samavāya is a unique concept of the Nyāya-Vaiśeṣika, which is criticised by all other schools of Indian Philosophy. Only the Prābhākara school of Pūrva-Mīmāṁsā admits *samavāya* , but the concept of *samavāya* of the Prābhākara school differs from that of the Nyāya-Vaiśeṣika in many respects.[35]

First, the Prābhākara holds that *samavāya* is both eternal, produced and unproduced. When *samavāya* holds between two eternal entities, it is eternal and that which holds between entities either of the two or both of them are non-eternal, is non-eternal. When an individual is destroyed, the relation of *samavāya*, that holds between individual and universal, is also destroyed. In other words, it subsists on perishable things also and, therefore, non-eternal.

It is produced and un-produced depending upon the condition of its occurence. It is not one, but as many as there are entities on which it subsists.

This position is not acceptable to the Nyāya-Vaiśeṣika, who holds that *samavāya* is eternal and hence is one, if it is held as non-eternal i.e. caused, the question of its occurence and many other complicacies would arise, which will negate the very peculiar nature of *samavāya*.

Veṅkaṭanātha while opposing the Nyāya-Vaiśeṣika concept of *samavāya* points out the incongruity if it is to be held as non-eternal i.e. produced. That a non-eternal relation between two inseparably related entities is brought about by their own nature, and that is not *samavāya*. He further asks–if *samavāya* is non-eternal, when it is produced? Before or after the production of the effect or simultaneously with it? Neither of the three alternatives is admissible for the obvious reason. He says that according to the Nyāya-Vaiśeṣika a substance, say a pot, is produced at the first moment of its existence, and quality is produced at the second moment *(utpannam dravyam kṣaṇam aguṇam... tiṣṭhati).* Thus both are related by their own nature. So the assumption of a non-eternal (caused) *samavāya*, in addition to the nature of the relata, is unwarrnted.[36] Anticipating such criticism the Nyāya-Vaiśeṣika holds that *samavāya* is eternal and on account of it it is one.

The Prābhākara further asserts that *samavāya* is perceptible and non-perceptible in accordance with the nature of things on which it subsists. Thus the Prābhākara's concept of *samavāya* is some-what different from that of the Nyāya-Vaiśeṣika.[37] It is evident that if *samavāya* is admitted by the Nyāya-Vaiśeṣika for explaining the theory of causality, *svarūpa* relation is adopted as a device to explain any unanalyzable entity.[38]

Notes and Referrences

1. *te eva tantavaḥ saṁsthāna-viśeṣasthitāḥ paṭākhyām labhante ityapaṭākhyās-tantavaḥ paṭaśabdena abhidhīyante ityuktam bhavati etacca viruddham mukhyāsambhavāt. nahi tantūnām apaṭānāṁ paṭena kiñcit sāmānyam asti. nahi asati sāmānye mithyāpratyayasya bījam asti* —NV., 2.1.33.
2. *yathā ekapalikasya svastikasya yo gurutva-kāryaḥ avanativiśeṣaḥ, adhikaḥ. na ca tat tantu-gurutva-kāryāt paṭagurutvasya kāryāntaram dṛśyate tasmād abhinnaḥ tantubhyaḥ paṭaḥ.* —STK., 9, p. 67.
3. *yad idam bhavatā manyate dvipalam dvipalam pañca palam iti nātra kārya-kāraṇa-gurutve avadhāryate kintu-ācaramād ā ca paramāṇor dravya-samāhāra umīyate.* —NV., p. 494.
   dravya-samāhāra iti kārya-kāraṇa-dravya-samāhāraḥ mṛtkaṇā-śarkarā-kapāla-kumbha-samāhāra ityarthaḥ. —NVTT., p. 494.
4. *pratītibhedād bhedo'sti deśabhedeastu neṣyate /*
   tenātra kalpyate vṛttiḥ samavāyaḥ sa ucyate //
   avayava-avayavinor guṇaguṇinoścāyameva vṛttir arthāntaratvam deśabhedaśca tayor nāstīti vispaṣṭam ayutasiddhatvāt. —NM.
5. *tantuḥ paṭe sthito yāvad upādānatayā tathā /*
   sarvopādāna-rūpatvāt sarvatnāyamavasthitih //

paṭādapyantaraṁ tantus-tanturapyaṁśurantaraḥ /
āntaratvasya viśrāntir yatrāsau anumīyatām // —Pa D., v.165-66

6. The identity of cause and effect is supported from the *Bhāgavata:*
kāryakāraṇa-bhāvas-tvaika-darśanam paṭa-tantuvat
avastutvād-vikalpasya bhāvādvaitvam taducyate. —Bha., 7
7. *Jātah sambandha-śa eti ekaḥ kālaḥ.* —NV
8. NV., 11.2.66
9. *piṇḍe sāmānyam anyatra yadi kārtasnena vartate /*
tatraivāsya samāptatvāt na syāt piṇḍāntare grahaḥ.//
ekadeśena vṛttau tu gotvajātir na kutracit/
samagrā' stīti go buddhiḥ pratipiṇḍaṁ katham bhavetṁ. —NM., p. 272
10. "*samavāyāgrahād akṣaiḥ sambandhādarśanaṁ sthitam.* —PV.,v. 148
Commenting on the above passage Manorathanandin says:
"*samavāyasya atīndriyasya agrahād akṣaiḥ akṣabhavaiḥ vijñāir jāti tadvatoḥ sambandhasya aviśiṣṭapratītyādarśanam sthitam niścitam, yadbalena yatpratītis tadabhāve na yuktā sā.*" —Ibid.
11. *apṛthak-siddhayoḥ samavāyākhyam svarūpādadhikam kalpyamānam sambandham na pratyakṣāmaḥ.* —SAS., p. 711
12. That universal is perceptible is testified by the Prābhākara:
jātirāśrayato bhinnā pratyakṣa-jñāna-gocarā. —PP.
13. The stand taken by the Vaiśeṣika that *samavāya* is not perceptible is due to the desire to meet the objection that "*samavāya* is perceptible yet without its own place of origin." That perceptibility is not concomitant with the heterogenous class of objects.
14. Praśastapāda states six kinds of sense-object relation. These are:
(I) *Saṁyoga* (contact), as in the case of the perception of a pot. The pot possessing quality is an object, and the visual organ is an object, the connection between the two is contact.
(II) *Saṁyukta-samavāya* (inherence in that which is in contact) as in the case of contact of the visual organ with the colour of the pot. The colour inheres in the pot which is in contact with the sense organ.
(III) *Saṁyukta-samaveta-samavāya* (inherence in the inherent which is in contact) as in the case of perception of 'blueness' of the blue colour which inheres in the pot, which is in contact.
(IV) *Samavāya* (inherence) as in the case of perception of the sound by the ear. The sound is the quality of the ether (*ākāśe śabda-saṁkhyādayaḥ)* and inheres in the ether. The earhole is also ether *(ākāśā)* hence its perception is on account of inherence.
(V) *Samaveta-samavāya* (inherent inherence) as in the case of the perception of universal of quality in 'soundness' in this case. This is perceived independently of the substance. Universal of sound inheres in the sound which inheres in the 'sky' of auditory organ.
(VI) *Viśeṣaṇa-viśeṣyabhāva* (qualifier-qualificandness) as in the case of

perception of absence of the pot on the ground. The visual sense organ is in contact with the ground, which is qualified by the absence *(abhāva)* of the pot.

15. *yathā sattādīnām prātyakṣeṣu artheṣu vṛttirasti tena te saṁyukta-samavāyād indrīyeṣu gṛhyante, naivam samavāyasya vṛttisambhavaḥ.* —PPBh. Faddegon compares the Vaiśeṣika concept of inherence with the reflective relation as classified by Sigwart, Windalband and others. The reason for this comparison lies in the fact that it is inferable *(iha buddhyanumeya)*. However, the comparison of inherence with the mid-dependent relation is not sound.
16. *yathā indriyeṇa saṁyoga-pratibhāso naivam samavāya-pratibhāsḥ sambandhinoḥ piṇḍībhāvenopalambhāt ataḥ apratyakṣaḥ.*
parasparopa-saṁśleṣo bhinnānām yat kṛto bhavet
samavāyah sa vijñeyaḥ svātantrya-pratirodhakaḥ. —NKa., p. 785
17. *etacca pañcavidha-sambandha-sambaddha-viśeṣaṇa-viśeṣya-bhāvād dṛṣyābhāva-samavāyor grahaṇam.* —NSa., p. 167
18. *samavāyasya tu kvacideva grahaṇam, yathā rūpa-samavāyavān ghaṭah, ghaṭe rūpasamavāyaḥ.* —Ibid.
19. *adṛṣṭa-viśeṣa eva sambandhas-tasyātīndriyatvāt."* —VV.
20. This nature of criticism of *samavāya* and for that matter of the Nyāya-Vaiśeṣika concept of relation is similar to the criticism of Bradley. —Ap. R., pp. 16-17.
21. *na punaḥ samavayāsya samavāyo' sti iha samavāya iti na syāt.* —NV., 2.1.33
22. *yathā dravya-guṇa-karmaṇām sadātmakasya bhāvasya nānyaḥ sattāyogo' sti evam avibhāgino vṛttyātamakasya samavāyasya nānyā vṛttirasti, tasmāt svātmavṛttiḥ.* —PPBh., pp. 784-85
23. *ata eva atīndriyaḥ, sattādīnāmiva pratyakṣeṣu vṛttyabhāvāt, svātma-saṁvedana-bhāvācca tasmād iha-buddhyanunayaḥ samavāyaḥ."* —Ibid.
24. *kṛtako hi saṁyogaḥ tasya vṛttyātmakasayāpi vṛttyantaramasti, kāraṇa-samavāyasya kārya-lakṣaṇatvāt. samavāyasya vṛttyantaram nāsti tasmādasya svātmanā svarūpeṇaiva vṛttiḥ na vṛttynatareṇa.* —NK., pp. 784-85
25. *ata eva sambandhasya sambandhi-bhinna-niyamatvena svarūpa-sambandham pare dūṣayanti.* —*Tattva-cintāmaṇi-āloka*, p. 715
26. —TC., p. 713
27. *Navya-Nyāya Doctrine of Negati on.*
28. *na ca jale gandha-nirūpitatva-viśiṣṭa-samavāyābhāvān na gandhavattā pratītiriti vācyam. viśiṣṭasya atiriktatvābhāvena jale 'pi tat sattvāt tathāvidha-viśiṣṭa-nirūpitādhikaraṇatayā atiriktatve kim aparāddham vibhinna-samavāyaih.* —PTN., p. 71
29. *taiḥ saha abhāvasya samavayāsya viśeṣaṇa-viśeṣya-bhāva ṣaṣṭhaḥ sambandhaḥ."* —NBS., p. 167

30. B.K. Matilal is of opinion that with the acceptance of *svarūpa* as a relation the position of *samavāya* becomes somewhat shaky. He thinks it is due to the influence of the Vedānta concept of idealism.
31. *sambandham antareṇa viśiṣṭa-pratyaya-janana-jogyatvasya svarūpa-sambandhatvāt* —TC., p. 713
32. *viśiṣṭa-pratyaya-janana-jogyatā-liṅgita-svarūpasya sambandhatvāt.* —TCA., p. 714
33. *nahyevam bhavati yat sambandham tad viśeṣaṇam, pādapīḍite śirasi dhārymāṇe vā daṇḍe daṇḍīti-pratyayānutpādāt.* —NM., p. 60
34. VS., 7.2.28
35. That acceptance of *samavāya* is one, among others, where the Bhāṭṭa school of Pūrva-Mīmāṁsā differs from that of the Prābhākara. The Bhāṭṭa enumerates those subjects on which the views of the Prābhākara are to be refuted.

    samavāyasya sāstitā ...

    Prābhākarā nirākāryā Bhāṭṭa-mārgānusāriṇā.
36. *gotvādi tattad-vastu-svabhāvād eva anyonya-niyame madhye samavāya-kliptir niṣphalā ityarthaḥ.* —SAS, p. 712
37. It is of interest to note that some of the views of the Prābhākara on *samavāya* found acceptance by the late mediaeval writers of the Navya-Nyāya, such as Raghunātha Śiromaṇi and others, who hold that *samavāya* is many. On the question of perceptibility of *samavāya*, the Prābhākara accommodates both the opposing views i.e. it is perceptible as held by the Naiyāyika, and knowable only by inference as held by the Vaiśeṣika, and avoids the debate. However, the views, of the Prābhākara that *samavāya* is non-eternal are not acceptable to none of the Nyāya-Vaiśesika school.
38. "... the Nyāya-Vaiśeṣika were forced to explain any irreducible, unanalyzable concept they come across as a *svarūpa* relation in order to avoid further hypothesis of relation." —NDN., p. 68

Chapter 8

Conclusion

The Importance of Samavāya

The importance of *samavāya* in explaining the world order as conceived by the Nyāya-Vaiśeṣika has been shown in the previous chapters while discussing the reality of the external world, the causation theory etc. The importance of *samavāya* has been aptly described by Bodas when he terms it as "the corner stone" of the Nyāya-Vaiśeṣika system of philosophy.

The system is known for its unique theory of causation on which the original concept of *samavāya* rests. That the effect is non-existent in its material cause but originates a new in it and thus is quite different from the cause but resides side by side along with it. The doctrine of origination *(ārambhavāda)* and the doctrine of manifestation of non-existent *(asatkhyātivāda)* are intimately linked with the causation theory. The cause and the effect so also the part and the whole are two distinct entities but being locked in inseparable relation of *samavāya* the two appear as an integrated one. Without the operation of *samavāya* the cause and effect would have been cognised as disintegrated entities, or, in the alternative they would have been admitted as identical.

If we go to the crux of the problem i.e. the theory of reality based on the desecrate ultimate particles which are real and innumerable the importance of *samavāya* in presenting those desecrate particles in the form of gross element can be understood.

The Nyāya-Vaiśeṣika is not only realist but pluralist too. As against the realist Sāṁkhya, to whom only *prakṛti* and *puruṣa* are eternal, the Nyāya-Vaiśeṣika admits innumerable atoms of different categories. These atoms are the material cause of the universe but themselves are not the universe. The universe, which originates in them, and not by them, is the result of the process of combination, which though a separate entity remains integrated with the cause due to *samavāya* . It is why *samavāya* , a relation, has been conceived as one of the six categories. "The Vaiśeṣika philosophy of reals based on the theory of atoms. According to this theory the effect is entirely different from the productive materials. It is immaterial whether effect produced is a substance or a quality or an action, in all cases it is a new thing altogether and distinct from the substance from which it arises. This view is the necessary corollary of *asatkāryavāda*. That the effect is found to inhere, so long it continues in the existence in its material cause and is not capable of separation from it, simply proves that there is an internal relation between the two and not that the two are identical."[1]

The idealist Vedantin admits only Brahma as the Ultimate Truth, the real and eternal, the world of our experience appears as real due to the erroneous cognition *(mithyā pratyaya)*. The objective world has no reality in the sense of the term that is applied to Ultimate Truth and has no separate existence of its own. Since the objective world has no separate identity and existence in the ultimate analysis there cannot exist a relation between the two which are identical. The apparently existent world resides in Brahma by its own nature.

The Nyāya-Vaiśeṣika cannot accept this position and to defend his theory of realism takes recourses to *samavāya* . In fact, the realism of the system and for that matter the world order can be explained only with the help of *samavāya* . The nihilist Buddhist holds that there is no whole as separate from the parts and there is no cause-effect relation between two entities, which are conceptual. With the rejection of distinct entity of *avayavī* the concept of *samavāya* as relating *avayava* and *avayavi*, into an integrated one stands rejected. In fact, with the refutation of *samavāya* by the Buddhists the architrave of the structure the universe as a whole as developed and established by the Nyāya-Vaiśeṣika tumbles down. The denial of which, the very concept of *dravya* as an agent entity round which all other categories–quality, activity, universal revolve or rather inhere in—is negated. Since without any relation of quality, activity and universal with their corresponding sustenance *(dravya)* which is their locus, the substance will be a misnomer and such categories as quality and activity etc. would have no locus to stand upon, hence the concept of *samavāya* is an inherent concept running through most of the categories and making them useful for our practical behaviours. Hence, to the Nyāya-Vaiśeṣika a logical explanation of the structure of the universe is rooted on the admission of *samavāya* as a distance relation and also a distinct unity because the universe to him is not an unqualified absolute unitary something but a related whole, a super structure or, more precisely, a systematic combination of diverse elements.

On the other hand, to the Buddhist every substance in the external world is momentary in nature and is self-evident *(sva-lakṣaṇa)* and the elements cannot combine since they are destroyed in the second moment of their production. Moreover, every eternal object is nothing but the cognition of mental imagination and hence acceptance of *samavāya* would be the very negation of their doctrine and lead to the acceptance of reality of objects.[2] It has been pointed out in the foregoing chapters that *samavāya* is a unique concept of the Nyāya-Vaiśeṣika, which is the key for the other theories such as *asatkāryavāda*, causation etc. and thus its importance lies in both ontological and epistemological aspects of the Nyāya-Vaiśeṣika philosophy. In short, *samavāya* has the same importance to Nyāya-Vaiśeṣika system of philosophy which the soul enjoys in the functioning of the body.

Notes and References

1. *M.M. Gopinath Kaviraj.* —*Sarasvatībhavana studies.*
2. *ekasya vṛttau sarvasya vṛttiḥ syādanāvṛttau dṛśyate rakte caikasmin rāgo' raktasya vā gatiḥ.* —PV., 2185-6

Appendix

The Jaina Critique of Samavāya

The Nyāya-Vaiśeṣika concept and the definition of *samavāya* have been severely criticised and refuted by the Jaina school of philosophy. Akalaṅka and Māṇikyanandin, the two pioneers of the school, have touched the subject in their works, but it is Prabhācandra, who in his *Prameya-kamala-Mārtaṇḍa*, the commentary on the *Nyāmukha-parīkṣā*, has dealt with the subject in great detail. Prabhācandra criticises the concept of *samavāya* and rejects it on the following grounds:

There is no perfect definition of *samavāya* and no valid proof, perception or inference, for the cognition of *samavāya*. The concept of *ayutasiddha* is erroneous and the cognition of "this is here" *(ihedam pratyeyam)* is a fallacious reason and thus it does not prove *samavāya*. The inference cited for proving *samavāya* is only the inference in absence *(vyatirekānumāna)* and in the absence of positive inference *(anvayānumāna) samavāya* can not be proved.

Samavāya is many and for its subsistence it needs another relation which leads to *regressus ad infinitum*. The relation which exists between the quality and the substance etc. is the self-linking relation *(tādātmya)* which does not require another relation for its existence. *Samavāya* is stated to be one of the six categories by the Vaiśeṣika, while the Naiyāyika admits sixteen. Moreover, there are another two categories—*pramāṇa* and *prameya;* therefore the assertion that *ṣaḍeva padārthāḥ* is not correct and *samavāya* stands rejected. Prabhācandra in order to reject, refute and demolish the concept of *samavāya* first quotes the definition of *samavāya* from Praśastapāda and meets the initial objections. He then examines the import of the term "inseparability" and the qualification "this is here" and "container-contained" relationship and justifies them only to refute them later on.

The objection to condition "this is here" *(ihedam)* is like this. In the instances, such as "trees are in the village" *(iha grame vṛkṣāḥ),* "birds are in the sky" *(iha ākāśe śakuniḥ)* also fulfil the requirement of the condition "this is here" and the definition will over-pervade these and other similar instances, which obviously are not the ground for *samavāya.* But it is shown that these will not be included in the provision of "this is here". Similarly, the provision of "*ayuta-siddha*" will exclude the instances such as "the berries are in the basket". To make out distinction he definies "*yutasiddha*" as the concept of having (a) separate substratum-super-stratumhood and also having (b) separate movement.[1]

Again, the concept of *vācy-vācaka-bhāva* (denotor-denotedship)[2] and that of *viṣaya-viṣayibhāva* (the subject-object relation of the knowledge) in the instances, such as "this is ether and this is the word ether *(ākāśa)* which denotes it", and "I know" or "the knowledge is in this self" cannot be cited to show the over-pervasion of the above definition. Because the relation which exists in such instances is covered by the concept of existence of the things which are separable.

The question arises if the provision of inseparable existence of the two relata serves the purpose of *samavāya,* why the provision of container-contained state of the relata is made obligatory to the definition? The intention, says Prabhācandra, may be to exclude the possibility of colour, small, etc. of being taken as mutually related through *samavāya,* although they reside in the same substratum *(āśraya).*[3] Because neither the colour nor the smell is container or contained of the either.

Therefore, it stands that the threads and the cloth, the quality and the quality-possessor are not the case of the relation of contact; because there is the inevitable concept of inseparable state and the container-containedhood and the instances are quite contrary to the instance of "the berries are in the basket".

Now *samavāya* must be distinguished from *saṁyoga.* There are two things which can be pointed out in this respect.

Samavāya is perceptible, because we cognise a piece of cloth as being related to the threads and the colour of the cloth in relation to the cloth. When remain unrelated, cannot be perceived as one.[4]

Samavāya can also be inferred. The inference is like this: the cognition of the relation that "the cloth is in the yarns" is like the cognition of "the barries are in the basket."

The cognition is neither without any reason, nor based on the cloth or the yarns. Again, the reason of such cognition cannot be said to be due to *vāsanā* (the present consciousness of the past perception or the latent impression) because it will lead to *ad infinitum.* Similarly it is also not based on the relation of identity or the relation of *saṁyoga.* It is simply based on a relation which is, later on, reduced to *samavāya.* Prabhācandra then quotes another definition of *samavāya* (discussed by Śrīdhara and Vādivāgiśvara) and meets the initial objection to the definitions.

Samavāya has been distinguished from *saṁyoga* on the ground that *saṁyoga* is many while *samavāya* is one. If it is presumed that inherence differs as the relata differ, there will not be consistent cognition of inherence, because inherenceness does not inhere in inherence. But contacthood can inhere in contact.

Further, no objection can be raised that inherence of substancehood on substance will create the cognition of qualityhood also, since inherence is one. Though inherence is one the power of container will restrict it to the substance or quality as the case may be.

The objection raised as to the fact that if the two relata of inherence do not exist before the relation takes place, there cannot be an inherence, because if the relata do not exist how there can be a relation. If on the other hand, it is persumed that they do exist, then the relation obtaining between them would be contact and not an inherence.[5] Again if the statement is this that inherence without being related to its relata unites them, such a cognition would be impractical; on the other hand if the assertion is this that inherence being related to its relata does relate them—the apparent question is—how does inherence exist in its relata? By itself or through some other agency? If the first alternative is admitted, that will overpervade contact, and if the second is accepted that will lead to *ad infinitum (anavasthā).*

Secondly, one which checks the movement of an object is called container *(ādhāra),* such as the pot in respect of water.[6] Consequently the thing they contain must have activity. But as quality have no activity obviously it cannot be the thing contained.

Thirdly, there cannot be an inherence between two entities having the same character, because in that case the entities will be one[7] and for a relation two entities are required.

Forthly, when one of the relata is not dependent on the other, there cannot be container-containedhood of the entities which are non-existent, on the other hand, if they exist on their own, the question of one being dependent on the other does not arise at all.[8]

Such objections are not valid, because inherence does not exist either between two existent entities or between two non-existent entities. They themselves are the cause of their being existent *(svakāraṇa-sattā-sambandhasyaiva niṣpattirūpatvāt).* The existence of the relata as being not different from the subsistence of inherence in them, hence there is no sequence of time between the two.[9] Thus the objection of identity *(rūpasaṁśleṣa)* and dependence *(pāratantrya)* has been met.

The question of inherence being related to its relata through another inherence does not arise. Such a proposition would lead to *ad infinitum.* Moreover, inherence is different from contact, hence the analogy does not apply. The relation between inherence and its relata is just like the relation which exists between fire and the heat. Thus the objection of dependence is not valid. That the quality *(rūpa)* resides in a substance, and as such is dependent on the existence of the substance no more holds good, because the cause of the residence of quality in the substance is the quality itself and nothing else.

Subsistence of inherence in the relata through some other relation cannot be brought in. It has been pointed out that acceptance of that position that "*samavāya* is related to its relata through some other relation" leads to *ad infinitum.* We do not cognise some other contact in the case of contact, similarly inherence also cannot be related to its relata through another inherence. As the hotness of the fire is related to fire by dint of its nature, similarly inherence is also related to its relata without the agency of other. But contact cannot be said to be related in this way, it requires some other relation.

The statement that in order to be a thing contained it must possess movement is not correct. Though quality lacks action, the substance, on which quality rests is full of action. The substance having action quality is also deemed to have possessed the same and they can be cognised as container and contained.

Thus stating the view of the Vaiśeṣikas on inherence Prabhācandra proceeds to refute, reject and demolish the entire edifice of arguments piece by piece. The summary of his forceful and detailed arguments is given below.

In the Vaiśeṣika Śāstra *samavāya* has been defined as inseparable relation *(ayutasiddha)*, says Prabhācandra. He asks what is this inseparableness?

(a) Has it been defined in the scriptures? or,
(b) Is it a matter of practical experience?

The first alternative is simply impossible because the inseparableness of the yarns and the cloth cannot be the subject-matter of definition in the scriptures.

So far the second alternative is concerned, inseparableness* *(ayutasiddhatva)* has been defined in the Vaiśeṣika Śāstra as the existence of entities having no separate locus *(apṛthagāśraya-vṛttitvam ayutasiddhatvam)*. But such a state of affairs is conspicuously absent in the above instance. While the yarns exist in their parts, the cloth subsists in the yarns, hence, the loci of the yarns and the cloth are different. In the same way, it will be seen that quality, activity and the universal have their locus which is different from the respective locus of their container *(ādhāra)*.

If it is, however, said that inseparableness, according to the conventional practice, is meant to be in the same container *(ekabhājanatva)* then the milk and the water, which are separable entities, will also be covered by the above definition, because they are seen to exist in the same container. A distinction is sought to be made that where the two relata of a relation have three aspects there lies the inseparable relation *(ayutasiddha)* and in case, the two relata have four aspects, the separable relation *(yutasiddha)* is there.

For instance, "the curd is in the can" *(kuṇḍe dadhi)*, the curd and the can are two separate entities and each of the two has got its separate parts *(avayava)*. And those parts of the curd and the can have got their respective parts *(avayava)*. Thus, the curd *(avayavin)* resides in its parts, and those parts in their respective parts. The parts of the curd is the locus of the curd and those parts reside in their own loci. Similarly, the can *(avayavin)* resides in its parts *(avayava)* which are its locus, and those parts reside in their parts. In this way, the two relata of the above-said relation have four aspects (the locus of the curd and the locus of the parts of the curd = two aspects; the locus of the can and the locus of the parts of the can = two aspects). The curd and the can have their respective loci and these loci have their loci. But in the instance of "the cloth is in the yarns" there are only three aspects, the parts of the yarns, the yarns and the cloth. The yarns become the things contained so far as they are related to the parts of the yarns, and also serve as the thing container so far as they are related to the cloth. In other words, the instance of, "the cloth is in the yarns", which is cited as a case of *ayutasiddha*, has only three aspects, while the instance of "the curd is in the can", which is cited as a case of contact (separableness), has four aspects, and hence, there is a difference between the two. Therefore, the definition of *yutasiddha* does not apply to the instance of "the cloth is in the yarns", and as such, it is a case of inseparableness. This leads to the acceptance of *samavāya*.

To this the opponents retort: The distinction which is sought to be made out above that the two relata of a *yutasiddha* relation have different loci, and, as such they have four aspects (two superstrata and two substrata) and *ayutasiddha* relation have only three aspects (two superstrata and one substratum) cannot be stated as a distinguishing factor between the two relations. If the criterion for *yutasiddha* as having separate container and contained be accepted, and absence of it as the case of *ayutasiddha*, that will overpervade ether and time *(ākāśa* and *kāla)*, self and direction *(ātman* and *dik)*, because these things are eternal and they have not separate locus for each of them. And as such, according to the above definition, they will fall within its orbit and constitute inseparable relation.

It also cannot, however, be said that the eternal entities have separate movement *(nityānañca pṛthag gatimattvam)* and this quality keeps the eternal entities out of the scope of inseparable relation, because the presumption of having separate movement *(pṛthaggatimattva)* cannot prevent the inseparable relation from occurring in all-pervasive entities. Of the two atoms *(paramāṇu)*, either of them may have separate movement of its own, both of them also may have separate movement. But unlike the atoms the all-pervasive entities *(vibhudravya)* cannot possess separate movement. If separate movement of all-pervasive entities by either one of them, or by both, is accepted the basic character of the entities, i.e. all-pervasiveness will be affected. A *vibhudravya* being all persuasive, in its character cannot move in compartment and does not leave room for others to move in.

Moreover, such presumption will lead to the conclusion that quality, action and the universal are mutually in inherence relation. Because in the absence of separate locus they reside in one and the same locus, like the ether, self, etc. and thus having been inseparably related constitute the basis of inherence. Subsistence of inherence between two such entities is not acceptable, because they lack the character of mutual dependence. In the absence of mutual dependence they have separate dependence and the relation occurring in them fall in the class of separable relation.

Nutual Dependence (Itaretarāśraya)

If it is, however, argued that the definition does not create a thing, but it distinguishes one from the others, which are already in existence, then it will lead to mutual dependence. The position of mutual dependence will be like this: That without knowing separability inherence as a relation of inseparability cannot be comprehended, and so long inherence is not known, no one will be able to make out what *yutasiddhi* is. Therefore, the definition of inherence is defective.

Further, the definition of *samavāya* will involve confusion of overpervasion. When we say ether, the word 'ether' is *vācaka* (denotor) and the substance ether is *vācya* (the thing denoted). Again in the instance, such as, "it is I" the self is the object, and the knower "I" is the subject, and the relation that exists between the two is of subject-objecthood *(viṣaya viṣayibhāva)*. In such instances there exists the relation of inseparability and that of container-containedhood. Thus the definition of *samavāya* based on inseparability and the container-containedhood will overpervade these instances.

It may be said that all the cases of denotor-denotedhood relation are not the cases of inseparable relation, some of them do exist as separable relation also. For instance, the word pot and the object of the word pot, they do not stand inseparably related and, therefore, the question of overpervasion does not arise.

Such argument has no force. Because the definition is not an all-inclusive one. If it covers even a part of the object which is not intended to be covered, or opposed to the things intended, the definition does not become all-inclusive. It exposes itself to the charge of "being capable of thus and not being capable of thus" *(anaikāntika)*. It is true that the relation that exists between the yarns and the cloth is not contact. We say it is self-linking relation *(tādātmya)*.

Samavāya is not perceptible

The statement that inherence is perceptible is not correct. An object in order to become perceptible must possess unique character *(asādhāraṇa-rūpatva)* and magnitude, just as the pot, which has a distinct character of its own and also magnitude. *(pṛthubudhnodarādyākāra-ghaṭādivat)*. But inherence is not such.

Let this position be examined in detail. In order to ascertain the position as to whether inherence possesses uniqueness or otherwise, the question is

"Is inherence an inseparable relation or simply a relation?"

The first alternative does not serve the purpose, because nobody (except you) recognises inseparable relation. Neither it can be stated as a class or genus, because it is one, and there is no second of it. There cannot be the cognition of universal in an object which has not second to it. If, on the otherhand, the universal is supposed to be cognised in respect of one entity also, then we shall have to recognise otherhood *(gaganatva)* as a universal.

Inherence is one and unique, because it differs from other relations, and as such it cannot be taken simply as a relation *(sambandhamātram).* If inherence be taken simply as a relation, the contact will also come within the purview of inherence.

For the perception of inherence three alternatives can be posed:

As a relation it may be perceived;

(a) through the cognition of the relation;

(b) in the cognition of "this is here"; or

(c) through the cognition of the concept of inherence.

Prabhācandra then has splitted up the first alternative into a number of alternatives, and every probability of perception of inherence is refuted.

(a) (I) If inherence is perceived as a relation, what is that relation? Is it a relation based on universal relationhood? No. There cannot be universal relationhood of inherence, because inherence is one. Inherence is neither substance, nor quality nor action. For the subsistence of the inherence there is no other inherence, therefore, the universal relationhood is barred *(sambandhatva-jāter-apravarttanāt).*

(II) Is it a relation caused by many constituents, just like the contact? No, it cannot be such, if it is accepted, the pot will also be covered by this proposition; pot also possesses many parts.

(III) Is it a relation which resides in many relata? No, that proposition has the defect of overpervasion and the potness will also come within the purview, and potness will be an inherent relation.

(IV) Is it a relation which generates the perception of the relation *(sambandha-buddhyutpādaka)?* No, this cannot be accepted. If this position is accepted, the eyes, the light, etc. also shall have to be taken as relation, because they generate cognition of the object.

(V) Is it a relation which is the object of a cognition of the relation *(sambandha-buddhiviṣaya)?* No, it cannot be accepted as such. If the relation and the relata be cognised as one, that is to say, they constitute one object of the cognition, the relata will also be cognised as relation. The argument that the cognition of every object is different cannot be advanced in this case, because if you hold that view that will lead to the non-cognition of darkness. The cognition of darkness is not different from the absence of the object.

(b) The second postulation, that is, inherence is perceived in the cognition of "this is here" *(ihedam)* also does not hold good. The cognition of "this is here" is in the locative. In a particular cognition where an object is cognised in a particular way it is not justified to accept the same otherwise. In other words, the cognition of an object in the locative cannot be cognised in the objective.

(c) The third postulation is also not sound. The said relation cannot be perceived in the cognition of inherence (*samavāya-buddhau*) because such an exclusive cognition is impossible. Nobody has separate cognition of the three, such as, "these are the yarns, this is the cloth and this is inherence." In fact, these three appear as one and not separately independent of each other.

It may be further argued that there is one characteristic which is common to all inherence and, therefore, the inherence could be perceived through that common characteristic. The question may be asked as to the nature of that common character. Whether this is a factor which can distinguish inherence from everything else; because such an extremity will reduce inherence to the state of "the lotus in the sky" and in such a state inherence will not be realised at all. Neither it can be a continued character (*anugataikasvabhāva*) which can be perceived. If the existence of the continued character is accepted in respect of inherence which is only one, the universal, which is also one, should be regarded as inherence.

Again this is also to be noted that for the perception of inherence its relata must be perceived. Now the position is: For the perception of the common character of inherence the relata of inherence are to be perceived, without perception of the relata, inherence cannot be perceived.

If the argument is that it is simply a relation which is different from the continued and distinguishing character *(anugata-vyāvṛttarūpa-vyatirekeṇa)* of the relation, and thus it is perceived simply as a relation, that is also impossible, because there is nothing as relation. This argument has been already refuted. Further, in the instance "the cloth is in these yarns" the cognition of "this is here" *(ihapratyaya)* is without contradiction and is similar to the cognition of "the curd is in the can," hence one can draw an inference to prove *samavāya*.

The above assertion is made without taking into consideration all aspects of the inference. For instance, the reason *(hetu)* has no proved locus here.

When you say "the cloth is in these yarns" the cognition of "this is here", i.e. the existence of the cloth in the yarns is neither proved nor cognised by us. In such instances the reason *(hetu)* of *ihapratyaya* is not known to anybody except you. Because the universal cognition is otherwise, such as, "the yarns are in the cloth", "the branches are in the tree, and not as you cognise. Hence the cognition of "the cloth is in the yarns" has been countered by the common cognition. Moreover, such cognition is self-contradictory, because when we cognise a piece of cloth, we do not cognise it as "the cloth is in the yarns" but the simple cognition is "this is a piece of cloth."

Further, the cognition of "this is here" *(ihapratyaya),* which is advanced as the reason *(hetu)* in the above inference is inconclusive *(anaikāntika)* to prove the inference. In such instances "the cloth is in the yarns" if the absence of cloth in the yarns is taken as the case of prior absence *(prāgabhāva)* it will lead to endlessness. On the other hand, if that is taken as the case of posterior absence *(pradhvaṁsābhāva)* then there will be no end to the posteior absence. Thus though the cognition of "this is here" is uncontradicted, there is no relation whatsoever between the yarns and the cloth. This also renders the reason inconclusive *(anaikāntika).*

It also cannot be said that here is a qualifier-qualificand relation (cloth is the qualifier and the yarn is qualificand), because without a relation there cannot subsist the qualifier-qualificand state. If such a qualifying principle is not accepted it will lead to the position that everything will be either qualifier or qualificand of everything. In other words, when there is a relation between the two, only then through that relaiton one thing may be construed as the qualifier and the other the qualified. On this premise only it is seen that among the substance, quality and activity one thing as the qualifier and other as the qualified.

If existence of qualifier-qualificand relation is accepted between two things which are in no way related, it will lead to overpervasion and the mountains of Sahya and Vindhya will stand in the said relation.

If the argument is like this—that in this case of prior absence (*prāgabhāva)* the relation is based on qualifier-qualificand *(viśeṣaṇa-viśeṣyabhāva)* and it can be termed as the relation of unseen *(adṛṣṭalakṣaṇa)* then this will be additional concept of relation over and above the six different ways, which are accepted by all.

Moreover it lacks the character of a relation. That in order to be a relation it must reside on two. This is an universally accepted principle and you yourself have admitted the same. The unseen *(adṛṣṭa)* being an attribute of self neither it can reside in the prior absence nor in the endlessness, and, hence it cannot reside in both. Thus the argument of *adṛṣṭalakṣaṇa* is open to debate. If, however, unseen itself is accepted as a relation, then on account of this, the quality and the quality-possessor etc. shall stand inter-related and what is the necessity for assuming inherence as a relation between the aforesaid two?

Again the question arises—what is going to be proved in the instance such as "the cloth is in these yarns?" The cognition of "this is here" being uncontradicted is a relation like in the cognition of "the curd is in the can." Whether by this simply a relation is sought to be proved or a particular relation? If the answer is, that the inference simply establishes the relation in general, nothing new has been proved. The existence of a relation in such cases, has already been accepted by us and that is the selfsame *(tādātmya)* relation.

An objection is raised to the selfsame relation that there shall be either the yarns or the cloth and not the both and the relata being one how the relation can exist there, which for its subsistence, requires two.

Such objection to the existence of selfsame relation is not valid. The relation is of two varieties, one exists in two and the other of the selfsame nature. Therefore, that the relation which exists in two, for obvious reason, cannot exist in one relatum, but the other relation, which is of selfsame nature does exist even when the relata are the same. The cloth is not a different entity from the yarns by its nature, because it is the yarns which existing in a given manner is cognised as the cloth.

Alternatively, if it is said that a particular relation is proved by inference. May we ask, what is that particular relation? Is it contact or inherence? If you say it is contact, we accept it; if, however, the answer is for inherence, that is not acceptable. Because the *dṛṣṭānta* (example) does not prove the *sādhya* (probandum). However, it may be stated that by inference neither contact nor inherence is sought to be proved but simply a relation is intended to be proved and when the existence of a relation is proved, by the logic of elimination inherence will ultimately be established. But this has been objected to on a number of grounds as has already been explained.

Here one may ask: What is this logic of elimination *(pariśeṣa)?* Is this is a case of rejection of all universally accepted relations, such as contact, self-linking, etc., and, when all these relations are rejected the remaining one will inevitably be the relation of inherence? From the premise further query arises: Whether this method of elimination is itself is a means of proving things? If it is not it cannot prove *samavāya*. In the alternative, if it is a proof, what is that, perception or inference? If cannot be a case of perception for the simple reason that perception helps us in knowing a thing having colour etc. which comes in contact with the sense organ. Inherence lacks these qualities and as such the question of its perception does not arise.

On the other hand, if inference is preferred, whether it is an exclusively negative inference *(kevala vyatiraki anumāna)?* But in that case the inference proving *samavāya* would be ineffective, because such inference cannot prove things without the assistance of the method of elimination. Hence, the Vaiśeṣika should have said that the method of elimination is alone able to prove *samavāya* without being assisted by the inference which proves *samavāya*. But the Vaiśeṣika has not stated that. Hence how can *pariśeṣa* prove *samavāya?*

Now the *samavāyavādin* may retort that unless *samavāya* is held responsible for the emergence of such cognition as "this is here", such cognition will be uncaused and as such its temporal existence *(kādācitkatva)* would remain unexplained. This argument is without force, says Prabhācandra. Because the cognition of "this is here" has been proved by constructing the self-linking relation as the reason for such cognition.

Another observation of the Vaiśeṣika is that the counter-inference of inherence which disproves it, should not be cited, because it wipes out all other inferences *(viśeṣa-viruddhānumānaṁ sakalānumānocchedakatvān na vaktavyam)*. This is not justified, says Prabhācandra.

Whether your objection to the said inference is for the reason that the counter-inference wipes out all other fallacious inferences (*anumānābhāsa*)? Or, it contradicts all other valid inferences?

The first alternative is not acceptable. Because such inference, which is based on a contradicted *hetu* is not a valid inference. There is no harm if fallacious inferences are contradicted by a valid inference. Even the upholder of inference cannot advocate the idea that the perception etc. which contradicts the fallacious inference should not be advanced as the proof. If such fallacious inference is accepted as proof, it will shake the foundation of perception.

The second alternative also does not stand on a sound footing. The existence of fire is inferred from the existence of smoke, and hence smoke is the reason *(hetu)* for the aforesaid valid inference. What is proved by such a valid inference, i.e. the existence of fire from smoke, cannot be contradicted either by a thousand of counter-inference or even by the perception.

Moreover, it cannot be said that such inference cannot be advanced, simply because it is opposed to a particular proposition, which is to be proved *(viśeṣa-viruddha)*. It is to be noted that the inference opposed to the particular proposition, which is to be proved, is not included in the list of fallacious reason *(hetvābhāsa)*. Thus, there is nothing which will preclude its *(viśeṣaviruddha)* by the propagandist of inference. Therefore, only the fallacious inference, which contradicts the particular thing, which is to be proved, should be avoided. For instance, "this place is not fire-possessing by the fire of this place, like the kitchen with the smoke![10] This inference is defective, and, as such cannot be accepted as valid, because the existence of fire can be cognised by the perception when one goes to that place.

Hereafter Prabhācandra refutes the statement that unlike contact the inherence is not many but one. Oneness of inherence is contradicted by inference. The inference will be like this:

"Inherence is many, because it generates the cognition of relation in different places, times and forms; whichever causes such different cognition, is many, like contact; inherence also generates such different cognition, hence it is many."[11]

It is well-known to all that the contact of the man with the stuff is different from the contact of the mat with the ground. Moreover, the cognition of contact differs according to varied nature of contact, such is "tight contact", "loose contact". Here the cognition of the tight contact is different from that of the loose contact, and on this ground contact is accepted to be manifold. Similarly, one has the different cognition of inherence, such as "eternal inherence", i.e. inherence between two eternal entities such as atom and its colour, "causal inherence", etc. Therefore let there be different inherence on the basis of different cognitions of inherence.

Moreover, it may be further argued that on account of the relata of the inherence being eternal or causal we may have the different cognition of inherence, namely, eternal and temporary; similarly, let there be different cognition of contact *(saṁyoga)* on being the contact-possessor *(saṁyogin)*, i.e. the relata, "tight" or "loose", and not on account of contact itself being "tight" or "loose". This leads to further complication. While it has somehow established the oneness of *samavāya*, contact will also fall in the same category, thus the Vaiśeṣika will find himself in an unenviable position.

"Inherence is many, because it is dependent on inseparably related substances having parts, like the number."[12] The plurality of number is due to the fact that number is dependent on entities and, accordingly, there is the use of two, three, four, etc. so also inherence on the basis of the entities should be many. By this inference also it is established that inherence is many. On the contrary, if inherence is taken to exist without being dependent on the entities, i.e. inherence does not require anything to reside in, it will contradict the assertion of Praśatapāda that the substance, quality, action, universal, particularity and inherence these six categories excluding the eternal substances have the character of dependence *(ṣaṇṇām āśritatvam).*[13]

Thus even when a particular substratum is destroyed the universality of dependence *(āśritatva-sāmānya)* being eternal, remains. This dependence serves as *hetu* and, therefore, on this analogy the direction etc. should have also possessed the character of dependence.

The direction *(dik)* is cognised in a manifested entity. The use is on the imposition of the direction on those entities, such as "this direction is in the east of this" *(idamataḥ pūrveṇa).* Similarly Time is also used as earlier, later, etc. In fact Time is one and undivided but since it is imposed on an entity, on that basis, this use is there. Therefore Time also have to be accepted as having the character of dependence.

The objection, in other words, is this: If the dependence of inherence on its substratum is not real but an assumed one, the direction, time, etc. will also fall in that category and on account of assumed dependence they must be treated as things dependent. Hence dependence of inherence must be real. On the other hand, if the direction, time, etc. are to be taken as dependent, the assertion of the Vaiśeṣika as to "entities other than eternal ones are of dependent nature" *(anyatra nityadravyebhyaḥ)* will be contradicted.

Prabhācandra says: Let inherence be non-dependent, that does not prove that it is one. Not withstanding this it is inevitable that inherence is many. We may cite an inference to prove this: "Inherence is many, because it does not depend on other entities for its existence like the atom *(parmāṇu).*"[14] This inference does not overpervade ether, because the ether is also regarded as many on account of its supposed association with different spaces. Thus inherence is proved to be many.

That inherence has many characters and the one differs from the other will be shown in the following paragraphs.

Let us examine the cognition "this is here". This cognition is not one and one only. It is our common experience that the cognition "the knowledge is in this self" is different from the cognition of "the colour is in the cloth." Thus being associated with different qualifier the cognition of "this is here" is bound to be many.

It may, however, be argued that since there is one continued cognition in all the cognitions of "this is here" inherence based on the said cognition is one. This argument is not valid says Prabhācandra. In the cognition of "cowness", "clothness", etc. and also that of substancehood, qualityhood, etc. the cognition is not one, but we have the continued cognition of those entities. The argument that "like the beingness" *(sattāvat),* i.e. to say that on account of the common notion that "it exists" as *sattā* is held to be one, inherence is also one. This example suffers from the defect of failure of proving the probandum (*sādhya-sādhana-vikalatā*), says Prabhācandra. The proposition as to oneness and the cognition of existence is also without distinction, and hence, not proved. If the cognition of existence is taken to be one and without any distinction in its nature, then when we cognise "the cloth exists" that cognition being the cognition of existence will leave no scope for the cognition of existence of other entities. Thus inspite of having the cognition of existence nobody will cognise that particular entity by the cognition. For instance, when we cognise a pot, we will cognise it as the existence of an entity and not as a pot. This will lead to the state of confusion in the cognition of entities, and for the removal of this confusion we must have particular cognition in respect of particular object. Thus the cognition is always qualified by its object. Hence, the qualified cognition is many, and it is to be accepted.

An argument may be advanced against this:

"The cognition that 'these are the substances related by inherence' is the cognition of the qualificand, because this cognition is proceeded by the cognition of the qualifier."[15] This is nothing but the outcome of ignorance, says the Jaina.

The anticipated qualified cognition, which is put as the reason for the qualificand cognition, is not proved as qualifier, and as such, the inference is fallacious. To be precise, in the absence of the stuff no one can have the cognition of a stuff-holder, similarly, in the absence the qualifier, i.e. inherence, there cannot be the cognition of inherent, the qualificand. The relation of inherence is not cognised and, therefore, the said reason is unproved.

Taking recourse to the inference for the cognition of inherence seems to be redundant. Who, after having cognised the objects related by inherence, will deny inherence? If the objects of inherence are cognised as the qualificand in the absence of the said inherence, then we may have the same even by the horns of an ass. Because, in fact, there is no difference between the absence of inherence and the horn of an ass.

If it is said that one may cognise the objects of the relation. Let him cognise what is of that so far inherence is concerned? It cannot be said that the relata are the relation, i.e. inherence. Such cognition, that is the cognition of the relation as identical with that of the relata is possible by the self-linking relation. This is similar to the cognition of the contact *(saṁyoga)*. After the cognition of the relata of the contact, the contact itself can be cognised.

Inspite of this position if you are eager for accepting *samavāya* why should you not insist on to have the horns of an ass?

Now you can say that inherence will appear simply as a relation to those who are not conversant with *samavāya* but it will appear as *samavāya* to those who know all about it. This will lead to the acceptance of one knowledge as two, and hence, is not admissible. However, it may be pointed out that to those who have no knowledge about this, it will be simply an object without a name for it, and the concrete knowledge is generated due to the name.

If this cognition is taken as the cognition of inherence and that is regarded as the reason, the reason will not be exclusive *(anaikāntika);* because the cognition of the qualificand does not require the assistance of a qualifier. If it is argued that the relata of inherence *(samavāyinoḥ)* such as the cloth and the yarns are the qualifiers of the cognition of inherence, that will be only partial.

When inherence of inherent relata *(samavāyinām samavāyaḥ)* is cognised, in such cases the relata of inherence may serve the purpose of qualifier. But in the cognition of inherence where is the qualifier?

It may be said that without the qualifier the knowledge of qualificand is impossible. And here in this context there cannot be any qualificand other than the relata of inherence. If that is denied, the knowledge of qualified will be impossible.

This argument, that is, the cognition of both qualificand and the qualified will not be possible is not correct. If it is accepted, the cognition of the cloth will also not be there, because the absence of the cognition of qualifier is the same in both the cases. If you say the "clothness" is the qualifier in the cognition of the cloth, what is the qualifier in respect of inherence? Is it "inherencehood"? No, such an entity is not accepted.

It may be however argued that by which the qualified cognition is generated, that is to be accepted as the qualifier. In the cognition of inherence, "inherencehood" is an unknown entity and as such it cannot take the place of qualifier and at the same time the relata of inherence (the cloth and the yarns in case of inherence of cloth in the yarns) are also not cognised. Therefore, the unseen *(adṛṣṭa)* is to be taken as the qualifier for the said cognition.

This is not justified, says Prabhācandra.

The question is—what is to be taken as the qualifier? Is it the qualifier for the existence of which one can have the cognition of the qualificand? Or, is it that whose relation is cognised in the qualificand? If the first alternative is preferred, then the eyes, the light, etc. in the case of perceptual cognition should have been regarded as the qualifier.

Acceptance of the second alternative will lead to the following position. In the cognition of the staff-holder *(daṇḍin)* the staff is the qualifier and through the cognition of the staff the cognition of the staff-holder is there.

If the relation of the staff with the person is accepted as the qualifier, then the word "staff" itself will serve the purpose. Even it is so, the utterance of the word *adṛṣṭa* would not generate the cognition of the relation. If inspite of the fact that *adṛṣṭa* is not cognised as the cause of the relation, it is assumed as the qualifier, then in the cognition of the staff-holder *(daṇḍin)* assumption of the same will hold good. What is the use of assuming the relata of inherence, viz. cloth and yarns etc. as the qualifier?

The statement that the emergence of the effect is nothing but the relation of the effect with the existence, existing in the cause, is not correct. If the effect is regarded as the same with its cause and, that is an inherence, it will make it eternal. On the assumption that it is eternal, the effect would never be destroyed because the cause will always be there.

The next point to be determined is: Whether it is an inherence of the existence in that what exists or does not exist? it cannot be the inherence in the non-existent entities, since in that case there will be inherence of *sattā* in the sky-lotus also. However, a distinction may be pointed out that the sky-lotus is an absolutely negative entity, but the quality and the quality-possessor are not so. Why it is so? If it is on account of inherence, then it is a case of mutual dependence. When inherence is proved, the absence of the absolute non-existence of the relata is proved and vice versa. Thus it involves mutual dependence.

It cannot be the inherence in that which already exists. Because the question will arise: Before inherence takes place their existence is dependent on another inherence or they exist per se. If you prefer to say that it is due to another inherence, then the proposition is contradicted by the admission of oneness of inherence. If on the other hand, inherence is accepted to be many, then for the existence of the relata of inherence another inherence is to be admitted, then again for that another inherence, and thus it will involve *regressus ad infinitum.*

On the other hand, if it is agreed that they exist by themselves, then there is no use for assuming inherence.

If it is said that before the cognition of inherence they are not cognised either as existent or non-existent, they will be cognised as existents due to the cognition of inherence.

This argument is not proper. When one of the two entities, which possess mutually contradictory qualities, is prohibited there by the other is not prohibited, because that will amount to prohibition of both, which is not possible. This existence and inherence are not mutually complimentary to each other, and, hence the presumption of a relation between two such entities is ruled out.

The definition of existence is non-pervasive, because this does not cover the existence itself, inherence and the ultimate particulars. That which generates the cognition of existence in three categories that is *sattā*. Moreover, it suffers from overpervasiveness, because it will cover the sky-lotus etc. It cannot be said that because they are non-existent, there cannot be inherence of existence; that will involve the defect of mutual dependence. Since they are non-exisistent, there is no inherence of existence and for want of this inherence, they are to be taken as entities of non-existence. Thus the mutual dependence is inevitable.

It also cannot be said that the inherence of the existence itself is the nature of existence, because one is different from the other. An entity which is different from the other, cannot be its nature. Presumption of identity of the two such entities will lead to overpervasion, such as in that case the cloth will be identical with the pot. Thus one will be no more treated as a different entity from the other.

Again, if from inherence of existence the existent entity is inferred, how the existence of existence and inherence could be ascertained? The assumption of relation of non-existent entities with inherence will overpervade the sky-lotus etc. If it is due to the relation of the existent entity with inherence, that will lead to the *regressus ad infinitum*. If it is presumed to arise from the relation itself, then there is no use of admitting inherence of existence let other entities also exist by themselves.

What has been stated that it is like the heat in the fire, i.e. inherence exist in the entities as the heat resides in the fire. This is mere a statement. That the fire possesses heat is a matter of common knowledge. When the nature of a thing is perceived everything regarding that nature should be confined to perception.

Inherence is related to its relata by itself, like the contact, but it is not established as a matter of perception. Inherence has been established as a non-perceptible entity.

If you cite the instances of being related by itself such as, the heat with the fire, the light with the lamp, the purity with the water of the Ganges and say, like these inherence is the cause of the relation between itself (inherence) and the other (the relata) *(svaparayoḥ sambandhahetuḥ)*, then why knowledge itself, on the analogy of this, will not reveal itself and its object? But everybody knows the knowledge cannot reveal itself. "Since the knowledge is a thing to be proved, it can be known only by another knowledge" *(jñānaṁ jñānāntara-vedyam prameyatvāt).*

Another argument regarding the nature of inherence that it does not need the help of any other relation to be related with the relata, is not valid. The inference is:

"To be related inherence does not stand in need of other relation, because it is related on is own; those which need another relation, they are not the relation to be related of their own, such as the pot etc.; it (inherence) is not that, it is related of its own, therefore, it does not require any other relation (for its subsistence)."[16]

In this inference the reason, i.e. 'being related on its own', is not proved *(hetorasiddheḥ).* When inherence itself has not been established, the reason (becoming related on its own) is not proved. Moreover, the said reason becomes non-exclusive, because becoming related on its own is equally applicable to the opposite inference.

Notes and References

1. It may be pointed out that Kumārila while dealing with *samavāya* has raised the question of separate movement *(pṛthag gatimatva)* and said that there are separate movement by the whole and the part, and as such on that premise *samavāya* does not and cannot exist between whole and part. The concept *yutasiddha* is not there in the instances such as "the cloth is in the yarns" because the cloth cannot remain without the yarns and hence both do not have separate substratum and separate movement.
2. ihākāśe vācye vācaka ākāśa śabdaḥ, ihātmani jñānam.
   —PKM., pp, 604.
3. ekadravya-samavāyinām rūparasādīnām ayutasiddhānāmeva parasparam samavāya-bhāvāt. —Ibid., p. 605.
4. sambandhābhāve Sahya-Vindhya-vad viśleṣa-pratibhāsaḥ syāt.
   —PKM., p. 605.
   (In Nyāya system samavāya is *pratyakṣa* (perceptible), according to the Vaiśeṣika *samavāya* can only be inferred).
5. na aniṣpannayoḥ samavāyaḥ sambandhinoranutpāde sambandhābhāvāt.
   —PKM., p. 608.
6. gatiprabandhakaśca ādhāraḥ jalādeghaṭādivat. —Ibid., p. 608.
7. na svarūpasaṁśleṣaḥ samavāyaḥ. —Ibid., p. 608.

8. svātantreṇa niṣpannayośca na pāratantryam. —Ibid., p. 608.
9. nahi niṣpattiranyā samavāyaścānyo yena paurvāparyam. —Ibid., p. 608.
10. ayam pradeśo' tratyenāgninā agnimān na bhavati dhūmavatvānmahānasavat. —PKM., p. 651.
11. anekaḥ samavāyo vibhinnadeśa-kālākārārtheṣu sambandha-buddhihetutvāt, yo ya itthambhūtaḥ so so' nekaḥ, yathā saṁyogaḥ, tathā ca samavāyaḥ tasmādaneka iti. —PKM., p. 616.
12. nānā samavāyo' yutasiddhāvayavi-dravyāśritatvāt saṁkhyāvat. —PKM., p. 616.
13. PPBH., p. 16.
14. anekaḥ samavāyaḥ anāśritatvāt paramāṇuvat. —PKM., p. 616.
15. samavāyini dravyāṇi ityādipratyayo viśeṣaṇapūrvako viśeṣyapratyayatvāt. —PKM., p. 617.
16. samvāyaḥ sambandhāntaraṁ nāpekṣate, svataḥ sambandhatvāt, ye tu sambandhāntaram apekṣante na te svataḥ sambandhāḥ yathā ghaṭādayaḥ, na ca ayaṁ na svataḥ sambandhaḥ, tasmāt sambandhāntaraṁ nāpakṣata iti. —PKM., p. 620.

Bibliography

Sanskrit Texts

Annaṁ Bhaṭṭa,

—Tarkasaṁgraha, ed. Rajaram Mahadev Bodas, Bombay Sanskrit Series, 2nd ed. Bombay, 1930.

Amarasiṁha,

—Nāmaliṅgānuśāsana, with Padārtha-candrikā of Rāyamukuṭa, Sanskrit College, Calcutta, 1973

Āpodeva,

—Mīmāṁsā-nyāya-prakāśa, ed. & trans. by Franklin Edgerton, Yale University Press, New Haven, 1929.

Arcaṭa,

—Hetubinduṭīkā, ed. Sukhlalji Sanghvi and Muni Sri Jina Vijayaji, Gaekwad's Oriental Series 113, Oriental Institute, Baroda, 1949.

Aśoka,

—Avayavinirākaraṇa, included in Six Buddhist Nyāya Tracts, ed. H.P. Shastri, Bibliotheca Indica, Calcutta, 1910.

—Sambandha-parīkṣā, (do)

Bādarāyaṇa,

—Vedānta-sūtra, with Śārīrakabhāṣya of Śaṁkara, and the sub-commentary Bhāmatī by Vācaspati Miśra, and with an abridged Bengali translation by Kālibara Vedānta-Vāgīśa, ed. M.M. Durgācaraṇa Sāṁkhya-Vedānta-tīrtha. Calcutta (Beng. script).

Bhāsaravajña,

—(I) Nyāyasāra, ed. S.C. Vidyābhūṣaṇa, Bibliotheca Indica, Calcutta, 1910.

—(II) Nyāyasara with Nyāyabhūṣaṇa, ed. Swami Yogindrananda with notes, Saddarsana Prakasana Pratishthana, Varanasi, 1968.

Bhartṛhari,
—Vākyapadīya, Vol. I-II, ed. G.D. Shastri, Banaras Sanskrit Series 6, Braja B. Das, Banaras, 1905.

Bhavānanda Siddhāntavāgīśa,
—Nañvādaṭīkā, included in Tattvacintāmaṇi, Part IV.

Bhīmācarya Jhalkikar, MM.,
—Nyāyakośa: an encyclopaedia of the technical terms in the Indian philosophy, Govt. Central Book Depot, Bombay, 1893.

Dharmakīrtti,
—(I) Pramāṇavārttika, ed. Rahul Sankritayana, with the commentary of Manorathanandin, Bihar and Orissa Resarch Society, Patna, 1938.
—(II) with Pramāṇavārttikabhāṣya of Prajñākaragupta, K.P. Jaiswal Research Institute, Patna, 1953.

Dharmottara,
—Nyāyabinduṭīā, included in Nyāyabindu, ed. Peterson, Bibliotheca Indica, Calcutta, 1929.

Deva, Rādhākānta,
—Śabdakalpadruma; an encyclopaedic dictionary of Sanskrit terms. Reprint. Chowkhamba Sanskrit Series Office, Banaras, 1961.

Diṅnāga,
—Nyāyapraveśa, Oriental Institute, Borada, 1968.
—Pratyakṣa-paricchea, ed. and translated, Massiki Hatori.

Gadādhara Bhaṭṭācārya,
—Vyutpattivāda, Chowkhamba Amarabhāratī Prakāśana, Varanasi.
—Gādādharī, a commentary on Tattvacintāmaṇi-dīdhiti, ed. Pt. Vāmācaraṇa Bhaṭṭācārya, Chowkhamba Sanskrit Series, Banaras.
—Viṣayatāvāda, (do)

—Nañvādavivṛti: a commentary on Raghunātha's Nañvāda, (do)

Gaṅgeśa Upādhāya,
—(I) Tattvacintāmaṇi, ed. with Māthurī, Motilal Banarsidass, Delhi, 1970.
(II) ed. with the commentary, Gādadharī and the Subcommentary Dīdhiti and Jāgadīśī, Patna.
—Vyāptipañcaka with commentaries, ed. Jibananda Vidyasagara, Calcutta, 1888.

Gautama,
—Nyāya-sūtra, with Vātsyāyana bhāṣya, Nyāyavārttika of Uddyotakara, Tātparyaṭīkā of Vācaspatimiśra and Tātparyapariśuddhi of Udayana, ed. Anantalal Thakur, Mithila Institute, Darbhanga.

Īśvarakṛṣṇa,
—The Sāṁkhyakārikā, ed. & trans. (English) S.S. Suryanarayan Shastri, Madras, 1930.
—ed. H.D. Sharma with English translation and the commentary of Gauḍapāda, The Oriental Book Agency, Poona, 1933.

Jagadīśa,
—Vyadhikaraṇa-prakaraṇa, Chowkhamba Sanskrit Series, Banaras.
—Jāgadīśa-sūkti, a commentary on *Praśastapāda-bhāsya*, ed. K. Tarkacharya, Calcutta.

Jayadeva (Pakṣadhara) Miśra,
—Tattvacintāmaṇyāloka, a commentary on Tattvacintāmaṇi.

Jaimini,
—The Pūrva Mīmāṁsā-sūtra of Jaimini, English trans. ed. Ganganath Jha, Pāṇini Office, Allahabad, 1916.

Jayanta,
—(I) Nyāyamañjarī, ed. G. Shastri Tailanga, VSS 10, Banaras, 1895.
—(II) With Vivaraṇa by Paṇḍitarāja Sūryanārāyaṇa Śukla, Chowkhamba Sanskrit Series, Varanasi, 1971.

—(III) Eng. Translation, Janakivallabha Bhattacharya, Vol. I, Motilal Banarsidass, Delhi, 1978.

Jñānaśrīmitra,
—Jñānaśrīmitra-nibandhāvalī, ed. Anantalal Thakur, K.P. Jaiswal Research Institute, Patna.

Kamalaśīla,
—Tattvasaṁgraha-pañjikā; a commentary on Tattvasaṁagraha of Śāntarakṣita, ed. with Sanskrit introduction E. Krishnacharya, 2 vols., Gaikwad Oriental Sanskrit Series 30-31, Baroda.

Kaṇāda,
—Vaiśeṣika-sūtra with Praśastapāda-bhāṣya and Nyāyakandalī, Varanaseya Sanskrit Visvavidyalaya, Varanasi, 1973.
—With the commentary, Upaskāra by M.M. Panchanan Tarkaratna (Beng. script), Calcutta.

Keśava Miśra,
—Tarkabhāṣā, Engligh translation, Ganganath Jha, Oriental Book Agency, Poona, 1949.

Kauṭilya,
—Arthaśāstra, ed. Vacaspati Gairola, Chowkhamba Vidyabhavan, Varanasi.

Kumārila,
—(I) Mīmāṁsā-ślokavārttika with the commentary Nyāyaratnākara by Pārthasārathi Miśra, Tara Publication, Varanasi.
—(II) Mīmāṁsā-ślokavārttika with the commentary Nyāyaratnakara of Pārthasārathi Misra, ed. Ram Sastri Tailang, Chowkhamba Sanskrit Series, Varanasi.
—(III) Mīmāṁāśloka-vārttika with the commentary Tātparyaṭīkā of Bhaṭṭombeka, University of Madras, 1940.

Laugākṣibhāskara,
—Tarkakaumudī, Bombay Sanskrit series XXXII, Bombay, 1886.

Mahādeva Puṇatamakāra,
—The Nyāyakaustubha, ed. Umesh Mishra, The Prince of Wales

Sarasvatibhavana Texts 33, Govt. Sanskrit Library, Banaras, 1930.

Mathurānātha,
—Māthurī or Tattvacintāmaṇirahasya, ed. Pt. Kamakhyanatha Tarkavagisa, Asiatic Society, Calcutta, 1901.

Mādhavācarya,
—Sarvadarśana-saṁgraha, ed. Vasudev Shastri Abhyankara, Government Oriental Sanskrit Series, Poona, 1924. (translation B. Cowell and A.E. Gough).

Nāgārjuna,
—Vigraha-vyāvarttinī, ed. E.N. Johnston and A. Kunst, Mādhyamika-sūtras with the commentary of Candrakīrtti, Bibliotheca Buddhica, St. Petersburg, 1908.

Nāgeśabhaṭṭa,
—Paramalaghumañjuṣā, ed. with Hindi Gloss by Kapildev Shastri, Kurukshetra University, Kurukshetra.

Nārāyaṇa,
—Mānameyodaya, ed. with English translation C. Kunhan Raja, Theosophical Publishing House, Madras, 1933.

Pāṇini,
—Aṣṭādhyāyī, Chowkhamba Sanskrit Series, Banaras.

Pārthasarathi Miśra,
—(I) Śāstradīpikā with the commentary Yuktisneha-prapūraṇī by Ramakrisna Miśra, Chowkhamba Sanskrit Series, Banaras, 1916.
—(II) Śāstradīpika with the commentary Prabhā by Vaidyanātha, Part I, ed. Pattabhiram Shastri, Lalbahadur Shastri Kendriya Sanskrit Vidyapeeth, New Delhi, 1978.

Patañjali,
—Pātañjala Yogasūtra with Vyāsa-bhāṣya and the subcommentary Bhāsvatī and Bengali translation, Calcutta University, Calcutta, 1962.

Praśastapāda,
—Padārthadharmasaṁgraha: the commentary on Kaṇāda-sūtra with Sūkti of Jagadīśa, ed. Kalipada Tarkacharya, Calcutta.

Prabhācandra,
—Prameya-kamala-mārtaṇḍa: a commentary on Māṇikyanandin's Parīkṣāmukhasūtra, ed. Mahendrakumar Shastri, Niranaya Sagar Press, Bombay, 1941.
—Nyāyakumudacandra (do)

Prabhākara Miśra,
—Bṛhatī: a commentary on Śabara-bhāṣya with Ṛjuvimalā of Śālikanātha Miśra, ed S.K.R. Shastri, Madras University Sanskrit Series, Madras University, 1934.

Raghunātha Śiromaṇi,
—Nañvāda, printed as an appendix to the Tattvacintāmaṇi of Gaṅgeśa in the Bibliothca Indica edtion, ed. Kamakhyanatha Tarkavagisa Part-IV, Vol. II.
—Padārthatattvanirūpaṇa with the commentaries of Raghudeva and Rāmabhadra, ed. Vindhyesvar Prasada Dvivedi, Banaras, 1916.
—Tattvacintāmaṇi-dīdhiti, a commentary on Tattvacintāmaṇi, ed. with Jāgadīśī (See Jagadīśa).

Rāyamukuṭa,
—Padārthacandrikā, a commentary on Amarasiṁha's Nāmaliṅgānuśāsana, Calcutta Sanskrit College, Calcutta, 1973.

Ratnakīrtti,
—Ratnakīrtti-nibandhāvali, ed. Anantalal Thakur, K.P. Jaiswal Resarch Institute, Patna.

Rucidatta Miśra,
—Prakāśa: a commentary on Tattvacintāmaṇiyāloka of Jayadeva Miśra (included in Tattvacintāmaṇi).

Śabara,
—Śābarabhāṣya on Jaiminisūtra, Bibliotheca India 45, Calcutta, Asiatic Socity of Bengal, 1889.

Sadānanda,
—Vedantasāra, ed. G.A. Jacob, Niranaya Sagar Press, Bombay, 1926.

Śālikanātha,
—Prakaraṇa-pañcikā, ed. Mukunda Shastri Dravida, Chowkhamba Sanskrit Series, Banaras, 1904.

Śaṁkara Miśra,
—Upaskāra: a commentary on Praśastapāda-bhāṣya, ed. Jibananda Vidyasagar, Calcutta, 1886.

Śaṁkarācārya,
—Śārīraka-bhāṣya: commentary on Vedānta-sūtra, with the sub-commentary Bhāmatī by Vācaspati Miśra, Calcutta.

Śāntarakṣita,
—Tattvasaṁgraha, ed. B. Bhattacharya, Central Library, Baroda, 1926.

Śrīharṣa,
—Khaṇḍanakhaṇḍa-khādya, ed. Lakṣmaṇa Śāstrī Draviḍa, Chowkhamba Sanskrit Series, Banaras, 1914.

Shastri, Haraprasad,
—ed. Six Buddhist Nyāya tracts, Bibliotheca Indica, Calcutta, 1910.

Śrīdhara,
—Nyāyakandalī with Hindi translation, Varanaseya Sanskrit Visvavidyalaya, Banaras, 1973.

Tarkavāgīśa, Kāmākhyānātha,
—ed. Tattvacintāmaṇi with gloss, Motilal Banarsidass, Delhi.

Tarkapañcānana, Jayanārāyaṇa,
—ed. Viśeṣika-darśana, with his own commentary, Calcutta, 1888.

Udayanācārya,
—(I) Kiraṇāvalī, with the commentaries, Kiraṇāvalī-Prakāśa of Vardhamāna and with the sub-commentary Kiraṇāvalī-prakāśa-

vivṛti of Rucidatta Miśra and also with the commentary (part) of Bhaṭṭa-Vādīndra, Asiatic Society, Calcutta, 1956.
—(II) Kiraṇāvalī, with Bengali translation and notes by Gaurinath Shastri, Calcutta.
—(I) Nyāyakusumāñjali, with the commentaries of Prakāśa and Makaranda, Chowkhamba Sanskrit Series, Banaras.
(II) With the commentaries of Āmoda and Viveka, Calcutta University, Calcutta.

Uddyotakara,
—Nyāyavārttika, ed. Vindhyesvari Prasad Dvivedi, Bibliotheca Indica, Calcutta, 1907.

Vallabha or Śrī-Vallabha,
—Nyāyalīlāvatī with the sub-commentaries of Vivṛti of Bhagīratha Ṭhakkura, Nyāyalīlāvatī-prakāśa of Vardhamāna and Kaṇṭhābharaṇa of Śaṅkara Miśra, Chowkhamba Sanskrit Series, Banaras, 1961.

Vallabhācārya,
—Brahmasūtrāṇubhāṣya: commentary on Vedānta-sūtra, with the sub-commentary Bhāṣyaprakāśa by Puruṣottama and sub-commentary Raśmi of Gopeśvaraji, Bombay, 1942.

Varadarāja,
—Tārkikarakṣā, ed. Vindhyeswari Prasad Dvivedi, Banaras, 1903.

Vardhamāna Upādhāyaya,
—Nyāyakusumāñjalīprakāśa (see under Udayana).
—Nyāyanibandha-prakāśa.

Vācaspati Miśra,
—Nyāya-vārttika-tātparyaṭīkā, Prakrit and Jaina Institute, Vaishali.
—Bhāmatī: commentary on Śārīraka-bhāṣya of Śaṁkarācārya, Calcutta.
—Tattvavaiśāradī: commentary on Yoga-sūtra, Pāṇini Office, Allahabad.

Vātsyāyana,
—Nyāyabhāṣya by Vātsyāyana, (see under Uddyotakara).

Vādivāgiśvara,
—Mānamanohara, ed. Svami Yogindrananda, Varanasi.

Viśvanātha Nyāyapañcānana,
—Bhāṣāpariccheda, with Dinakarī and Rāmarudrī, Niranaya Sagar Press, Bombay.

Viśvanātha,
—Nyāya-sūtra-vṛtti, ed. Ashubodh and Nityabodh, Calcutta, 1919.

Vijñānabhikṣu,
—Śāṁkhyapravacana-bhāṣya, Harvard, Cambridge.

Vyāsa,
—The Mahābhārata, Bhandarkar Oriental Research Institute, Poona.
—Śrīmad Bhāgavata, Gita Press, Gorakhpur.

SECONDARY SOURCE

Alston, William P.,
—Philosophy of Language, Eagle Wood Cliffs, New Jersy; Prentice Hall Inc., 1964.

Aristotle,
—The Basic Works of Aristotle, ed. by Richard P.McKon, Random House, New York, 1941.

Atreya, Bhikhanlal,
—The Element of Indian Logic with the text and Hindi and English translation of Tarkasaṁgraha, 2nd edn., the Indian Book Shop, Banaras.

Bagchi, Sitansusekhar,
—Inductive reasoning: A study of tarka and its role in Indian logic, Calcutta Oriental Press Ltd. Calcutta, 1953.

Barlingay, S.,
—A Modern Introduction to Indian Logic, National Publishing House, Delhi, 1965.

Bhaduri, Sadananda,
—Studies in Nyāya-Vaiśeṣika Metaphysics, Bhandarkar Oriental Research Institute, Poona, 1947.

Bhattacharya, D.C.,
—Bange Navya-Nyāya-carcā (Bengali), Bangiya Sahitya Parishad, 1952.
—History of Navya-Nyāya in Mithilā, Mithala Institute of Post-Graduate Studies and Reseach in Sanskrit Learning, Darbhanga, 1958.

Bhattacharya, G.,
—Studies in Navya-Nyāya Theisim, Calcutta Sanskrit College Research Sẹries, No. XIV, Sanskrit College, Calcutta, 1961.

Bradley,
—Appearance and Reality, Clarendon Press, Oxford, 1930.

Burrow, T.,
—Indian Theories of Meaning (summary), London, 1966.

Burough, John,
—Theories of general linguistics in Sanskrit Grammarians, Oxford, 1951.

Chatterjee, S.C.,
—The Nyāya theory of knowledge a critical study of some problems of logic and metaphysics, 2nd edn. (rept.), Calcutta University, Calcutta, 1965.

Chatterjee, T.C.,
—The Hindu Realism: being an introduction to the metaphysics of Nyāya-Vaiśeṣika system of philosophy, Indian Press, Allahabad, 1912.

Datta, D.M.,
—The Six Ways of Knowing, George Allen & Unwin, London, 1932.

Dasgupta, Surendranath,
—History of Indian Philosophy, University Press, Cambridge, 1957.

Geokoop, C.,
—The Logic of Invariable Concomimtance in the Tattvacintāmaṇi of Gaṅgeśa, D. Reidle Publishing Campany, Dordecht, Holland, 1967.

Guha, D.C.,
—Nyava-nyāya System of Logic, Bharatiya Vidya Prakasana, Varanasi, 1968.

Hall, Fitzeward,
—Index to the Bibliography of the Hindu philosophical systems.

Hattori, Massiki,
—Dignāga on perception: being pratyakṣa pariccheda of Dignāga's Pramāṇa Samuccaya from the Sanskrit fragments and the Tibetan version, Translated and annotated, Harvard University Press, Cambridge, 1968.

Hiriyana, M.,
—Outlines of Indian Philosophy, Madras.
—Indian Philosophical studies, Madras.

H.UI.,
—The Vaiśeṣika Philosophy, Tokyo, 1917.

Ingalls, D.H.H.,
—Matreials for the Study of Navyanyāya Logic, Harvard Oriental Series 40, Cambridge, Mass., 1951.

Jacobi, H.,
—Dates of the philosophical sūtras of the Brāhmaṇas, JAOS XXXI, 19U.

Jha, Ganganath,
—English translation of Tarkabhāṣā of Keśava Miśra or Exposition of reasoning, Oriental Book Agncy, Poona, 1924.

—English translation of Tattvasaṁgraha of Śāntarakṣita and the commentary Tattvasaṁgraha-pañjikā of Kamalaśīla, G.O.S., Vol. XXX, Baroda Oriental Institute, Baroda, 1937.
—The Pūrva Mīmāṁsā school of Prabhākara, Allahabad.

Jhunkara, N.S.,
—Gautama: The Nyāya philosophy, Motilal Banarsidass, Delhi, 1978.

Kaviraj, Gopinatha,
—Gleanings from the History and Bibliography of Nyāya-Vaiśeṣika literatures, The Princes of Wales Sarasvatībhavana studies III, Banaras.

Kane, P.V.,
—History of Dharmaśāstra (4 Vols.), Bhandarkar Oriental Research Institute, Poona, 1930.

Keith, A.B.,
—Indian Logic and Atomism: an exposition of the Nyāya and Vaiśeṣika systems, Oxford, 1921.

Kunjuni Raja, K.,
—Indian Theories of Meaning. The Adyar Library Series, Vol. 91, Madras, 1963.

Mill, John Stuart,
—A System of Logic, Relation inactive and inductive, Longmans Green & Co., London, 1965.

Mishra, Umesha,
—Conception of Matter according to Nyāya-Vaiśeṣika, Allahabad, 1936. ed. Nyāya-Kaustubha, Banaras.

Motilal, Bimal Krishna,
—The Navya-nyāya Doctrine of Negation, Harvard University Press, Cambridge, Mass., 1968.

Moore, G.E.,
—Some main problems of philosophy, George Allen & Unwin, London, 1966.

Mukherjee, Satkari,
—The Buddhist Philosophy of Universal Flux: an exposition of the philosophy of critical Realism as expounded by the school of Dignāga, Calcutta University, Calcutta, 1955.

Murti, T.R.V.,
—The Central Philosophy of Buddhism, George Allen & Unwin, London, 1965.

Patti, G.,
—Der samavāya in Nyāya-Vaiśeṣka system, Scripta Pantifici Institute Biblica, Rome.

Potter, H. Karl,
—ed. The Encyclopedia of Indian Philosophy: Nyāya-Vaiśeṣika, Motilal Banarsidass, Delhi.

Quine, W.V.,
—From a logical point of view, Logic-philosophical essays, Harvard University Press, Cambridge, 1964.

Radhakrishnan, S.,
—Indian philosophy, Vol.I & II, George Allen & Unwin, London, 1931.

Randle, H.N.,
—Fragments of Dignāga, The Royal Asiatic Society, London, 1926.

Shastri, D.N.,
—The Philosophy of Nyāya-Vaiśeṣika and its conflict with Buddhist Dignāga School (Critique of Indian Realism), Bharatiya Vidya Prakasan, Delhi, Reprint, 1976.

Shastri, Gaurinatha,
—The philosophy of Word and Meaning: Some Indian approaches with special reference to the philosophy of Bhartṛhari, Calcutta Sanskrit College, Calcutta, 1959.
—ed. Kiraṇāvalī of Udayana with explanatory notes & trans. in Bengali, 3 Vols.

Shastri, Kuppuswami,
—A Primer of Indian Logic according to Annambhaṭṭa's Tarkasaṁgraha, Madras, 1932.

Sinha, Jadunath,
—Indian Realism, Kegun Paul, Trench, Trübener & Co. Ltd., 1930.

Staal, J.P.,
—Negation and the Law of Contradiction in Indian Thoughts: a comparative study, BSOAS, 25, 1962.

Stcherbatsky, Th.,
—Buddhist Logic, 2 Vols. Bibliotheca Buddica XXVI, Leningrad, 1930-32.

Sen, Saileswara,
—A Study on Mathurānātha's Tattvacintāmaṇi-rahasya, Wageningen, 1924.

Tarkavāgīśa, MM Phaṇībhuṣaṇa,
—Nyāyaparicaya (Bengali), Jatiya Siksa Parisat, Calcutta.

Tārānātha Tarkavācaspati,
—Vācaspatiyam; an encyclopaedic dictionary of Sanskrit terms, Chowkhamba Sanskrit Series, Banaras, 1957.

Tucci, G.,
—Pre-Dignāga Buddhist Texts on Logic from Chinese Sources, Gaikwad Oriental Sanskrit Series, No. XLIX, Borada, 1929.

Varadachari, K.C.,
—Samavāya: a critique included in the Essays in philosophy, Ganesh & Co., Madras, 1962.

Vidyabhusana, S.C.,
—trans (Eng.) Nyāyāvatāra: The earliest Jaina work on pure Logic by Siddhasena Divākara, Indian Research Society, Calcutta, 1909.
—A History of Indian Logic, ancient, mediaeval and modern schools, University of Calcutta, 1921.

—trans. The Nyāyasūtra of Gautama, Panini Office, Allahabad, 1930.

Vesey, G.N.A.,
—Ed. Body and Mind, George Allen & Unwin, Lodon, 1946.

Index